Natural Rights and the Right to Choose

Over the last thirty years the American political class has come to talk itself out of the doctrines of "natural rights" that formed the main teaching of the American Founders and Abraham Lincoln. With that subtle shift, it has talked itself out of the ground of its own rights. It is no longer in a position to give a coherent account of those rights or to mount a moral defense of those rights for others. Ironically, this transition has been made without much awareness, with a serene conviction that constitutional rights are being expanded. In the name of "privacy" and "autonomy," vast new claims of liberty have been unfolded, all of them bound up in some way with the notion of sexual freedom. Hadley Arkes argues that the "right to choose an abortion" has been the device that has shifted the political class from doctrines of natural right. This new right overturned the liberal jurisprudence of the New Deal and placed liberal jurisprudence on a notably different foundation. And so, even if there were a right to abortion, that right has been detached from the logic of natural rights and, in that way, stripped of its moral substance.

Professor Hadley Arkes is Edward Ney Professor of American Institutions at Amherst. He has published many books on moral philosophy and constitutional law, including *First Things* (1986). A writer for periodicals such as *The Wall Street Journal*, *The New Criterion*, and the *Weekly Standard*, he has influenced public policy as an architect of the Defense of Marriage Act and the Born-Alive Infants Protection Act.

Natural Rights and the Right to Choose

Hadley Arkes

 CAMBRIDGE
UNIVERSITY PRESS

PUBLISHED BY THE PRESS SYNDICATE OF THE UNIVERSITY OF CAMBRIDGE
The Pitt Building, Trumpington Street, Cambridge, United Kingdom

CAMBRIDGE UNIVERSITY PRESS
The Edinburgh Building, Cambridge CB2 2RU, UK
40 West 20th Street, New York, NY 10011-4211, USA
477 Williamstown Road, Port Melbourne, VIC 3207, Australia
Ruiz de Alarcón 13, 28014 Madrid, Spain
Dock House, The Waterfront, Cape Town 8001, South Africa

http://www.cambridge.org

© Hadley Arkes 2002

First published 2002

Printed in the United States of America

Typeface Galliard 10/12 pt.   *System* QuarkXPress [BTS]

A catalog record for this book is available from the British Library.

Library of Congress Cataloging in Publication Data
Arkes, Hadley.
  Natural rights and the right to choose/Hadley Arkes.
      p. cm.
  Includes bibliographical references and index.
  ISBN 0-521-81218-6 (hc.)
      1. Law – United States – Moral and ethical aspects.   2. Justice, Administration of –
  United States – Moral and ethical aspects.   3. Abortion – United States.   4. Natural
  law.   I. Title.
  KF384 .A89 2002
  340′.112 – dc21   2002016550

ISBN   0 521 81218 6   hardback

For
    Michael Martin Uhlmann

Contents

Acknowledgments and Dedication

The work on this book was undertaken and essentially completed during a year of academic leave. That leave was supported, for the most part, by Amherst College, but the Lynde and Harry Bradley Foundation provided an additional generous grant, which made it practicable to devote a year of work to this and other projects. I would like to thank yet again my own college, of 36 years, and my ever-supportive dean, Lisa Raskin. And I would record a special gratitude to Michael Joyce, the former president of the Bradley Foundation, for support over the years that has been sustaining. The year of leave was spent mainly in Washington, and I had the benefit there of an office and supporting staff provided by the Ethics & Public Policy Center (EPPC). The Center proved to be the most congenial and productive of places for this work. For that kind of support, both material and moral, I would like to thank Elliot Abrams, the former president of EPPC, now special assistant to the President of the United States for human rights, and Michael Cromartie, for a while the Acting President of the Center. Michael Cromartie has been a remarkable source of energy and judgment, as he manages to connect people and projects, and find a way of "putting wind in the sails" of many people. He has had that rare combination of political experience, joined to the passion of an academic to read everything in the literature that bears on the questions of consequence. He weaves it all together with a religious sensibility, always affected by humor and playfulness, but always serious at the core.

That sense of things pervaded the character and style of the Center. It was reflected then in many staffers, who proved not only persistently helpful, but enduringly buoyant, in their interest in this project. In that respect I would especially like to thank Ethan Reedy, the Administrative Director of the Center, for his frequent, timely, and saving aid in dealing with computers and printers and their inevitable lapses.

Two of the chapters in this book were first published in other places, as the argument in the book unfolded in different phases. I would like to thank the editors of *The New Criterion*, Hilton Kramer and Roger Kimball, for their permission to draw heavily on the essay that first appeared in their series on The Betrayal of Liberalism. My own essay, "Liberalism and the Law," appeared in the issue of January 1999. For Chapter 6, I drew in a similar way on an essay I did as part of the defense of the Symposium in *First Things* (the journal) on "judicial usurpation" and a crisis in the American regime. The original sym- posiasts were invited to respond to their critics in a meeting at the law school at Loyola University in New Orleans, and my own essay was called "Prudent Warnings and Imprudent Reactions." That essay appeared in *The End of Democracy II: A Crisis in Legitimacy*. I am grateful to Mitchell Muncy, the editor, and to Thomas Spence of Spence Publishing in Dallas, for their permission to make use of that essay here.

The final word is for Michael Uhlmann. Man of letters, counsel without peer, raconteur with limitless range, sustainer of families, runner to the rescue, devoted son of the Church, maddeningly self- effacing. For matters of moral consequence, enduring alertness; for pretension, unremitting jest. And in friendship, untiring, with the touch of grace that lifts everything. I write here with a free hand, not holding back, because I fill in a story that the principal himself will ever be too modest to set down. He immersed himself in Elizabethan literature at Yale, then went back for a while to teach at his beloved Hill School. But then to the law, at the University of Virginia, with the same depth of engagement, this time in jurisprudence and phi- losophy. Following philosophy out of the clouds, he moved thence to political philosophy, to earn his doctorate, studying with Leo Strauss and Harry Jaffa in Claremont. His natural – or supernatural – gifts of teaching kept him for a while in the academy, until the academy turned upside down in the turmoil of the late 1960s. He had done a master work on the Electoral College, and he was drawn away to

Washington, to Senator Hruska, to save the Electoral College, when it was subject again, in the 1970s, to another bootless campaign to end it. The recurring melodrama would play out once again: the affectation of shock that we should be governed in modern times by such an anachronistic device, followed by an awareness, slowly setting in, that every practical alternative was notably worse or unworkable. The passion for reform would usually exhaust itself before Michael could go on to show that this arrangement, devised by the likes of Gouverneur Morris, might actually have something to do with preserving constitutional government in a continental republic. Staying in Washington, Michael would join the staff of Senator James Buckley, where he wrote the first Human Life Amendment. He would be recruited to the Department of Justice under President Ford, where he would shepherd John Paul Stevens to confirmation at the Supreme Court, and eventually persuade a young Clarence Thomas that he could find his vocation in judging. With the advent of the Reagan administration, Michael became counselor to the president, where he argued compellingly, and dealt deftly, on matters freighted with a moral significance. He took an active lead in propelling the administration into action, in dealing with the Baby Doe cases that arose in the 1980s. In those cases, parents sought to withhold medical care from newborn infants afflicted with Down's syndrome and spina bifida. If there was a federal presence, casting up alarms, standing against the trends, it was there mainly as a function of his own art.

At one moment, he was persuaded by his friends to let himself be appointed to the federal court of appeals in the District of Columbia. But that was also the moment when the rigors of teenage years began to be felt keenly in a family of five children, and he came to the judgment that his energies and wit had to be absorbed more fully in the family at that moment than in the courthouse. For his friends it has been a lasting source of disappointment that he did not take that appointment – as it has been a source of pride among the same friends that he made the decision he did. But in public office, or in private practice, returning to teaching, or to the life of a private foundation, his counsel has been sought by people at every level in the country, from Attorneys General and presidents to kids in the shipping room. He continues to be, at every turn, the sustainer of everyone else. I have pleaded with him never more to write an essay or speech with the willingness to put, in place of his own name, the name of a figure in public office. In the judgment of his friends, he has been too inclined to efface himself, with rationales too public-spirited: namely, that the byline of a public figure will draw more attention to the argument, and the argument may be far more important than the name attached to it. With the same temper, he is apt to spend Thanksgiving Day working at a kitchen in the parish or painting walls for nuns. And on Christmas morning, his friends are likely to find gifts laid at the doorstep, from a messenger evidently sweeping past in a Mercury station wagon rather than a sleigh. When he returned to teaching, with a stint back in Claremont, one of his students wrote in a review that "Professor Uhlmann could read the telephone book and make it compelling." He could also, no doubt, lead the students into its deeper implications and find, somewhere in that prosaic thing, the lurking premises of modernity.

In the course of this book I describe the proposal I had shaped as the most modest first step of all on abortion: to preserve the life of the child who *survived* the abortion. When it appeared to be the moment to revive that proposal in 1998, Michael made the rounds with me on Capitol Hill, meeting with senators, congressmen, and their staffs. He would take himself out of any of his projects to join me, with a keen sense of what staffers on the Hill would find helpful. With the right blend of respect and familiarity, and with the authority of one who had been there before, he would make the case, and no one made it better. Along with Robert George, of Princeton, he knew the logic of that bill as well as the one who devised it. The sparest account of Michael, and the one most readily recognized, might well be that account, in *All's Well That Ends Well*, of Helena's late father, a man legendary for his wisdom in council. Of him the poet writes that

> . . . his honour
> Clock to itself, knew the true minute when
> Exception bade him speak, and at this time
> His tongue obeyed his hand.

Governed by that hand, this account would have ended far earlier. But I plead again for a certain license when the principal figure in the story will never broadcast it himself. Lincoln, as a young politician, in his taut style, defended his course and said, "If I falsify in this you can convict me. The witnesses live, and can tell." In this account, I would make the same claim, and the venture is even more warranted here because the chief witness would never tell, or speak of what he has done. His friends know, and so they must tell. Judy Arkes and Susannah Patton would no doubt skip the embellishment, but they would confirm the judgment, and they would join me, with deep affection, in dedicating this book to Michael Martin Uhlmann.

One

Introduction

Backing into Treason

I had been asked to do a piece, for a magazine, on the Holocaust Museum in Washington, and I asked my wife to come along with me. But she had lost family in the camps, and she was not ready to see the scenes played out in vivid pictures, still and moving. I asked then my friend Alan Greenberg, the architect, to come with me, and as we walked through the museum, he offered his commentary on the building, and his reflections, formed over many years, on the characters and politics brought back again in the tableaux set before us. But then we took a turn, and we suddenly came upon a scene that must have been encountered by many other visitors to the museum: a vast vat filled with shoes. They were the shoes of the victims, collected by the Nazis, as they sought to extract anything they could use again or sell. And what came flashing back instantly, at that moment, were those searing lines of Justice McLean, in his dissenting opinion in the Dred Scott case: You may think that the black man is merely chattel, but "He bears the impress of his Maker, and is amenable to the laws of God and man; and he is destined to an endless existence."[1] He has, in other words, a soul, which is imperishable; it will not decompose when his material existence comes to an end. The sufficient measure of things here is that the Nazis looked at their victims and thought that the shoes were the real *durables*.

I have several colleagues, in the academy, who have taken as their own signature tune that line from Nietzsche, amplified by

---

[1] McLean in *Dred Scott v. Sandford*, 19 Howard 393, at 550 (1857).

Dostoyevsky, that "God is dead" and everything is permitted. They are people of large natures, with sensitivities cultivated to the most exacting liberal temper, and so they are prepared to engage their sympathies for all species of hurts suffered by the mass of mankind. When the conversation turns, say, to a homeless man in the gutter, they are quick to insist that there is, about that man, even in his diminished state, an irreducible human dignity. There is still, about his life, a certain *sanctity* that commands our concern. And we ask, "Sanctity?" Do they mean, of the sacred? Does that not rather point to – well, You-know-who?

We find ourselves in a curious situation in which so much of our language of politics and law is rooted in layers of moral understanding and religious persuasion, which have departed from the recognitions of most of our people. My colleagues in the academy speak firmly of "rights," or of the "injuries" done to "persons," and they seem serenely unaware that their language here is grounded in understandings that they have professed, at least, to have rejected long ago. They have, as I say, the most generous reflexes, but whatever can be said on their behalf, even they would have to concede this point: that they cannot possibly give the same account of the wrong of slavery, or the wrong of the Holocaust, that McLean was in a position to give. Some of those homeless characters, living in the streets, might have broken their own lives, and the victims of racism might be reduced and abased; and yet, McLean could look through it all and see beings who were made in the image of something higher. The modern liberal will proclaim his social sympathy and strike a militant posture in defense of rights, but he can no longer explain why that biped who conjugates verbs should be the bearer of "rights."

The malady I am describing here is not confined to those rare quarters of the academy, where professors, swollen with "theories," may talk themselves into brands of imbecility so exquisite that they elude the common man. But in our own day, that imbecility has been imparted to the common man, taught now by his betters. The man on the street may know nothing of Nietzsche, to say nothing of Heidegger and "post-modernism." And yet, over the last 25 years, that man on the street, and the members of the political class, have absorbed the moral relativism retailed in the academy. It is not, of course, the sophisticated relativism or nihilism of Heidegger; it is a "soft" relativism, a receding from "judgmentalism," or the casting of judgments, but it is hardly without consequence. One result is that many of our people who take an interest in matters of politics and law have gradually talked themselves out of the ground of their rights, without being quite aware of it. For like those professors in the academy, they can no longer offer a moral defense of those rights; and worse than that, they have talked themselves into premises quite at odds with the premises of the American Founders. To put it another way, they have talked themselves out of the premises on which their own freedom rests.

It might even be said then, of that common man, interested in politics, that he has been drawn, with a benign haze, into a kind of inadvertent treason: He cannot be counted on to preserve the regime of freedom left to him by the founders. He cannot give an account any longer of the premises of this regime, and therefore he cannot offer a moral defense of that regime and the rights it was meant to secure. He cannot vindicate then his own rights, and for the same reason, *he is not in a position any longer to vindicate the rights of anyone else.* He has become then, in effect, an undependable ally, or even an unwitting enemy, of the regime established by the American Founders and preserved by Abraham Lincoln.

The common man acts through inadvertence, and moves in channels that have been carved out by others. He gives voice, in sentiments grown common, to maxims shaped by leaders of the bar and politics, who should have known better. As the classical philosophers recognized, the law teaches. When the law forbids, say, acts of racial discrimination, it removes those acts from the domain of private choice or personal taste, and forbids them to people generally or universally. It treats those acts, in other words, as matters of moral consequence. As the public absorbs the understandings of right and wrong contained in the laws, the character of the public becomes shaped, for better or worse. That, as Aristotle understood, was the vast promise and the vast danger of politics; and it was the condition that could never be removed. The law could never stop teaching lessons of right and wrong, for human beings could never repress the inclination, built into their natures, to form judgments on the things that were right or wrong, just or unjust. Law there must needs be, and the men and women who shape the laws must be, perforce, teachers of morality, even when they profess to teach that there is no morality. In fact, we have discovered in our own time that judges and political men are never more rigid and moralistic in their teaching as when they are ridiculing moral judgment and professing to free people from the tyranny of moral truths.

The public has been schooled now to a different temper because it has been schooled, quite deliberately, by lawyers and jurists with serious pretensions to philosophy, but schooled in a philosophy that attacks at the root the teachings of the American Founders. At the very beginning of the American law, in *Chisholm v. Georgia* (1793),[2] Justice James Wilson observed that the law in America would be placed on a strikingly different foundation from that of the law in England. That law in England, made familiar by Blackstone, began with the notion of a sovereign issuing commands. But the law in America, he wrote, would begin "with another principle, very different in its nature and operations":

> [L]aws derived from the pure source of equality and justice must be founded on the consent of those, whose obedience they require. The sovereign, when traced to his source, must be found in the *man*.[3]

As we shall come to see, judges in our own time have shifted radically from the understanding of the founders because they no longer profess to understand, in the same way, just what constitutes a "man." They affect the skepticism of the age, or an uncertainty about all "settled truths," including the understanding, settled among the founders, that one could know the difference between a man and a horse. And so, as Jefferson remarked, anyone who rejected the notion of government by consent would suggest that the "mass of mankind" had been "born with saddles on their backs," and that a privileged few had been born, "booted and spurred, ready to ride them legitimately."[4] The judges, in our own day, profess to be far less certain about the meaning of "nature" and "man." As we shall see, they are more disposed to leave to the "political process" the power to resolve that question of what constitutes a person or a human life. But in the name of philosophic

---

[2] 2 Dallas 419.   [3] *Ibid.*, at 458.
[4] Jefferson, letter to Roger Weightman (June 24, 1826), in *The Works of Thomas Jefferson*, Paul Leicester Ford, ed. (New York: Putnam, 1905), p. 477.

doubt, the judges back into an arrangement quite ancient: Since there is no "objective" standard of what constitutes a human being, the decision will be left in the hands then of people with political power. And when they flex their power, in reaching a judgment, that judgment will be tested by no standard of right or wrong *apart from power itself.* That may sound quite portentous, and yet the moves are all familiar to us, and we have heard them, in different forms, over the years: "Are those black people, held in slavery, really human beings, or are they creatures falling somewhere between human beings and animals? And those creatures in the womb – they are conceived by human beings, but does that mean that they are human at all times? Can we not rid ourselves of them if they strain our interests, just as we may rid ourselves of certain animals, with discomfort, perhaps, but without moral strain? But who is to say?" Indeed, who is to pronounce on the question if there are no right answers? And who is to say that self-interest may *not* be a sufficient and defensible ground for the taking of a life, even the life of an innocent being, if there is no ground on which to say that self-interest is any better or worse as a standard of judgment than anything else?

As the judges advance in their work, at the end of the century and the beginning of a new millennium, they have removed from our law any fixed notion of what constitutes a "man" or a human being. But they have removed that part of James Wilson's understanding precisely as they have removed the rest: Human beings were stamped as different because they could give and understand reasons over matters of right and wrong. As Aristotle observed, in the first lines of *The Politics*, animals may emit sounds to indicate pleasure or pain, but human beings may do something notably different. They can "declare what is advantageous and what is the reverse, . . . what is just or what is unjust."[5] But if there are no moral truths, no standards of judgment in matters of right and wrong, then that difference between men and animals dissolves: If "right" and "wrong" simply mean "I like it, or I dislike it," then the giving of reasons over matters of right and wrong is no different in substance from emitting sounds to indicate pleasure or pain.

---

[5] Aristotle, *The Politics*, 1253a.

And yet, if that were the case, we may merely take the matter one step further: If there are no moral truths, no ground of right and wrong, then law itself turns simply into a system of power, without the least pretense of finding a moral justification for itself. That sense of the matter, stated directly, may still shock the sensibilities of common folk. But it is no longer a shock to the professors in the law schools, who teach the doctrines of Critical Legal Studies or Legal Realism, or the legal version of postmodernism. They know that the law is about power, and they insist that there are no "foundations" for moral judgment. Their aspiration then is to become possessed of political power, or the powers of the law. And once possessed of that power, the object is to use it for their own ends, without moral inhibitions, or without at least those fairy tales that were offered in the past to the gullible as "the moral law."

Just after the Battle of Gettysburg, General Meade had not realized the full depth of the victory won by the forces of the Union under his command. He was still, in the aftermath of that battle, shaken by the severity of the casualties. He was given, quite understandably, to the task of assembling the men who had survived, and taking stock of his army in its reassembled state. But President Lincoln did grasp the depth of the victory – and its potential significance – if the moment were not lost. Lincoln understood, as not all of his generals did, that the tactical objective was not to "take Richmond" but to destroy Lee's army, the military force that alone sustained that "pretended government" known as the Confederate States of America. With a proper delicacy, but with the sense of the moment, Lincoln sought to jar Meade from the haze that engulfed him. Lee and his forces could not yet cross the Potomac River while the tide was high, and Lincoln urged Meade to strike at Lee before the general could get back across the Potomac into Virginia. Meade, however, held back, and in holding back, lost the moment. He telegraphed to Lincoln and remarked that they could take consolation at least in this: that the army had been successful in "driving the invader from our soil." His dispatch could not have had, though, for the president, a consoling effect. Lincoln remarked to his secretaries, John Nicolay and John Hay, that it was just like McClellan all over again – the same spirit that led the general to proclaim a great victory because "Pennsylvania and Maryland were safe." Lincoln wondered how he could convey the point to his officers: "Will our generals never get that idea out of their heads? The whole country is our soil."[6]

It must be the most sobering thing when one's own people begin to absorb the premises of the other side. I would take that incident, or vignette, as an analogy for the kind of lesson I would try to convey in this book: I would suggest that, in the most affable and serene way, many Americans, and especially, members of the political class, have come to talk themselves out of the premises of the American Founders and Lincoln. They have done it without the least awareness, and indeed they have done it even while they have had the impression that they have been expanding their constitutional rights. In the name of "privacy" and "autonomy," they have unfolded, since 1965, vast new claims of liberty, all of them bound up in some way with the notion of sexual freedom. In the first steps, there was a liberty, for married couples, but then soon for unmarried persons, to have unregulated access to contraceptives. Next, the claim of privacy was extended into a private right to end a pregnancy, or destroy a child in the womb, at any time in a pregnancy, for virtually any reason. That same claim of privacy was soon extended to the freedom to end the lives of newborns afflicted with Down's syndrome or spina bifida. After the briefest interval, that same doctrine of personal autonomy was applied to the other end of the scale of age and converted into a claim to assisted suicide.

Ironically, this unfolding scheme of liberation has advanced even while privacy, in other domains, has been progressively crimped and disrespected by the law. Private corporations, private clubs, private households, have found themselves under thicker regulation, and the overhanging threat of lawsuits. The combined effect has been to remove the attribute most prized about privacy: the freedom to arrange one's own association, or private enclave, according to one's own, private criteria. But this recession of privacy and freedom seems to count for very little when set against the expansion of rights associated with sexual freedom. The dismantling of restraints on sexuality has evidently been taken as far more liberating, even exhilirating, perhaps because it has been taken as a matter of the most irreducible

---

[6] John Nicolay and John Hay, *Abraham Lincoln: A History* (New York: Century, 1886), v. 7, p. 278.

"personal" freedom. And yet these freedoms, celebrated as pre-eminently "personal," have required the assistance or intervention of surgeons and counselors, and they have quickly annexed to their cause the demand to have the support of *public* monies, drawn from tax-payers with the coercions of the law. It must surely count, too, as one of the paradoxes of this new phase in our law that people seem to identify their well-being, not with an obligation to preserve life or go to its rescue, but with the creation of vast new franchises to destroy human life, for wholly private reasons, without the need to offer a justification.

Each step in liberation has been marked, then, by a further detach-ment of people from the traditional restraints of the law. The corol-lary, of course, is that, as restraints have been removed, persons once protected by those restraints have been removed from that protection. Vast new liberties come along with vast new injuries – unless, of course, the victims no longer count. In any event, there is little doubt that these alterations in our law over the past thirty years have been taken as the hallmarks of a new regime of personal freedom; a freedom so vital to those who savor it, that any threat of having it qualified or diminished in any degree is taken as nothing less than an assault on the constitutional order itself. For them, it would seem, an America without the right to abortion would simply no longer be America. For them, there has been little doubting that each step in the receding of the law has brought a deepening of their freedom. But they seem blithely unaware that, with each step, they have been talking them-selves out of the premises of the founders and Lincoln. And if I am correct, they have done nothing less than talk themselves out of the grounds of their own rights. As a consequence, we are less able as a people, than we were even 25 years ago, to vindicate our own rights, or the rights of the people around us, the people who thought they were joined with us in this political community.

I don't mean to offer in these pages an historical account of how we got here. My burden is to show us that we have, and I would do that by looking at the doctrines that have been put in place as a result of the arguments that have been woven into our law, in some of the most significant cases, over the past 25 years. The story of this shift is really a story about the notable changes that took place in the fur-nishings of mind of American judges. But that in turn is a reflection of the changes that took place in the schools, and especially the schools of law, that formed the sensibilities of those judges. The heart of the matter is that the schools sought to mark off a new genius in philosophy by undercutting the false certitudes that were thought to have enthralled an earlier generation. The most celebrated minds at schools such as Harvard began to teach a new variety of moral skepticism. As those teachings carried over from the nineteenth century, as they were translated in the 1930s and converted into caricatures, they made their way into the minds of men and women who would come to exercise judicial power in the 1970s and 1980s. And when they began to find expression in our law, those shifts began to describe a judicial mind of matchless vulgarity. The playwright Tom Stoppard had one of his characters, a professor of moral philosophy, offer this candid account of his career: that he had managed to take a subtle thesis and traduce it into a proposition of "staggering banality." So much could be said for several justices of the Supreme Court in our own time if they could stand back, with a comparable detachment, and give us the same, pithy summary of their lives' work. The main difference, however, is that this banality comes at a serious cost in lives. For the men and women engaging in these affectations of philosophy have done that while they have been wielding the powers of the federal government.

But my point, again – my point, ever – is that this alteration is not to be taken as a shift merely in style. The sensibility engaged is a moral sensibility, which encompasses the understanding of moral things. That is not merely the knack of having finer intuitions, but of grasping propositions. James Wilson observed, in that first case to elicit a set of opinions from the Supreme Court, that the jurist who would grasp the first principles of law must be able to grasp, at the threshold, the principles of understanding themselves, or what Wilson called, following Thomas Reid, the "philosophy of mind." The change in the judges has to do precisely with the shift away from judges who could engage the problem at that level and explain the ground of natural rights. The shift involves then a move away from the understanding of what the founders regarded as the "axioms" or the "first principles" of a government of law.

That first generation of jurists understood that they could not speak seriously of the things that were truly rightful, and the things that stood in the class of "rights," unless they could speak seriously of "truths" in matters of right and wrong. They could not grasp or explain the principles of justice unless they could grasp the grounds on which any proposition could claim to be true. That first generation of jurists saw no disconnection then between the world of law and the most demanding work in philosophy. For them, "natural law" was not one "theory" among several to be chosen. What they understood as the natural law was bound up with "the laws of reason," or the very grounds of judgment. To gauge the depth of change in our own times is to measure a shift, then, away from the understanding of "natural rights," and a drift into one form or another of legal "positivism." In our own day, that drift has carried so far that observers, looking back, may be stunned when they find, say, Alexander Hamilton, without the least strain, striking off axioms, or first principles, in the sweep of an essay on the politics of the day. Suddenly, there comes an awareness of how truly elegant, how deeply accomplished, that first generation of lawyers was. The evidence, almost springing from the page, is so plain that it cannot be gainsaid; it can merely invite our admiration. The attempts to reconstruct those understandings are condemned to look clumsy in comparison. But any attempt to understand the nature of our current discontents must take, as a standard of comparison, the understandings that furnished the minds of that founding generation. It would offer the most sobering commentary on the state of our law, and the condition of our own citizens instructed by that law, if we cast a look back for a few moments and reminded ourselves, even briefly, of what that first generation of judges happened to know.

Two

The Drift from Natural Rights

Blackstone, that venerable commentator on the English law, insisted that it was a chimera or an oxymoron to suggest that the law may contain a principle of revolution. Laws were settled rules; revolutions involved the overturning of the deepest rules, the unsettling of that which had been most deeply settled.[1] And yet, what Sir William Blackstone regarded as a contradiction in terms, James Wilson regarded not only as plausible, but as an understanding that ran to the foundation of the law in America. In his first lecture on jurisprudence, in 1790, Wilson insisted that "a revolution principle certainly is, and certainly should be taught as a principle for the constitution of the United States, and of every State in the Union."[2]

As paradoxical as that may sound, Wilson recognized that it was simply an implication that flowed from the understanding of natural rights or natural justice. For *natural right* implied an understanding of what was just or right apart from the positive law, the law that was "posited," enacted, set forth in official statutes and decrees. Built into the logic of natural rights, one might say, was a recognition that the positive law, a "law" established in a thoroughly legal manner, may

---

[1] Sir William Blackstone, *Commentaries on the Laws of England* (Oxford: Clarendon Press, 1765), bk. I, p. 157. I am using here the edition published by the University of Chicago Press in 1979, with a copy of the original plates and preserving the same pagination.

[2] Wilson, First Lecture on the Law, in *The Works of James Wilson*, Robert Green McCloskey, ed. (Cambridge: Harvard University Press, 1967; originally published in 1804), v. I, p. 79.

nevertheless be wanting in the substance of justice or lawfulness. For that reason, a statute might not be "lawful" in the strictest sense even if it were passed with a thorough respect for the forms of law. To put the matter another way, the American law would begin by taking as profoundly serious the existence of the natural law, as the measure of the positive law, and the ultimate guarantor of a right to revolution.

That did not mean, of course, that the man on the street would claim a facile license for disobeying a law duly enacted. For as George Washington remarked, of what avail was it to establish the right of a people to govern itself, if the laws, now made by the people and their representatives, need not be obeyed?[3] From the perspective of natural law, there were compelling reasons to obey the positive law, and bear even serious ills before moving outside the law. For one thing, there was the danger of setting, for the less thoughtful, an example that might be read as a warrant for lawlessness. By any reckoning, the Declaration of Independence has to be regarded as the most dramatic invoking of natural rights; and yet, the drafters cautioned, even in that revolutionary text, that "Prudence, indeed, will dictate that Governments long established should not be changed for light and transient causes."

By the very principles of natural law, laws should be made and changed only for the most compelling reasons. That maxim is not merely a sentiment, but the expression of a deeper ordering principle: Only a ground of "reason" can justify anything with the properties of a "law," binding on other creatures of reason.[4] The ground that justifies the law makes it entirely reasonable, or even necessary, that there should be such things as "positive laws." And it is the underlying principle – the principle anchored, we might say, in the natural law – that alone justifies the regulations of the positive law. For example, we may be aware of a principle that enjoins us not to risk life for casual reasons

---

[3] See Washington, Sixth Annual Message to Congress (November 19, 1794) in W. B. Allen, ed. *George Washington: A Collection* (Indianapolis: Liberty Classics, 1988), p. 493.

[4] As Kant argued, the idea of law is "present only in a rational being," and "since moral laws have to hold for every rational being as such, we ought . . . to derive our principles from the general concept of a rational being as such." Immanuel Kant, *Groundwork of the Metaphysics of Morals* [1785], Lewis White Beck, trans. (Indianapolis: Bobbs-Merrill, 1956), p. 69 (p. 401 of the edition of the Royal Prussian Academy), and p. 79 (p. 412 of the edition of the Royal Prussian Academy).

by driving vehicles at reckless speeds on the highways. But it may be quite useful to have regulations of the positive law, which can apply that kind of principle to the circumstances of our daily lives. In the case of the speed limits, the positive law applies these principles to our local terrain and winding roads. The sign "55 mph" marks no natural law, but behind that regulation of the positive law is a deeper principle, which tells us why we would be justified in restraining the liberty of people to drive unencumbered, unregulated, on the highways.

From another angle also, the tradition of natural rights made a distinction between the rights that arose from nature, and the rights that arose from governments, or from local associations.[5] The "right to use the squash courts at Amherst College" can be taken as one of those local rights. It can be created and extended – and justly confined – to the people who sustain that particular entity called Amherst College. But to recognize this species of rights does not foreclose another set of rights that applies to all persons everywhere, even those who did not attend Amherst College. The visitor from Britain gets off a plane in New York, and he will not have to show his passport before the police will protect him from a lawless assault in the street. His "right" not to suffer that kind of lawless attack does not depend at all on his citizenship, or his membership in this polity. Any government that calls itself a government of law should seek to protect him from that species of unjustified harm. But on the other hand, that visitor from England may not take a cab over to the City College of New York and expect to be admitted under the rules, and the special rate of tuition, that the people of New York will make available to one another. One class of rights inheres in all human beings as a species of natural right; the other set of rights grows out of a particular association.

All of this is quite compatible with the traditional understanding of natural rights – that there is a need and justification for positive law and

---

[5] As a notable example, during the debate over the Civil Rights Act of 1866, Senator Saulsbury of Delaware cautioned that the Thirteenth Amendment had recognized the natural right of black people to the ownership of themselves; but in his reading, that amendment could not have authorized the federal government to interfere in the rights of citizenship conferred by the separate states. "What are civil rights," he asked. "What is the basis, the foundation of them all. They are divisible into two classes; one, those rights which we derive from nature, and the other those rights which we derive from government." Quoted in Horace White, *The Life of Lyman Trumbull* (Boston: Houghton Mifflin, 1913), p. 268.

more distinct clusters of "positive rights." But that is not the radical understanding that we associate with the people who style themselves these days as "legal positivists." That bit of self-labeling usually goes hand in hand with the expression of a deep skepticism about the sources of law. The positivist is more likely to register a profound doubt that there are moral truths, holding steady from one place to another. In our own time, there has been more of an inclination to say that there are merely "opinions" of right and wrong, which will always be "relative" to the feelings of the person who holds them, or to the opinions that are dominant in any place. Positivism becomes more truly radical as it becomes more deeply "skeptical" or relativist, and the mystery is just why this stance does not shock people more than it does. The most likely answer is that it fails to shock because most people neglect to draw out the plainest implications that arise from that doctrine: most notably, that there would be nothing in principle wrong with making slaves of other men, and carrying out policies of genocide. For whether these things are right or wrong would depend entirely then on the opinion that is dominant in any place. In that case, the right not to be enslaved, or subjected to genocide, would stand on the same plane as the right to use the squash courts at Amherst: It would depend on the sufferance, or the generosity, of the ruling majority.

There is not, in all of this, the slightest exaggeration, for this is precisely the way in which the issue of slavery was conceived by Stephen Douglas in his celebrated debates with Abraham Lincoln in 1858–59. That was our "crisis of the House divided," and in that crisis the issue of natural right and "positive" law was expressed in this way: When the founders proclaimed in the Declaration of Independence that "all men are created equal," did they really mean all men, black as well as white? In Lincoln's understanding they did. The founders had taken the occasion of that revolutionary moment to articulate a truth extending well beyond the moment: That "proposition," as Lincoln called it, that "all men are created equal," articulated an abstract truth "applicable to all men and all times."[6] But for Douglas, that "truth" had to be read through the prism of what we would call today "cul-

---

6 *The Collected Works of Abraham Lincoln*, Roy P. Basler, ed. (New Brunswick, NJ: Rutgers University Press, 1953), v. III, p. 376 (Letter to Henry Pierce and others, April 6, 1859).

tural relativism": In Douglas's understanding, the founders could not
have meant "all men," black as well as white, for they clearly knew
that black people were being held in slavery in almost all of the States
at the time. "I hold," said Douglas, "that this government was made
on the white basis, by white men, for the benefit of white men and
their posterity forever, and should be administered by white men and
none others."[7] When the founders declared then that "all men are
created equal," they really meant, in Douglas's construal, "all white
men," or all men who shared the rights of Englishmen. As Harry Jaffa
remarked, this translation would imply that when the founders proclaimed the right of all men everywhere to be governed with their own
consent, they were suggesting at the same time "that all true men are
by nature British!" As Jaffa rejoined quite aptly, "such a proposition
might find its place in some undiscovered operetta by Gilbert and
Sullivan," but it would not make sense of what the founders were
pronouncing to the world.[8] In the same way, Lincoln thought that
Douglas's version of the Declaration and its central truth would suffer
the problems of any other attempt to deny a necessary truth or axiom
– it would fall into a shambles of contradiction. And so, Lincoln
would twit Douglas by trying out a reading of the Declaration of
Independence on the new premises supplied by Douglas:

> My good friends, read that carefully over . . . , and ponder well upon it
> – see what a mere wreck – mangled ruin – it makes of our once glori-
> ous Declaration.
>
> 'They were speaking of British subjects on this continent being equal to
> British subjects born and residing in Great Britain!' Why, according to
> this, not only negroes but white people outside of Great Britain are not
> spoken of in that instrument. The English, Irish and Scotch, along with
> white Americans were included [in the terms of the Declaration] to be
> sure, but the French, Germans, and other white people of the world are
> all gone to pot along with [Douglas's] inferior races.[9]

What was in dispute then between Lincoln and Douglas was the
question of whether the rights mentioned in the Declaration of

---

[7] *Ibid.*, p. 112 (from the third debate, in Jonesboro, Illinois, September 15, 1858).
[8] See Harry V. Jaffa, *Crisis of the House Divided* (Chicago: University of Chicago Press,
    1982; originally published, 1959), p. 317.
[9] *Supra*, n. 6, v. II, p. 407.

Independence had a "natural" foundation, or whether they were rights merely of the positive law. If they were rights that arose from nature, then those rights would be the same in all places where that nature remained the same. As the understanding ran, no man was by nature the ruler of other men in the way that man was by nature the ruler of dogs and horses, and God was by nature the ruler of men. If some men were in the position then of exercising power over others, that state of affairs could not have arisen from "nature"; it had to arise from convention or *consent*. James Wilson had been clear that the law in America would not begin with the notion of a superior issuing commands. Yet, as he acknowledged in his lectures on jurisprudence (in 1790), there were circumstances under which the rule of a superior would be eminently justified, and that was the rule of "Him who is supreme." But among those sublunary beings, those beings somewhere between the angels and beasts, there could be, said Wilson, "neither superiority nor dependence."[10]

Even in this age of "animal liberation," we do not sign labor contracts with horses and cows. Nor do we seek the "informed consent" of our household pets before we authorize surgery for them. But we continue to think that beings who can give and understand reasons deserve to be ruled in a different way – with the rendering of reasons, in a regime that seeks to elicit their consent. Lincoln would show his own genius at expounding natural rights by drawing on the strands that ran back to Aristotle and those differences that separated human beings from animals. And so his teaching would take this form:

> Equal justice to the south, it is said, requires us to consent to the extending of slavery to new countries. That is to say, inasmuch as you do not object to my taking my hog to Nebraska, therefore I must not object to you taking your slave. Now, I admit this is perfectly logical, if there is no difference between hogs and negroes.

> [And later, in the same speech, he continued:] The doctrine of self-government is right – absolutely and eternally right – but it has no just application, as here attempted. Or perhaps I should rather say that whether it has such just application depends upon whether a negro is *not* or *is* a man. If he is *not* a man, why in that case, he who *is* a man

[10] "Of the Law of Nature," in *The Works of James Wilson, supra,* n. 2, pp. 126–47, at 126.

may, as a matter of self-government, do just as he pleases with him. But if the negro *is* a man, is it not to that extent, a total destruction of self-government, to say that he too shall not govern *himself?*. . . . If the negro is a *man*, why then my ancient faith teaches me that 'all men are created equal;' and that there can be no moral right in connection with one man's making a slave of another. (Speech at Peoria, Illinois, October 16, 1854)[11]

With his deft political sense, and with his arts as a writer, Lincoln performed nothing less here than the tasks of classic statesmanship: Without being tutored explicitly in Aristotle or Aquinas, he nevertheless managed to incorporate an understanding that was distinctly philosophic; and he managed to bring the logic of natural rights to bear on the most vexing issue in our politics. The ordinary citizen, not exactly tutored in these things, can still be moved and instructed by the force of the argument. It would require then a special genius to explain why this understanding, set forth so movingly by Lincoln, has so offended the professoriate of our own time. That it has offended them, that it elicits their hostility and condemnation, is now clear beyond cavilling. The news has been out for a long while, and yet it still comes as a surprise to many alumni of our leading colleges and universities: that the understandings held by Lincoln and the American Founders stand in an *adversarial* relation to the orthodoxies that are now dominant on the campuses. Those orthodoxies have been shaped by an array of groups clustered in the same family: Some are called "postmodernists," some are radical feminists; they are almost all exponents of "multiculturalism," and they stridently reject, as a form of colonialism or "ethnocentrism," the claim to know moral truths holding across cultures. They put themselves forth under different labels, but as Henry James might say, they form merely chapters in the same book. For what runs most deeply and commonly among them is a commitment to moral relativism in all its forms, including cultural relativism and "historicism" (the disposition to hold that truth is always relative to the epoch in which the action takes place or in which the writer is casting judgments). But of course, as I have had the occasion to point out myself, there is nothing the least "relative" about the doctrines of cultural relativism and historicism. Those doctrines

[11] Lincoln, *supra*, n. 6, v. II, pp. 264, 265–66.

are held to be true in all places, and across all epochs. They may be afflicted by self-contradictions, and yet on the campuses of the country this catechism of relativism remains unsinkable. There may be a willingness to tolerate the differences that come into play among the followers of Heidegger, Nietzsche, or Michele Foucault, but the people who "form the regime" in the academy come together readily to resist any relic of another age who would profess to take seriously the doctrines of the American Founders on "natural rights."

To the family of the Left now on the campuses, the notion of "natural rights" is simply an "ideology," and in this case an ideology of a particulary vicious strain. In their construal, "natural rights," as it was used in the founding generation, was merely an ideology of "patriarchalism," which covered over the rule of white men. In the understanding of the postmodernists there is no objective "nature" of human beings, and no settled moral truths that arise from that nature: What we call "human nature" is "socially constructed" from one place to another according to the vagaries of the local "culture." Even the differences of sex are regarded as differences in perception, which may be shaped in different settings by the way in which people come to view the matter of "gender."[12]

And yet the curious thing is that the people who profess these views so stridently in the academy persist themselves in casting moral judgments across cultures. They have offered the most emphatic judgments, for example, on the evil of the regime of apartheid in South Africa, or the regime of repression in China, and more recently, on the wrongs of ethnic cleansing in Kosovo. The radical feminists do not betray the least diffidence about their capacity to detect the wrongs done to women, even in most remote places and the most exotic cultures. And in fact it appears that they have no trouble in detecting, or identifying, "women" in all cultures. They do not start by asking just who is *regarded* as a woman. They seem to take it for granted that there really are "women" out there, beings who have a certain ontological standing in nature. When we sum up these things, we arrive, as I say, at the most curious result: In the world of the Left on the

---

[12] See, as a notable case in point, Judith Butler, "Contingent Foundations: Feminism and the Question of Postmodernism," in Judith Butler and Joan W. Scott, eds., *Feminists Theorize the Political*, pp. 3–21.

campuses, there are "human rights" to be vindicated all over the globe; but strictly speaking, there are no "humans," for there is no such thing as human nature. And because there are no moral truths, there are no "rights" that are *truly rightful.*

The burlesque flows without strain when we simply take the postmodernists at their word. For the burlesque marks the flaws in the argument, and it is the telling mark of the fact that people are trying to make a living in the academy under the burden of having nothing new to say. After all the affectation, and the springing of new words ("postmodernism," "deconstruction"), there is only a pretense of novelty. There is merely an attempt to dress up in a new form, with a new choreography, the old slogans of "relativism" or moral skepticism. There is nothing in the current scene that had not been prefigured quite precisely by Leo Strauss after the Second World War, when it was evident that the ethic of "social science" was taking hold in American universities and bringing with it the premises of relativism. There was the distinction, most notably, between "facts" and "values": the insistence that we can have no rational knowledge of right and wrong, as we can have about empirical "facts." We would speak then of "value judgments" in place of moral understandings: statements about morality were irreducibly personal and subjective, cut off from judgments of truth and falsity. With premises of that kind in place, it was but a short step to add the further refinements of cultural relativism and historicism. The doctrines with an edge seemed to emanate in the main from Nietzsche, Weber, Heidegger, and the early Wittgenstein. They came, curiously, from German philosophy. Strauss remarked then, in *Natural Right and History* (1953) that "this would not be the first time that a nation, defeated on the battlefield . . . , has deprived its conquerors of the most sublime fruit of victory by imposing on them the yoke of its own thought."[13]

But we may forget just how early it was that academics began to reject the doctrines of the founders, and they did not apparently require help from the Germans. Woodrow Wilson thought that the founders were simply pre-Darwinian: They worked on the curious assumption that human nature was fixed. But science would now

---

[13] Leo Strauss, *Natural Right and History* (Chicago: University of Chicago Press, 1953), p. 2.

inform the enlightened that the nature of human beings was a work in progress, open to the wondrous future of evolution. Wilson was a Hegelian, and so he was disposed to think that our understanding of politics and even nature would be unfolded and enlarged as the laws of history worked to their end, disclosing more with each epoch.[14] He could not credit then the notion of a human nature that would remain essentially the same from one period to another, and he was certainly quite dubious about the prospect of knowing moral truths that would hold in all epochs. The American Constitution was a useful instrument, marred by one or two notable defects, but with a few salutary changes, bringing it closer to the model of parliamentary government, it could remain quite serviceable. Not to be considered seriously for a moment was the suggestion that the Constitution bore a logical relation to the understandings held by the founders about "natural rights." Nor could Wilson take seriously the notion that the understanding of natural rights furnished both the ground of the Constitution and its telos, or end.

And yet, that was precisely how the founders understood the matter. In his famous lectures on jurisprudence, James Wilson argued, as a

---

[14] "All that progressives ask or desire," wrote Wilson, "is permission – in an era when 'development,' 'evolution,' is the scientific world – to interpret the Constitution according to the Darwinian principle. . . .

"Some citizens of this country have never got beyond the Declaration of Independence, signed in Philadelphia, July 4th, 1776. Their bosoms swell against George III, but they have no consciousness of the war for freedom that is going on to-day.

"The Declaration of Independence did not mention the questions of our day. It is of no consequence to us unless we can translate its general terms into examples of the present day and substitute them in some vital way for the examples it itself gives, so concrete, so intimately involved in the circumstances of the day in which it was conceived and written." (Woodrow Wilson, *The New Freedom* [Englewood Cliffs, NJ: Prentice-Hall, Inc., 1961; originally published, 1913]).

This book is a compilation of speeches Wilson delivered in the course of his presidential campaign in 1912. It must be remarkable – and not in any flattering way – that Wilson could write these lines when the crisis of the Civil War was still in living memory. Had it somehow escaped his attention that Lincoln had crystallized the issue of principle precisely as he sought to defend the principles of the Declaration and their bearing, in the most concrete way, on the issue of human freedom in our own time? Was there any issue of freedom, addressed by Wilson, that could possibly run deeper than the issue that Lincoln had addressed in the most sublime and compelling way? And could Wilson have achieved any larger end of freedom in disdaining the Declaration and its principles than Lincoln had achieved in ending slavery and bringing about "a new birth of freedom"?

central point, that the purpose of government was not to create new rights. The aim, rather, was to secure and enlarge the rights that we already possessed by nature.[15] The purpose of any legitimate government – and the purpose then of any constitution devised for a legitimate government – was to secure those natural rights. Even in the state of nature, there was no "right to do a wrong."[16] We had never possessed then a "right" to kill or rape. And so the laws that restrained us in the freedom to kill or rape did not restrain us in anything we ever had a rightful liberty to do. At the same time, human beings possessed, even in the state of nature, a right not to suffer those kinds of wrongs. That right did not arise, then, when men and women entered into civil society; it was not a right created by the government. Again, the function of the government was not to invent rights of this kind, but as Wilson said, to secure and enlarge them.

When the matter was understood in this way, the protection of "natural rights" would not be assigned then to a Bill of Rights, tacked onto the Constitution as an afterthought. In fact, one concern of the Federalists was that the move to add a so-called Bill of Rights would distract people from the understanding that the protection of natural rights was in fact the central, animating purpose of a constitution.[17] And so, as the Declaration of Independence had asserted, governments ceased to be legitimate when they became destructive of those ends for which governments were instituted in the first place. But for Woodrow Wilson, the Constitution could be detached entirely from these moral doctrines of the founders about natural rights. It could be regarded simply as a device that could be used for all manner of ends that may spring from the inventiveness and imagination of political men. And those schemes could spring more readily, with a more

---

[15] See Wilson, *supra, n. 2*, "On the Natural Rights of Individuals," v. II, pp. 585–610, at 585, 586–87, and 592. "What was the primary and the principal objection in the institution of government? Was it . . . to acquire new rights by a human establishment? Or was it, by a human establishment, to acquire a new security for the possession or the recovery of those rights, to the enjoyment or acquisition of which we were previously entitled by the immediate gift, or by the unerring law, of our all-wise and beneficent Creator" (585). And again: "It will, I think, be found, that wise and good government . . . instead of contracting, enlarges as well as secures the exercise of the natural liberty of man" (586–7).

[16] *Ibid.*, at 587.

[17] For a fuller statement of this argument, see my *Beyond the Constitution* (Princeton: Princeton University Press, 1990), ch. 4.

expansive field, if they were not confined by those legal aphorisms that described a "limited government," inhibited in its reach, constrained in its powers. Behind that design of limitation lay an understanding of the ends of government that were *by nature* rightful and wrongful. The emancipation of politics could be more truly complete if political men were delivered from such fables about nature, and such emphatic notions of right and wrong.

Woodrow Wilson reflected nothing so much as the world of higher education at the end of the nineteenth century, with its leading figures tutored, as he was, in the advanced scholarship of Germany. But in that respect, he would be more reflective of the orthodoxies that would come to dominate the universities in our own time. Not long after Wilson retired from the White House, Carl Becker published his notable book on *The Declaration of Independence* (1922). Very quickly, Becker's "line" on the Declaration came to represent the orthodox view in the American academy, lasting to our own day. This distinguished historian could offer a close analysis of the several drafts of the Declaration of Independence – while detaching himself utterly from the question of whether the doctrine in the Declaration, its central teaching, was true or false. But the moral argument in the Declaration was absolutely essential to any judgment on whether it finally made sense in its own terms: Did it offer a true account of the character of legitimate government, and the grounds on which governments could be legitimately overthrown? And did it actually explain, in this particular case, whether the revolution in America had been *justified*? It was the conceit, not only of Becker, but of his profession as well, that all of these matters could be treated as entirely beside the point. "To ask whether the natural rights philosophy of the Declaration of Independence is true or false," he wrote, "is essentially a meaningless question."[18] It was a meaningless question, that is, from the standpoint of the doctrines of "logical positivism" then taking hold in the academy: In this view, moral propositions had no "cognitive" standing; they were essentially emotive statements, which could not be judged, or verified, for their truth or falsity. And so, as Becker wrote:

[18] Carl Becker, *The Declaration of Independence* (New York: Alfred Knopf, 1942; originally published in 1922), p. 277.

When honest men are impelled to withdraw their allegiance to the established law or custom of the community, still more when they are persuaded that such law or custom is too iniquitous to be longer tolerated, they seek for some principle more generally valid, some 'law' of higher authority, than the established law or custom of the community.[19]

The revolutionary generation was breaking away from the law made by the British government, and so it was predictable that the Americans would appeal to a law beyond the positive law of Britain. But that was quite separate from the question of whether there was in fact any such "higher law" that was anything more than a fiction or a rhetorical ploy. With a wink to his readers, Becker made it clear that he, of course, knew better, just as other urbane people, schooled in the colleges, knew better. But behind that familiar facade of urbanity or skepticism was the most serious *defection* from the doctrines of the Founders. Becker was hardly detached or open-minded himself; his detachment revealed his own settled judgment that the doctrines of the Declaration were not indeed truths, because *there were no moral truths*.

Almost twenty years after Becker's book had been published, Becker was induced by Alfred Knopf to reissue the book with a new, summoning introduction. For it was now a time of crisis in the West: War had broken out in September 1939, and by the summer of 1940, France had fallen to Nazi Germany. By the time Becker would pen the preface to the new edition, it was June 1941, and Hitler had turned his armies on the Soviet Union. If Hitler had succeeded, the survival of Britain and the United States as free countries would be gravely endangered. At this moment of peril, then, for the democracies, Becker found himself observing that the only chance for the democracies depended on the possibility that people could still be recruited to risk their lives for those sentiments, sounded so compellingly in the Declaration of Independence:

The incredible cynicism and brutality of Adolf Hitler's ambitions, made every day more real by the servile and remorseless activities of his bleak-faced, humorless Nazi supporters, have forced men everywhere to re-appraise the validity of half-forgotten ideas, and enabled them once more to entertain convictions as to the substance of things not evident to the senses. One of these convictions is that 'liberty, equality, fraternity' and

[19] *Ibid.*

'the inalienable rights of men' are phrases, glittering or not, that denote realities – the fundamental realities that men will always fight for rather than surrender.[20]

The fate of the West depended, that is, on the summoning of support once again for those "truths" of the Declaration of Independence – the truths for which men were evidently still willing to risk their lives – though Becker himself did not take them seriously for a moment as *truths*.[21]

But around the time that Becker had offered the first edition of his book, the most notable contrast with Becker did not come from anyone inside the American academy. It came from a figure outside the academy, a man in political office, who had the advantage, however, of a tutored mind. It came from the President of the United States, offering a meditation on the meaning of the Declaration of Independence, on the occasion of its 150th anniversary, in 1926. This was still a time before presidents had at their disposal speechwriters, and Calvin Coolidge remarked that his own speeches had to be restricted in number because he was much more restricted, as president, in the time available to do research for the speeches. From the writings he has left us on political history and other subjects, it is apparent that his thoughts, set down here, reflected his own, matured judgments. And what he had to say was this:

> About the Declaration there is a finality that is exceedingly restful. It is often asserted that the world has made a great deal of progress since 1776, that we have had new thoughts and new experiences which have given us a great advance over the people of that day, and that we may therefore very well discard their conclusions for something more modern. But that reasoning can not be applied to this great charter. If all men are created equal, that is final. If they are endowed with inalien-

---

[20] *Ibid.*, preface, p. xvi. I am grateful to Harry Jaffa for recalling this preface, and the time at which it was written.

[21] Faced with the chilling reality of the Nazis, Becker could now make this acknowledgment in the new preface: "Certainly recent events throughout the world have aroused an unwonted attention the immemorial problem of human liberty." To which Jaffa tellingly rejoins with a talmudic question: "If the problem of human liberty is 'immemorial,' might not the principles of human liberty also be immemorial." See Harry V. Jaffa, *A New Birth of Freedom: Abraham Lincoln and the Coming of the Civil War* (Lanham: Rowman & Littlefield, 2000), p. 99. On the close, critical reading of Becker, see 83–6, 96–102, and 105–7.

able rights, that is final. If governments derive their just powers from the consent of the governed, that is final. No advance, no progress can be made beyond these propositions. If anyone wishes to deny their truth or their soundness, the only direction in which he can proceed histori- cally is not forward, but backward toward the time when there was no equality, no rights of the individual, no rule of the people. Those who wish to proceed in that direction can not lay claim to progress. They are reactionary. Their ideas are not more modern, but more ancient, than those of the Revolutionary fathers.[22]

When Carl Becker conceded that the truths proclaimed in the Declaration of Independence had a plausible claim to be reappraised, for whom was there a need for such "re-appraisal"? For whom did those "half-forgotten ideas," as he called them, need to be called back? And who bore the need to consider again their "validity" with a new seri- ousness? Clearly, not the Calvin Coolidges of the world, for they had never let them fade from memory, to a domain "half-forgotten." Nor had they need to think again on the "validity" of the Declaration, for they had never doubted the standing of those truths as truths. The only ones who were undergoing the crisis of conviction were the aca- demics, the intellectuals who had talked themselves out of the truths of the Declaration by talking themselves into an arty and dubious epis- temology: They could slide, with Becker, into the assumption that the truths of the Declaration could not be true because they were not "empirical" – not dependent wholly on data from "the senses."

In a strange turnabout, Calvin Coolidge happened to be ahead of his time, for what he managed to anticipate, with a certain acuity, was this: In the name of "progress" or "science," people persuaded of the newness of their doctrines, or the novelty of their insights, would seek to detach themselves from those "outmoded" doctrines of the founders and the constraints of the founding principles. And yet, they would persistently find themselves reinventing something quite old and reactionary in the name of something new. As they backed away from one version or another of government by consent, they would talk themselves into one form or another of the "rule of the strong." For the Marxists, it would involve a detachment from the principles of

---

[22] Calvin Coolidge, "The Inspiration of the Declaration," (Speech delivered on July 5, 1926, around the 150th anniversary of the Declaration of Independence) *Foundations of the Republic* (New York; Scribner's, 1926), pp. 441–54, at 451–2.

"bourgeois constitutionalism." What followed then was the discovery that what was right or just was that which served the interests of the proletarian revolution. And what served the interests of the revolution were the interests defined and declared by the dominant class – that is, by those men who now ruled in the name of the proletariat.

As Coolidge recognized, there was no advance, no going forward from the principles of the Declaration, and he could say that only if he understood that the truths of the Declaration were indeed, as the founders thought, "self-evident" truths. Again, not truths that were "evident" to every "self" who happened down the street, but truths that were indeed closer to "first principles," or axioms, as the founders understood them. There was no advance beyond the truth of the Declaration of Independence as there could be no advance, say, beyond the law of contradiction. The man who sought to "transcend" the law of contradiction would not soar off into the stratosphere of novelty; he would float into a delusion of his own making. He might fancy that he was attaining a new world with rights even more sublime and exquisite, but he would find that what he regarded as a "right" would be, for other people, a misery; and what he regarded as a deliverence would be, for others, a descent into tyranny.

That, I take, not merely as a metaphor, but as a sober account of our current condition. For a new generation of professors in our schools of law, jurisprudence moved into a different register around 1965, with *Griswold v. Connecticut* (on a right to "privacy" and contraception), and later, in 1973, with *Roe v. Wade* (a "right to abortion"). It was rather as though American law had been born anew. One young professor remarked to a colleague that any theory of jurisprudence that produced the "wrong" outcome in Griswold and Roe would identify itself instantly as a *wrong* theory of jurisprudence. It was as though the inventory of cases, the literature produced by the judges in the past, counted for nothing. Everything would be redone, everything would be seen anew, through the lens of the Fourteenth Amendment. And that device would also give to judges a vast new leverage in overturning the laws in the separate States in the name of whole new ensembles of rights. They were rights that would begin with "privacy," but more precisely, and more narrowly, a privacy that meant sexual freedom. It was not the "privacy" of private businesses and corporations and universities to arrange their affairs, in hiring and firing, according to their own, private criteria. Nor was it the privacy of private clubs to define their own character and exclude people of another race, religion, or gender. These claims of privacy, in regard to private businesses and colleges, were decisively rejected in the 1960s and early 1970s, with the Civil Rights Act of 1964, and its additions in 1972. Private clubs would come increasingly under the pressure of local laws, which reflected in turn a climate of opinion ever more hostile to the notion of private enclaves, with their private discriminations. These dimensions of privacy, once the anchor of a "liberal" society, would fall to their nadir, and they would not claim, in our own time, even a shadow of the respect they once held in our law.

But while those claims of privacy were radically disparaged, the law became remodeled around the privacy of sex. And that too, did not mean privacy, so much as sexual liberation. It meant, foremost, a receding of the law from the casting of moral judgments on the rightful and wrongful forms of sexuality: There would be no rightful authority recognized for the government in forbidding contraception, first to married couples, then to unmarried couples. There would be a denial of any authority in the political community to "privilege" marriage, or a relation of commitment, as the most justified and salutary framework for sexuality. But then there would be a denial that the government could pronounce on the meaning of sexuality – that it could refuse to honor homosexuality, or any other form of sexuality, by treating any style of sexuality as less desirable, less legitimate, than that sexuality "imprinted in our natures." The next step, already in litigation, is to deny that the law can confine marriage to a man and a woman. By the summer of 1999 jurists were meeting in an international assembly in London to sound the call for the next step: to deny, finally, that the law may do anything as invidious as enact a law of marriage, with a "privileged" standing given to couples. Already, the argument has been heard that the law falls into the same patterns of discrimination when it refuses to honor the love of a man with a boy, for it refuses to honor their profession of love and their "sexual orientation."

That one member is not an adult may not be, after all, a decisive concern. In many instances, the law allows adults to give permissions for youngsters who are not yet adults. In most cases that authority is ceded to parents, and yet in some cases (notably, abortion ordered by a minor), it is thought fitting to hide those decisions from parents and

assign the authority to a judge. If there is no moral purpose surrounding and confining sex, the child would know as much as any
adult just what gives him pleasure. But if a decision has to be made
for the child, the question might be posed, Why not let the decision
be made by the adult who loves him, and who is loved by him in turn?
Why do we incline to the parents in these cases? Is it an enduring
attachment to "nature"? But is it not exactly "nature," and the implications of nature, that have been so persistently called into question
in this entire chain of cases dealing with sexuality?

As I say, these kinds of arguments have already been sounded, and
they prepare the way for arguments, and steps, even further yet. The
professors of law who have endorsed these moves, or used their arts
to give Providence a Helping Hand, may not be clear themselves on
the end to which all of this is tending. But they seem clear that the
design unfolding before them sets in place the legal ground for an
unparalled regime of personal freedom. At the beginning of the republic, the securing of freedom meant the securing of religious liberty
and the freedom to engage in a public criticism of the government.
Yet, for the new jurisprudence, the first freedoms are no longer the
freedom of expression and religion. The anchor of personal freedom
is to be found, rather, in the freedom of sexuality, less and less encumbered by the constraints of law and nature. Nature worked to place
on women the burdens of pregnancy, but women could be placed on
the same plane as men if they were as free as men to walk away from
a pregnancy. Sexual freedom seemed to mandate, then, as a necessary
annex, a right to be emancipated from the unwanted effects of sex,
and so it would entail the right to destroy an unborn child in the
womb. That is not the way, of course, that proponents of abortion
would describe what takes place. In fact, the right to abortion seems
to require, as a corollary, the right to purge any trace of moral significance from our language on this matter, along with any concrete sense
of what is being done. The assertion of the right seems to entail a
flight to euphemism, and the benign haze of abstraction: What was
being defended, then, was not the right to dismember or poison the
body of another being, but the right to "terminate" a "pregnancy."

But it could hardly be an unimaginable notion, even to the cham-
pions of these new rights, that they may come at a cost of diminish-
ing, quite dramatically, the freedom and "rights" – and even the

privacy – of others. And so, in the name of vindicating the right to privacy in sexual freedom, the authority of the law will be invoked to punish people, in private settings, if they express an adverse judgment on homosexuality. A couple who are reluctant to rent space in their home to a gay couple are brought under a local ordinance barring discriminations based on sexual orientation. A woman in Boulder, the wife of a shopowner, leaves a pamphlet with one of their employees, a gay man, offering counseling in a religious vein in "dealing" with his homosexuality. For that expression of her moral sentiment, grounded in her religious tradition, she is made the object of a complaint under a law on gay rights and compelled to undergo a regimen of "counseling." The case for gay rights began with a demand that people recede from casting judgments with the force of law. But it advances now precisely by annexing the power of law and punishing people for expressing, or even honoring, in private settings their own moral judgments on homosexuality. First we are told to recede from judgments, to keep our moral judgments to ourselves in a private domain. And then we are told that people are not even entitled to their private judgments when they run counter to the new ethic of gay rights. First we are told that styles of sexuality are so irreducibly personal and subjective that they cannot rightly be the objects of moral condemnations cast by others. But then, as the argument takes hold, we are told that we can cast, however, the most severe moral judgments on those people who persist in casting moral judgments!

We are instructed, under the catechism of the Griswold case, that the law has nothing to pronounce in restricting the access of adults or even minors to the liberating wonders of contraception. Senator Joseph Biden could strike a rhetorical pose then, during the hearings over Robert Bork in 1987, when he asked,

> Does a State legislative body, or any legislative body, have a right to pass a law telling a married couple, or anyone else, that behind . . . their bedroom door, telling them they can or cannot use birth control? Does the majority have the right to tell a couple that they cannot use birth control?[23]

---

[23] *Hearings on the Nomination of Robert H. Bork to the Supreme Court of the United States,* Committee on the Judiciary, U.S. Senate, 100th Cong., 1st sess. (1987), pt. 1, p. 116.

But Biden was evidently lulled into incredulity by a want of imagination. For women had already engaged in lawsuits over the injuries produced by the Dalcon shield. When juries pronounced judgments in these "tort cases" and inflicted serious penalties, then the law, in effect, punished people for manufacturing contraceptives. It provided then a powerful incentive to remove those devices from the marketplace. Yet, many women had used that Dalcon shield without adverse effects, and they were quite prepared to argue that they should be free to make decisions about the things they were willing to do, or the risks they were willing to run, with their own bodies. But the law worked, in effect, to bar even to consenting adults a form of contraception they were pleased to have.

When it comes to the matter of abortion, the melancholy paradox should be even closer to the surface of things. For after all, the reigning aphorism on this issue has been "the woman's choice." The proponents of abortion have steadily held back from proclaiming abortion as a positive good; they have defended abortion only as a regrettable "choice," which must be preserved for the woman who is pregnant. But why the holding back? The ground of reluctance has been plain: There cannot be any serious scientific doubt that the offspring of homo sapiens is anything other than homo sapiens. The partisans of "choice" cannot pretend that abortion does anything but extinguish an organism that is living and growing – otherwise there would be no need for this surgery. Nor can they pretend that the life growing in the womb of a woman is anything other than a human life. Hence, the conclusion, announced with the proper gestures of strain: that this is a hard decision, a judgment that brings to bear all of our moral hesitations and sensitivities, and yet a judgment that should be, in the end, the woman's choice to make. The accent on choice, the strain to cast the problem in that neutral way, makes sense only with the awareness that a human life is at stake. Even if the proponents of choice will not admit the evidence of embryology, they concede at least that it is quite plausible for others to think that these surgeries destroy human lives. Let us take, then, that concession offered implicitly: If it is reasonable to conclude that human lives are destroyed in these surgeries, and if 1.25 to 1.5 million of these surgeries have taken place each year, for the past 29 years, then should this much not be clear?: For the 30-plus million human beings killed in these procedures, the "right to abortion" has not been liberating. Clearly, it has not enlarged their personal rights. Nor has it demonstrated that the Constitution brings a stiffening of procedures, a casting up of obstacles, before whole classes of persons can be removed from the class of "rights-bearing beings" and placed beyond the protections of the law. If *Griswold* and *Roe* have brought about a new regime of personal freedom, that regime has had the effect of closing down the protections of the Constitution for vast numbers of human beings. Whether one sees, then, an America with a happier lilt, with people soaring now in their personal freedom, turns entirely on the question of whether we screen out, from our vision, any recognition of the victims as persons, whose injuries somehow count.

That is not actually so hard to do, as we can now plainly see; and indeed the reflex to do it might itself spring from our moral natures. People of ordinary sensibility will feel sheepish before claiming a right to take the life of an innocent human being for their own self-interest. It is far easier to talk oneself into the notion that the small being in the womb is not really, or not yet, human, not human as you and I are. After all, it doesn't yet look like a child, or have what looks like human form: it may be genetically homo sapiens, but is it fully human? It requires no elaborate theory to bring off that maneuver in rationalizing. People with college degrees, and pricey educations, have been doing it with ease now for over 25 years. But what is harder to recognize is that, as people talk themselves into that rationale, they are subtly, but decisively altering what James Wilson and the founders understood as the very ground of their natural rights – and the ground of our entire law. If we can arbitrarily alter the definition of a "man" as it suits our convenience, if nature provides no definition of a human being that we are obliged to respect, then – as we shall see – we remove the distinct ground of our claim to "natural rights." But if we do that, if we remove "natural rights," we would convert all rights into rights of "positive law." With that subtle shift, we would have removed, in effect, the very logic and substance of rights. For what we call "rights" then are simply the things declared to be right by the opinion that is dominant in any place. In that event, the "rights" enacted into law are merely the rights that a majority is willing to confer. But what the majority may confer, the majority may also remove when it no longer strikes the majority as right or convenient.

As Harry Jaffa remarked on this same problem, when it was played out on the question of slavery, the question of what is a human being cannot be a "value judgment": What is a human being cannot depend, that is, on whether any of us is inclined to impute "value" to the life of any other human being. If we happen to be owners of slaves, there may be no "value" to us in acknowledging that some of these mammals bearing burdens for us happen to be human. To say that the question, What is a human being?, depends on a value judgment, is to say there is no objective truth or standing that attaches to a human being. The founders assumed, as Lincoln did, that we could tell the difference between a man and a hog: They thought that the difference was fixed in nature, in a way that we were obliged to accept, not in a way we were free to manipulate. If we were free to shade that definition of a human being, we were free to deny people the standing of "men" or moral agents. The point warrants restating without apology: If there is no "nature," there can be no "human" rights springing from that nature. But in that case – as I will try to argue more fully later – there would be no "rights" at all, in the hardest and strictest sense.

There is no harm then in telegraphing, as we used to say, or signaling in advance, the conclusion that I think will settle in as the argument in this book unfolds. And that conclusion may be stated with a fuller force if I suspended, just for a moment, my most settled moral convictions on abortion. For the purposes of this argument we could work on the assumption that the right to abortion is indeed thoroughly right, fully defensible. What we would discover, however, is that this "right" – the right that so many learned people consider now the anchoring right of their freedom – can be put into place only by denying, at the root, the logic of natural rights. In that event, this grand "right" is evacuated of its moral substance. It ceases to be a right that can command the respect of a majority, when the majority is no longer pleased to sustain it. It ceases then to be a right in the deepest sense, for it is not a right that can be vindicated against the vote of a majority. The people who have talked themselves into the premises of that right to abortion will not only be incapable then of vindicating that right to abortion; they will no longer be in a position to vindicate *any* of our rights, for in the grandest sweep, with the most expansive confidence, they would have overthrown the very ground of their "rights." That drift, of course, is barely noticeable to them. It can be seen for what it is only when it is measured against the understanding held by the founding generation about the grounds of our rights.

Three

On the Things the Founders Knew – and How Our Judges Came to Forget Them

The city of Cincinnati can be an engaging place, but federal judge Arthur Spiegel also found, in the mid 1990s, that it could be quite a vexing place. The city council of Cincinnati passed what was called the Human Rights Ordinance of 1992, which barred virtually all species of discrimination – including discrimination on the basis of "Appalachian origin." But the bill also encompassed a bar on discriminations based on "sexual orientation." That kind of bill, in other places, had been turned into a club to be used against evangelical Christians, who might refuse, on moral grounds, to rent space in their homes to gay or lesbian couples. And so a movement arose in Cincinnati, modeled on a similar movement in Colorado, to override the ordinance passed by the council: This would not be a referendum merely to repeal the law, but a move to amend the charter of the municipal government and remove, from the hands of the local legislature, the authority to pass bills of this kind. In effect, it was a move to override an ordinary statute by changing the constitution of the local government.

The amendment did not seek to make homosexual acts the grounds for criminal prosecutions. It sought rather to bar any attempt to make gay and lesbian orientation the ground for special advantages or quotas or the standing of a preferred "minority." The framers objected to the tendency to treat gays and lesbians on the same plane as those groups that suffered discriminations based on race, religion, or gender. The proposal, known as Issue 3, drew wide support and passed in a referendum in 1993. It was, of course, challenged in the courts, which is why it found its way into the hands of Judge Spiegel.[1]

But to a case amply supplied with philosophic puzzles, Spiegel added a complexity that no one had anticipated: The Human Rights Ordinance, passed by the council, was rather sweeping in its proclamation of "rights," and in Judge Spiegel's manual of construction, a measure that proclaimed more rights was more authoritative than a measure that proclaimed fewer rights, or refused to grant, to certain claims, the standing of rights. And so, turning on their head the canons of constitutionalism, Spiegel was inclined to regard the *constitutional amendment* in Cincinnati as invalid *because it ran counter to a local ordinance*, far more liberal. On this matter I would speak from direct, personal experience, since I was called in as a consultant on this case precisely for the purpose of addressing that argument.[2] It fell then to the attorneys and professors defending the referendum to remind the judge of the lessons taught by Chief Justice Marshall in *Marbury v. Madison*: Behind the ordinary laws were the "basic laws," the laws that told us, in effect, just what constitutes a "law." The fundamental law of a constitution bears then a *logical precedence* over the statute or the ordinary law.

Spiegel seemed to appreciate that the public at large in Cincinnati was far more conservative in its reflexes than officials elected in the city. Politicians were far likelier than ordinary citizens to cultivate a sensitivity to virtually any group with a presence or visibility in the

---

[1] The policy engaged here, framed as a constitutional amendment, would come to describe a rather strange course: the amendment in Colorado would be struck down in the Supreme Court in a rather dazed opinion, while the same policy, in Cincinnati, would be upheld by the court of appeals. See *Romer v. Evans*, 134 L Ed 2d 855 (1996).

[2] At the trial in Cincinnati, I unfolded the arguments that I restate here, in the paragraphs to follow. Their record, in the transcript of the trial, can be found on pp. 652–60, and *passim*. By the time the judge came to write his opinion, he backed away from that remarkable argument, and there was only a muted reflection left in the record. See *Equality Foundation of Greater Cincinnati v. City of Cincinnati*, 838 F. Supp. 1235 (S.D. Ohio 1993), at 1238. In the style of legal positivism, it was claimed, as a ready excuse for Judge Spiegel, that his task was to "predict" what the appellate courts above him would do. But Spiegel's decision could not be rescued in that manner either, for he would be overruled twice by the court of appeals, even after the *Romer v. Evans* in 1996. See *Equality Foundation of Cincinnati v. Cincinnati*, 54 F. 3d 261 (1995), and *Equality Foundation of Cincinnati v. Cincinnati* [Equality Foundation II], 128 F. 3d 289 (1997).

politics of the city. Politicians would be far more averse to measures that promised to irritate any blocs of voters. The judge thought there was something immanently suspect, then, in appealing to the public in a referendum, when it was clear that the public was likely to be far more illiberal in its reluctance to install or confirm new brands of "rights." But in taking that line, he had to suggest that there was something faintly disreputable, or illegitimate, about a people framing a constitution that puts limits on the use of political power. His understanding then would have left the local legislature as the sole, legitimate source for shaping or amending the constitution. What seemed to have vanished from the understanding of the judge were the deepest premises of government by consent, anchored in the understandings of natural rights. Spiegel seemed to have forgotten the instruction of James Madison, George Mason, and James Wilson: namely, that a legislature was itself the artifact or creation of a constitution; it could not be its source. As Madison observed, it was a "novel & dangerous doctrine that a Legislature could change the constitution under which it held its existence."[3]

John Locke once put the matter in this way, in his *Second Treatise*, in an instruction that really did run to the root: "the constitution of the legislative being the original and supreme act of the society," it had to be "antecedent to all positive laws." That there is a "legislature" with the power to make positive laws is a matter established in the Constitution. *But the Constitution itself cannot spring then from the positive law.* It had to find its origins, as Locke said, in that understanding "antecedent to all positive laws," and that authority was "depending wholly on the people," on their natural right to be governed with their own consent.[4]

It is one of the mysteries of our time that even conservative jurists and writers on law seem to have forgotten these ancient lessons, that the difference between positive law and natural law does not depend simply on a theory: that it is bound up, rather, with the canons of propositional logic. Alexander Hamilton drew on that reservoir of

---

[3] Max Farrand, ed., *Records of the Federal Convention of 1787* (New Haven: Yale University Press, 1911; 1966 edition), v. II, p. 92.

[4] See Locke, *An Essay Concerning the True Original, Extent and End of Civil Government*, Sec. 157.

understanding, and made points quite telling in the Federalist papers. It would appear that those passages have disappeared from the edition of the Federalist papers read by many lawyers, and so they are worth recalling. In the *Federalist* #78, Hamilton noted the rule that guided the courts in dealing with statutes in conflict: The statute passed later is presumed to have superseded the law enacted earlier. The same rule does not come into play, of course, with the Constitution, for a Constitution framed earlier would have to be given a logical precedence over the statute that came later. Were that not the case, the Constitution would lose its function, or its logic, as a restraint on the legislative power. But these rules for the interpretation of statutes are nowhere mentioned in the Constitution. As Hamilton remarked, they were "not derived from any positive law, but from the nature and reason of the thing."[5]

Somewhat later, in the *Federalist* #81, he went on to point out that the notion of "parliamentary supremacy" in Britain had never been taken to mean that the legislature was empowered to overturn a verdict rendered in a court. The understanding seemed to be settled that the legislature might act instead to "prescribe a new rule for future cases." But here, too, this understanding was not expressed anywhere in the *positive* law of the Constitution. And so what made it valid or authoritative, as an understanding woven into the Constitution? As Hamilton explained, this understanding was simply anchored in "the general principles of law and reason."[6]

Blackstone had written in a similar way about "the law of nature and reason"; and when jurists of the founding generation spoke in these accents, it seemed to be understood that they were pointing beyond the positive law to the principles of natural justice. But what seems to have fled from the understanding of jurists in our own day is that the principles of moral judgment, like the principles of natural law, are bound up with those "laws of reason." It seems to come persistently as a surprise to jurists and writers in our own time that the "natural law" could be composed in part of the canons of logic. Even more surprising is that those canons of logic could bear, with the most pronounced effect, on the practical judgments of the law. And yet, the

[5] *The Federalist Papers* (New York: Random House, n.d.), p. 507.
[6] *Ibid.*, p. 526.

very understanding of "nature" ran back to Aristotle and the first book
of political science: The polis was marked by the presence of "law," or
the authority to make decisions binding on everyone within the territory. Man alone, among the animals, was suited by nature for the polis,
for human beings could do more than emit sounds to indicate pleasure or pain; they could give reasons over matters of right and wrong.[7]
Immanuel Kant is not readily or easily identified with the tradition of
natural law, but Kant understood that moral principles were accessible only to creatures of reason. And so, Kant could remark, in a passage
that should be set down in all the primers, that "since moral laws have
to hold for every rational being as such, we ought . . . to derive our
principles from the general concept of a rational being as such, and
on this basis to expound the whole of ethics. . . ."[8]

Some of the confusion here has arisen from the conviction, long
planted, that natural law must be confounded with matters of religious
belief. As the positivists understand law, it is the command of a sovereign, of one who has the authority to issue commands with the force
of law. But even the religious would understand that the authority of
the Ten Commandments, or biblical law, would rest on the conviction that they emanated from a divine Lawgiver. That issue of the lawgiver is a plausible concern, which has endured in legal philosophy,
but there seems little awareness of the nuances that have altered the
cast of the problem: Several of the American Founders, like James
Wilson, leaned importantly on the teachings in natural law of Jean-
Jacques Burlamaqui, especially his treatise on *The Principles of Natural
Law and Politic Law* (1748). In that engaging work, Burlamaqui
managed to settle, in the most delicate way, that enduring question
about the source of the law or the grounds of obedience: Even if the
law commanded what was right and forbade what was wrong, what
commanded our obligation to respect that judgment? The most familiar answer was that the law emanated from a Lawgiver; we were
obliged to obey the one who commanded. The other answer was that
the law was grounded in the laws of reason, in propositions that we
were obliged to respect because they had the sovereign attribute of

[7] See Aristotle, *Politics*, 1253a.
[8] Immanuel Kant, *Groundwork of the Metaphysic of Morals* [1785], H.J. Paton, trans.
(New York: Harper & Row, 1948), p. 79, p. 412 of the edition of the Royal Prussian Academy.

being true. The clearest example was the "law of contradiction": that two contradictory propositions both cannot be true. It was not like the law of gravity, in the sense that people could "violate" this law without the consequences coming instantly or the ceiling falling in. In what respect then was it a law? Solely on the grounds that it was true of necessity, that it could not be contradicted without falling into contradiction. And therefore it rightly claimed to govern our judgments in the domain of reason.

As Burlamaqui put it, the authority of the Lawgiver may provide the external *incentive* to obey the law. But that external incentive is given a further, *internal* support, when the law is in accord with the laws of reason. The compelling force of the reason behind the law may augment our confidence that the law must indeed be in accord with the intentions of the Lawgiver. Burlamaqui remarked that the Roman polytheists were guilty of a "vincible error" – that is to say, what was implausible in their theology could have been exposed through a relentless use of reason – much in the way that Augustine subjected these notions to the stringency of his own reason, and the caustic of his wit, to make clear their incoherence. As Augustine wrote,

> The god Juganitus is brought in when a man and a woman are united in the "yoke" (iugum) of marriage. . . . The god Domiducus is employed to "lead her home" (domum ducere). . . . The goddess Manturna is called in . . . to see that she will "remain" (manere) with her husband.

And so Augustine asks, with mock wonder, "Why fill the bridal chamber with a mob of divinities, when even the bridal escort retires."[9] The lesson here is that the divine gift of reason may deliver us from gullibility and alert us to some of the more extravagant and spurious claims that are offered up to us in the name of the Lawgiver. An earlier generation of jurists understood, then, that they were *doing* natural law when they were making strenuous use of the laws of reason in settling the grounds of their judgments. In a comment made in passing in one of his opinions, John Marshall apologized to his readers for "much time . . . consumed in the attempt to demonstrate propositions which may have been thought axioms."[10] Marshall apparently took it for granted

---

[9] Augustine, *The City of God*, bk. VI, ch. 9.
[10] *Gibbons v. Ogden*, 22 U.S. 1 (1824), at 221.

that every literate reader would know that axioms cannot be demonstrated, and that they need not be. Anyone tutored in logic would have understood that "first principles" were indemonstrable in the sense that they depended on certain truths that had to be grasped, as Aquinas said, *per se nota*, as things true in themselves, and true of necessity. Consider, as a brief example, that we wished to conduct an "experiment" on the variables affecting the speed of a ball rolling down an inclined plane. Our hypothesis is that the rate of acceleration will quicken as the angle of inclination is made steeper. But that proposition can be tested only by altering the angle of inclination while everything else is kept constant. Only in that way could we test the significance of alterations in that one variable, the angle of inclination. Now, how are we to understand the aptness of that procedure – that it is necessary for us to keep everything constant apart from the variable whose significance we wish to measure? Evidently, we must be able grasp at once that differences can be attributed then to the component (or "variable") that is allowed to vary. And how do we know that, when we altered the angle, from state A to state B, these two states are different, that A does not equal B? Are those things, quite critical for the experiment, things that we have come to understand *through experiments*? Or do they depend simply on grasping the "law of contradiction" – in this instance, that two things cannot be at the same time different and the same? Clearly, we cannot do an experiment unless we understand these postulates or axioms already. They must be in place then – we must be capable of grasping them as axioms – before we are in a position to conduct an experiment or carry out a demonstration.

That the founders understood the matter precisely in this way was nowhere expressed with more elegance and clarity than by Hamilton, in the opening paragraph of his essay in the *Federalist* #31. The paper was about taxation, and in the course of the essay, he did not reach any conclusion that would not have been reached in our own day, say, by Bob Dole. But any disinterested reader would notice at once some striking difference in the furnishings of mind. Hamilton put it in this way:

> In disquisitions of every kind there are certain primary truths, or first principles, upon which all subsequent reasonings must depend. These contain an internal evidence which, antecedent to all reflection or combination, command the assent of the mind. . . . Of this nature are the

maxims in geometry that the whole is greater than its parts; that things equal to the same are equal to one another; that two straight lines cannot enclose a space; and that all right angles are equal to each other. Of the same nature are these other maxims in ethics and politics, that there cannot be an effect without a cause; that the means ought to be proportioned to the end; that every power ought to be commensurate with its object; that there ought to be no limitation of a power destined to effect a purpose which is itself incapable of limitation.

Just as Bob Dole might have put it. The contrast may become even deeper – and even more telling – when we realize that this was the kind of prose that Hamilton struck off at a moment's notice, writing for a deadline as a political essayist. That first generation of American jurists contained minds of the first order, but Chief Justice Marshall and some of his colleagues were heard to remark on one occasion that "Hamilton's reach of thought was so far beyond theirs that by his side they were schoolboys – rush tapers before the sun at noon day."[11] Of Hamilton, and his comparison with jurists of our own day, there will be more to say in a moment. But my point is that Hamilton was a preeminent figure in a circle of jurists who were tutored in the best things said and done in philosophy and literature, and these men moved with an uncommon ease when they had to move back to first principles in the course of settling a practical judgment. They would do that in the course of resolving cases, but what seems to be curiously overlooked is that they made that move to first principles, not only in the matter of settling a particular case, but in shaping the whole frame of the government. After all, the very appeal to "first principles" as the ground of a constitution, or as a guide to its content, is itself a move of the natural law.

The task of "founding" a new constitutional order draws one back to the root, or to the questions that stand at the beginning of the law. But the founders also stood in that rare position rather hard for the rest of us to imagine: Their experience encompassed an America, and a world of law, without the Constitution. And if they moved to establish a constitutional government, it was precisely because they understood, in the first place, certain principles that enjoined them to

[11] Quoted by Forrest MacDonald, *Alexander Hamilton: A Biography* (New York: Norton, 1979), p. 314.

establish a government restrained by law rather than a despotism. It requires but a moment's reading, in any of the legal texts of the founding, to become aware instantly of the vast differences that separate the furnishings of mind of that first generation of jurists from the sensibilities more typical of judges in our own day. Two snapshots, drawn from the two periods, may tell the story.

In that first case to elicit a set of opinions from the Supreme Court, *Chisholm v. Georgia* (1793), James Wilson and his colleagues understood that this was a moment of teaching, for they were at the beginning of the law under the Constitution, with no cases to draw upon as precedents. Before Wilson would speak about the text of the Constitution, he found it necessary to speak then about "the principles of general jurisprudence." But even before that, something else had to be set in order: Before the judges would begin expounding the principles of legal judgment, they found it necessary, as Wilson wrote, to acknowledge something of the laws of reason and "the philosophy of mind." And so, before Wilson would invoke the authority of any case at law or any commentator on matters jural, he would invoke the authority of "Dr. [Thomas] Reid, in his excellent inquiry into the human mind, on the principles of *common sense*, speaking of the sceptical and illiberal philosophy, which under bold, but false pretensions to liberality, prevailed in many parts of Europe before he wrote."[12]

Wilson would begin then by rejecting "scepticism," as the fount of all forms of relativism in morality and law. If we had to offer a contrast, as a quick snapshot, it would be hard to find anything more redolent of our age than the famous "mystery passage" in *Planned Parenthood v. Casey* in 1992. Before the judgment in that case had been announced, it had been anticipated that the Court might overrule *Roe v. Wade*, the decision in 1973 that established a constitutional "right to abortion." But instead, three judges appointed by Presidents Reagan and Bush went over to the other side, in an opinion that seemed to entrench even further the holding in *Roe v. Wade*. In fact, Justices Sandra Day O'Connor, Anthony Kennedy, and David Souter wrote a plurality opinion in which they enjoined the country to cease its agitation over this issue, lest that challenge to the law, tumultuous and steady, begin to erode the authority of the Court. But in restat-

[12] 2 Dallas 419, at 453–4 (italics in the original).

ing the claim for a "right" to abortion, the three judges sought to soar to a level poetic, and deliver themselves of this profundity: that "at the heart of liberty is the right to define one's own concept of existence, of meaning, of the universe, and of the mystery of human life."[13]

The founders began by rejecting "scepticism," or relativism, in philosophy and morality, and the modern judges, the products of the best law schools in the land, affirm the right of a person to make up his own version of the universe. But what of that person himself, the one who was conceded now the right to define his own relation to the universe? Was there any reality or truth attaching to *him*? And what was there about him that commanded the rest of us to respect these decisions he reached about himself and the universe? Why were the rest of us not entitled, in turn, to *make him up*, or to conceive of him in a different way, far more diminished as a bearer of rights? What if we found that scheme far more consonant with the sense of *ourselves* and our own scheme for the universe?

By the time we attribute to anyone the standing to have his judgments about himself respected, we are, at the very least, acknowledging his "existence" as an objective fact, not something dependent on the vagaries of our perceptions. We would seem to be attributing to him also the attributes of a "rational agent." To respect his account of himself, or the meaning of his life, is to suggest that we regard him as a thoughtful or reasonable being, whose claims about himself come to us with a certain momentum of respect. We assume, that is, that he is a creature who is capable of reflecting seriously about the grounds of his own well-being. We are probably assuming then that he is, as Madison said, a "moral agent," who has access to an understanding of "right" and "wrong." But as a moral agent, who has at least some rudimentary sense of right and wrong, we would expect him to know that it is unreasonable for him to demand, as part of his own freedom

---

[13] *Planned Parenthood v. Casey*, 505 U.S. 833, at 851 (1992). As an exemplar of what might be called "postmodernist jurisprudence," this passage stood alone until the summer of 2000 – and the contribution suddenly bestowed upon the country by federal judge Maryanne Trump Barry. Judge Barry, with her colleagues, struck down the law on partial-birth abortion in New Jersey and "explained" that the law was addressing a mirage: There was, in reality, no child to be born, and no "delivery" of a baby, because "a woman seeking an abortion is plainly not seeking to give birth." See *Planned Parenthood v. Farmer*, 220 F. 3d 127, at 143 (July 26, 2000). But on all of this, more later.

or his own rights, things that do injury to others, and possibly even to himself. We may become aware again of the notion of an "unalienable" right, a right we are not competent to waive or violate even in relation to ourselves. Of course no one would think of making these attributions to all of the other animate creatures who pass before our visual screen. As I noted earlier, even in this age of animal liberation, no one suggests that we ought to sign labor contracts with horses and cows, or seek the "informed consent" of our household pets. These modes of acting become sensible, and appear wholly "natural," only when we are dealing with beings who can give and understand reasons. We may move chairs in a room without the need to give reasons to the chairs. But when we govern human beings, when we displace their own private choices or restrict their freedom, we are obliged to deal in a different way with creatures who are animated by reasons of their own, and who are capable of weighing the justifications that are offered for the restriction of their freedom.

Once we have put in place all of these reactions grounded in "common sense," we would have explained that "proposition," as Lincoln called it, on which the American regime was founded: "All men are created equal." That was, as Lincoln said, "the father of all moral principle" among us.[14] And yet, of course, as Lincoln explained, the authors of the Declaration of Independence "did not mean to say all were equal in color, size, intellect, moral developments, or social capacity."[15] People were not equal in all respects, and we understand ourselves that moral discriminations are justified at all levels: We would not be obliged to treat all persons with the same affection or respect, regardless of their character, and the law would affect a position of mindlessness if it made no discriminations between the innocent and the guilty. As Lincoln understood, that "proposition" in the Declaration referred to those differences anchored in nature between human beings and animals. Those differences were so decisive and enduring that they could furnish an axiom: namely, that beings capable of giving and understanding reasons over matters of right and wrong deserve to be ruled only with their consent. In a telling passage in his speech

[14] Lincoln, Speech in Chicago, July 10, 1858, in *The Collected Works of Abraham Lincoln*, Roy P. Basler, ed. (New Brunswick, NJ: Rutgers University Press, 1953), v. II, p. 499.
[15] Lincoln, Speech on the Dred Scott case, June 26, 1857, in *ibid.*, pp. 405–6.

at the Cooper Union, Lincoln noted those black slaves who had the wit not to throw in with John Brown during the raid by the abolitionist at Harper's Ferry. As Lincoln remarked, "John Brown's effort was peculiar. It was not a slave insurrection":

> It was an attempt by white men to get up a revolt among slaves, in which the slaves refused to participate. In fact, it was so absurd that the slaves, with all their ignorance, saw plainly enough it could not succeed.[16]

These were not lettered or educated men. But they understood that the scheme of this white man, touched with fanaticism, would not work to their advantage. It would not conduce to their well-being. Even the slave untouched by education had the understanding then to reason about the conditions of his well-being; and for that very reason, he did not deserve to be made an annex to the purposes of other men, without the need to gain his consent.

Harry Jaffa has stated, with an illuminating compression, the axiom contained in that proposition, "all men are created equal": No man is by nature the ruler of other men in the way that God is by nature the ruler of men, and men are by nature the ruler of horses and dogs. And therefore, as the argument ran, if we find about us today a situation in which some men are put in the position of ruling over others, that state of affairs cannot arise from nature. It must arise from convention or consent.[17]

In many documents and resolutions of the revolutionary period, we find these understandings reflected. The Town of Malden, Massachusetts, in 1775 declared in a resolution in May 1776, that

> [W]e are confirmed in the opinion, that the present age would be deficient in their duty to God, their posterity and themselves, if they do not establish an American republic. This is the only form of government which we wish to see established; for we can never be willingly subject to any other King than he who, being possessed of infinite wisdom, goodness, and rectitude, is alone fit to possess unlimited power.[18]

---

[16] Lincoln, Address at the Cooper Institute, New York City (February 27, 1860), in *ibid.*, v. III, p. 541.

[17] See Harry V. Jaffa, *Equality and Liberty* (Claremont, 1999; originally published in 1965), pp. 137, 177–8.

[18] Instructions from the Town of Malden, Massachusetts, for a Declaration of Independence, May 27, 1776, in Henry Steele Commager, ed., *Documents of American History* (New York: Appleton-Centry Crofts, Inc.; 6th ed.), pp. 97–8.

John Locke had famously argued in the same cast in the Second Treatise on Civil Government:

> For men being all the workmanship of one . . . wise Maker . . . , and being furnished with like faculties, sharing all in one community of nature, there cannot be supposed any such subordination among us that may authorize us to destroy one another, as if we were made for one another's uses, as the inferior ranks of creatures are for ours.[19]

James Wilson had insisted, in *Chisholm v. Georgia*, that the law in America would not start with the notion of a superior issuing commands; but he also acknowledged that, under certain conditions, the rule of a superior would be eminently fitting. And that was the rule of "Him who is supreme." But among human beings, there could be, as Wilson said, "neither superiority nor dependence."[20] From many angles, then, and many sources, we find a confirmation of this understanding. And yet, my own students, children of their age, cannot make themselves speak the language of the founders when they turn to give an account of their work. The students tend to fall into the expression that the American founders "believed" that "all men are created equal." But that proposition was not put forth as a matter of belief or "opinion," which may vary from one person to another, with the variations in beliefs and opinions. The same students would find it queer if anyone said that he "believed" in the validity of the Pythagorean theorem. They will also laugh instantly when the question is posed, "Do you think that the Pythagorean theorem was about *Greek* triangles?" And yet, why are we so inclined to rule out the notion that the theorem was meant to deal mainly with things Greek? For after all, the Pythagorean theorem was articulated by a Greek, and Pythagoras was able to draw on the distinct achievements in his own culture, in the work of Greek mathematics. But once we grasp the theorem and its ingredients – that the square of the hypotenuse is equal to the sum of the squares of the two adjacent sides – we seem to grasp at the same

---

[19] Locke, Second Treatise on Civil Government, bk. I, ch. II, in *Social Contract*, Sir Ernest Barker, ed. (Oxford: Oxford Univerity Press, 1960), pp. 5–6. And for a fuller treatment of this matter, see my book, *First Things* (Princeton: Princeton University Press, 1986), pp. 33 ff.

[20] "Of the Law of Nature," in *The Works of James Wilson* (Cambridge: Harvard University Press, 1967; originally published in 1804), v. I, pp. 126–47, at 126.

time that the validity of the theorem is contained in the axioms and the reasons that bring it forth, and no one seems to presume that those reasons and axioms are confined to Greece. In the same way, the founders would have regarded it as quite as queer if anyone had remarked that he "believed" that "all men are created equal" – that human beings are radically different from animals. They would have found it, also, quaint or unintelligible if anyone had suggested that this proposition was distinctly "American" or "English," or that it should not hold true, as an axiom, anywhere else in the world.

By now it should not require any special burden of demonstration to show that lawyers and jurists of our own day simply do not have the same awareness of first principles and axioms that were incorporated, in that first generation, by jurists and lawyers of the caliber of Hamilton, Marshall, and Wilson. For lawyers in our own day seem serenely inattentive to the fact that they are running afoul of those axioms. They can often be found, then, backing into propositions that are self-contradictory, even as they offer them up as postulates that they apparently regard as self-evident. The most dramatic example here would have to be the proposition that has become, by now, the most well-traveled fallacy in politics and the law, in the West or the East. In this new popular refrain, offered in commentaries on the law by people in the know, the proposition runs esentially in this way: "If there were moral truths that held in all places, they would be universally recognized. But the very fact that there is such widespread, even universal, disagreement over the nature of the 'good' and the 'just' must itself stand as prima facie evidence that there are no such truths."

I have pointed out, in other places, that this argument is built on what the philosophers would call a self-refuting proposition: namely, that in the absence of a consensus, or the presence of a disagreement, there is no truth, and therefore no valid propositions that would justify legislation. I have made the simple point that I would myself object to *that* proposition, and by its own terms, that should be enough to establish its falsity.[21] If we were timing things, we would discover that this proposition self-destructs in about 10 seconds. And yet, it has been incorporated by many writers and jurists as the anchoring premise

[21] For an elaboration of the argument, see my book, *First Things* (Princeton: Princeton University Press, 1986), pp. 51–9, 132–8.

of their theories of justice. More than that, Justice Blackmun managed to found a whole new branch of our jurisprudence on this self-refuting proposition. With Blackmun's drafting, the proposition came out in this form:

> We need not resolve the difficult question of when life begins. When those trained in . . . medicine, philosophy, and theology are unable to arrive at any consensus, the judiciary, at this point in the development of man's knowledge, is not in a position to speculate as to the answer."[22]

That proposition, cast in a slightly different way, has been invoked by feminists in Ireland to "explain" why it is no longer tenable to have laws restricting abortion – for opinion is now so divided in Ireland on this question as it has not been in the past. But long before feminists in Ireland had picked up the refrain, the theme had been sounded in a central place by Professor John Rawls in *A Theory of Justice*: Liberal society should confirm a large degree of liberty by avoiding the temptation to legislate on those contentious moral questions that inspire a deep division in the country.[23] And on the other side, politically, I have more than one friend, among the judges, who have offered a "conservative" variation on this theme as part of a rejection of natural law. In this construal, we are faced with *contending moralities*, and the problem with natural law is that it does not elicit a universal acceptance. As the argument then goes, it should become necessary for the law to base itself on premises that enjoy a consensus, for any law that does not reflect a consensus is not apt to be enforceable as "law." In the meantime, the liberal commentators go on to draw the conclusion that people should be left free to follow their own, personal choices, in any matter of moral controversy.

All of these writers are no doubt aware that, in the middle of the nineteenth century, this country was deeply divided over slavery, and that a hundred years later it was divided over the Civil Rights Act of 1964. Are we to suppose that, under those conditions, it was somehow wrong for anyone to have formed moral judgments about slavery or

---

[22] *Roe v. Wade*, 410 U.S. 113, at 160.

[23] This critical premise runs, as a strand, through Rawls's book, and it is especially prominent in the first chapter, when he sets in place the groundwork for his argument and explains the so-called "original position." See John Rawls, *A Theory of Justice* (Cambridge: Harvard University Press, 1971), pp. 5, 12, 16, 18, 21.

racial discrimination, and deeply wrong to have legislated upon those judgments? But I raise the matter for the sake of taking it from a slightly different angle, expressed by one of my friends, a conservative jurist: that we do not have tenable grounds on which to legislate in the absence of a consensus. The question that the natural lawyer would raise at this point is, Do we have a *consensus on that proposition* – the proposition that we may not legislate in the absence of a consensus? Had the conservative jurist taken a survey and discovered that this rule of construction was itself voted in by the *consensus* of the public? If that is the claim, I'd have to report that I never received my ballot. I would not have voted for this proposition, and it would not, then, have garnered a "consensus." But the question merely points up the fact that the conservative judge did not derive this rule from any consensus, achieved in any survey of the public. He offers this rule because he apparently thinks it valid on its own terms; that it is true, as we used to say, *per se nota.* To borrow language from Hamilton, that proposition seems to contain, for him, "an internal evidence, which antecedent to all reflection or combination, commands the assent of the mind." In other words, the proposition is treated by the conservative jurist as though it has the properties of an axiom or a first principle. Without being quite aware of it, we would have backed into the logic of "first principles"; we would be speaking again the language of natural law. I happen to think, of course, that my friend's construction of the first principle here cannot be tenable. Still, it is cheery to note that, on his construction, we would have access to certain truths that did not depend in the least on a consensus, or agreement, in the country. And if there is at least one proposition of that kind, which may form the ground of our judgments in the law, there seems to be a lively possibility of discovering others.

But when did it begin, this drift of lawyers away from that vivid awareness of axioms and first principles that was a common trait among the founders? The irony is that it began just at the moment when the understanding of natural rights achieved its most telling victory, in the gravest crisis of our politics, the crisis of our "house divided." In the classic debate between Abraham Lincoln and Stephen Douglas, Lincoln had represented the tradition of natural law, while Douglas expressed the purest form of legal "positivism," with all of its shadings of moral relativism: For Douglas, there were no truths grounded in the "nature" of human beings, truths that would hold their truth in all places where human nature remained the same. And therefore, there were no "rights" arising from that nature wherever "human" beings might be found. The measure of morality would be found in the understandings that were dominant in any place, so dominant that they could be "posited" or enacted into law by the people with the power to rule. But less than 30 years after Lincoln's cause had triumphed on the battlefield, the intellectual currents among the educated were running in quite another direction. The end of the nineteenth century would find the advent of law schools, and Douglas's positivism would become the reigning orthodoxy in these new schools, teaching a "science" of law. By our own day, the lawyers and judges who emerged from those schools would hardly be aware that there had ever been a serious debate on these questions.[24] In this movement, Justice Oliver Wendell Holmes had been a representative figure, both reflecting and shaping this change in the legal culture, with his lectures at Harvard and his writings on the bench. With his characteristic terseness, or his lunge toward aphorism, Holmes marked the new sensibility, and in one revealing sentence he seemed to define the character of the modern project in the law. Holmes thought it would be a notable gain if "every word of moral significance could be banished from the law altogether, and other words adopted which should convey legal ideas uncolored by anything outside the law."[25]

This perspective, so startling in its expression, has become remarkably unnoticeable as it has worked itself into the reflexes of legislators and politicians, where it takes forms of this kind: The authorities in

---

[24] This sobering point was brought home to me quite concretely and personally several years ago, when Professor Robert George invited me to participate in some seminars he was running for federal judges at Princeton University. The "students" in the seminar were given, among other things, an exchange I had with Robert Bork over the problem of natural rights and positivism. Two of the judges, evidently quite taken by the exchange, were candid enough to remark that this was the first time they had ever encountered a statement of the argument for natural rights. And there was ample reason to suspect that they were not alone among the judges.

[25] See Holmes, "The Path of the Law," in *Collected Legal Papers* (New York: Harcourt Brace and Co., 1920), p. 179. For a recent commentary on this address by Holmes, as the beginning of a new phase in the philosophy of law, see Robert P. George, "What is Law? A Century of Arguments," in *First Things* (April 2001), pp. 23–9.

New York City are pressed to do something about the culture of prostitution, blighting several neighborhoods, but in a liberal city, they do not wish to say that consenting adults may be condemned in the law for their sexual relations. It becomes important, that is, that the law not utter, officially, any words of distinct "moral" significance. Instead, the legislators try to discourage brothels by insisting that any establishment calling itself a "massage parlor" must contain a swimming pool or a squash court. And more than that, the squash court must have these dimensions: 25 feet wide, 45 feet long, 20 feet high. As I have had the occasion to put it elsewhere, these are the kinds of rituals of empty exactitude that legislators produce when they cannot name the real object of their concern, or explain why the law is justified in addressing a distinctly "moral" issue.[26] In this way, the Holmesian perspective turns itself into a routine burlesque in the law. But as soon as the law offers a parody of itself, we find a jurist who proclaims these doctrines quite earnestly. In our own time, that jurist turns out to be Justice David Souter, who had done his undergraduate thesis at Harvard on Holmes. For Souter, as for Holmes, it is critical that the law never invoke, as the ground of its action, any distinctly "moral" concern. And so, when Souter turns to the question of prostitution, or nude dancing in public, he insists that the law can reach these matters only when they produce harmful "secondary effects": The presence of prostitution or tawdry entertainments may become baneful for a community as they draw muggers and pickpockets, and foster a climate of violence. But then again, pickpockets and muggers may be drawn by games at Yankee Stadium, or by the prospect of crowds gathered at Grand Central Station on Fridays. Yet, the predictable rise in crime, associated with these scenes or entertainments, has not supplied us with any ground for banning the ball games or the commuting. At a certain point the law may make sense only if it could say, in the voice of Justice Scalia, in a case about nude dancing in bars, that the legislators of Indiana meant to ban the public display of genitals, not because of any speculation about "secondary effects," and "not because they harm others but because they are considered, in the traditional phrase, 'contra bonos mores,' i.e., immoral":

---

[26] The reader may wish to consult, on this point, my book, *The Philosopher in the City* (Princeton: Princeton University Press, 1981), pp. 399–406.

> The purpose of the Indiana statute is to enforce the traditional moral belief that people should not expose their private parts indiscriminately, regardless of whether those who see them are disedified.[27]

At the turn of the century, young Learned Hand, as an undergraduate, would be affected by the same currents felt by Holmes before him, and by the currents at work in the teaching of philosophy at Harvard. From William James and Josiah Royce and others he would incorporate a kind of genteel skepticism, dressed up with "pragmatism," and a new vocabulary with academic trappings. But what was produced was a new kind of affectation among the intellectual classes: the writers, the judges, would mark their sensibility by professing, at every turn, their doubts, their uncertainties, about "truths," and especially the truths that marked "first principles." They would be left then, of course, with the intuitions that sprung from their own exquisite sensibilities. Learned Hand would become the most accomplished of judges, widely respected, and rightly admired as a common law judge. When he concentrated his genius on issues of copyrights and patents, he would write with a remarkable spareness, and with a literary craft that could claim its place in the guild of professional writers.[28] But when this highly tutored man would turn to questions of constitutional law, or become more self-consciously philosophic, he would be marked by a mannered aversion to "absolutes." And that

---

[27] *Barnes v. Glen Theatre*, 115 L Ed 2d 504, at 517, (1991). Scalia pointed out also that the Holmesian view of morality and law had never been incorporated in the Constitution. "Our society," he wrote, had never shared that " 'you-may-do-what-you-like-so-long-as-it-does-not-injure-someone-else' beau ideal," and much less had it ever thought that position to be "written into the Constitution." He went on to remark that "In American society, such prohibitions have included, for example, sadomasochism, cockfighting, bestiality, suicide, drug use, prostitution, and sodomy. While there may be great diversity of view on whether various of these prohibitions should exist (though I have found few ready to abandon, in principle, all of them), there is no doubt that, absent specific constitutional protection for the conduct involved, the Constitution does not prohibit them simply because they regulate 'morality.' "

[28] In this respect, one could hardly find a better example of the judicial craft, or even an example of the craft of writing, than Hand's opinion in *Sheldon v. Metro Goldwyn Pictures*, 81 F. 2d 49 (1936), a case in which Hand offered three precis covering two plays and a motion picture, and then wove his judgment with an acuity that was distinctly philosophic.

reflex would produce in him a shallowness that reflected the public philosophy of his age.

That theme of recoiling from "absolutes" has been picked up by his most recent biographer, a professor of law who had been a clerk to Hand. The result was that Professor Gerald Gunther began to see the cases, and the world, through the same cliches that acted as a screen to Hand, and prevented that urbane man from seeing what was before him.[29] The screening was quite instructive, and it was illustrated in a telling way in the account offered both by Hand and by Gunther of George Sutherland's opinion in *Adkins v. Children's Hospital.* In that case, Sutherland, a leader in the cause of votes for women, saw himself as acting on the same principles when he struck down a law mandating minimum wages for women in the District of Columbia. But when Hand (and Gunther) characterized Sutherland's argument, they viewed the opinion through the lens of positivism: Sutherland's distinctly jural argument, arranged in layers, was entirely flattened into the conclusion that Sutherland was merely being wilfull, that he disliked the legislation at hand, or that the legislation collided with his predilections. The reasoning offered by Sutherland was never reported or addressed, and along with everything else lost from view in this case were the circumstances of the injured party. Nowhere in the account of Hand or Professor Gunther was there any mention of Willie Lyons, forced out of her job at the Congress Hotel, as a result of the law on minimum wages for women in the District of Columbia. In other words, the teaching had taken hold: What Hand had screened from view was now screened from the sight of his admirers. In the story of Hand and the judges around him, the villains for Professor Gunther were marked by the judges who were "never tortured by doubt." Hand might differ strongly at times with Holmes, and yet, as Gunther remarked, "they shared a common philosophic outlook," quite representative of the circles, and the schools, from which they had sprung. "Neither," said Gunther, "believed in absolutes or eternal truths."

Hand never made it to the Supreme Court, but he would later recommend to President Eisenhower the appointment of his colleague on the federal court of appeals for the Second Circuit (in New York), the redoubtable John Marshall Harlan. Harlan was the grandson of a

---

[29] See Gerald Gunther, *Learned Hand, the Man and the Judge* (1994), pp. 374–5.

famous justice of the Supreme Court bearing the same name, the man who had offered the ringing dissent against racial segregation in *Plessy v. Ferguson* ("the Constitution is color-blind"). The original John Marshall Harlan had come from Kentucky, but the grandson came from the schools and the corporate world of the east coast, and he would be as reflective of those circles as Hand. Toward the end of his career, this supposedly conservative judge would help advance the cause of sexual liberation by helping to strike down the laws on contraception. But he would astound observers, in 1971, with an opinion on "political speech" that would bring jurisprudence on the First Amendment into a new register. And yet, in that famous case of *Cohen v. California*, Harlan had simply advanced the strands of moral skepticism that he had inherited from Hand and Holmes.

It is one of those ironies of our own times that Harlan could gain a reputation for novelty and inventiveness in the law when he simply "discovered," for the courts, the doctrines of "logical postivism" about 30 years after they had been refuted in the schools of philosophy. Still, they had been much in fashion when Harlan had been in school, and he could draw upon them now with all of the freshness of his own youth. As the key to the case, Harlan offered the cliche that would become, for many judges, their signature tune on matters of the First Amendment: "One man's vulgarity is another's lyric."[30] Speech on matters of moral and political significance was all "subjective" in nature. For, as logical positivism had instructed Harlan's generation, there were no "truths" that could anchor our judgments on matters of morality and justice. Statements about the things that were right or wrong, just or unjust, were essentially "emotive" in character. There was nothing "cognitive" about them, no propositions that could be weighed for their truth or falsity.

And so restrictions on speech simply reflected the passions and the emotions of the people who made the laws. In *Cohen*, a young man, in the turbulent days of 1968, had walked into a crowded courthouse in Los Angeles, wearing a jacket that bore the inscription "Fuck the Draft." The intention was clearly to provoke, with the conscious use of a shocking, gross expression, not part of civil discourse – or not at least yet. But Harlan, with an affectation of philosophy, professed now his

[30] 403 U.S 15 (1971), at 25.

want of surety in unlocking the meaning of the words. "How is one to distinguish this [word]," he asked, "from any other offensive word?" He insisted that there was "no readily ascertainable general principle" by which one could draw distinctions. That is to say, there were no principled grounds on which the authorities, or anyone else, could distinguish between the speech that was assaulting or innocent, threatening or inoffensive. And for that sovereign reason, Harlan declared now with his colleagues that the decision as to what language is fit for a public place must be left "largely [in] the hands of each of us."[31]

It was understood in the past that when people ventured into public, they had an obligation to restrain themselves out of a respect for the sensibilities of others in a public place. But now Harlan and his colleagues, with their relativism, had switched the presumptions and the burdens: People who used uncivil gestures and assaulting words would have a presumptive "right" to speak. The burden would fall now on the victims, or the passersby, to avert their eyes or develop tougher skin. For years, urbanists had been urging planners to arrange cities in such a way that they would facilitate the encounter of strangers: They preferred public transport to the privacy of automobiles; they would contrive parks and benches where strangers could meet while at lunch. But now Justice Harlan and his colleagues, with this access of novelty, had undermined the moral framework for these policies of urbanism. For the teaching in *Cohen* would make it hazardous for people to venture out, especially at night, into public places. Throughout the country it suddenly became harder for the police to enforce the laws on loitering, to remove the aggressive hawkers and beggars who would virtually take over prominent corners in the city. In Washington, restaurants would go out of business on Connecticut Avenue near Dupont Circle as their customers finally became reluctant to move through the gauntlet of exotic characters, importuning and insulting them as they made their way along the public paths.

With this small move, Harlan would trigger nothing less than a minor revolution in our civic life and the jurisprudence of the First Amendment. And yet, there was the most telling discord between the argument he was forced to make for the subjective nature of offensive or assaulting speech, and the argument he had to put in place to

---

[31] *Ibid.*, at 24.

establish the claim of this speech to constitutional protection. Harlan assumed that the "speech" contained on Cohen's jacket had a claim to constitutional protection because it was "political"; it conveyed a sentiment dealing with a matter of public controversy. According to Harlan, what Cohen was doing with his jacket was "asserting [a] position on the inutility or immorality of the draft."[32] But there was a point to be made by taking Harlan at his word and asking just which one, exactly, he thought Cohen meant. Was "Fuck the Draft" merely a shorthand expression for: the draft was "inutile"? Or that the draft was "immoral"? A tenable point was served in pointing out that the sign did not necessarily mean either one: The profanity on the jacket was meant to mock with its grossness; it lacked the precision of analytic prose, particularly when it was applied to matters of public policy, where it mocked by its gross lack of relevance. Yet, in one respect Harlan's reading was correct, but on grounds that contradicted his argument at the root: What we knew of Cohen's sign was that it condemned or denounced the draft. But we knew that mainly because he drew upon a word that was established, in the currency of ordinary language, as a term of condemnation, derision, or profane insult. We knew it, that is, because the meaning of words was not subjective and arbitrary. And in the same way we knew that he was referring to the military "draft." Someone who had taken Harlan's argument with literal seriousness might have turned around and insisted that all the words were entirely "subjective," and so how could we know that Cohen was not referring to a "draft" in the sense of wind? How did we know then that Cohen was not enjoining us, perhaps in a spirit of paganism, to "make love to the wind"?

But we could know that Cohen was making a political speech precisely because words are not subjective in their import, and we could know these things for the same reasons that were brought forth, years earlier, to refute logical positivism: The functions of condemning or commending, of deriding or applauding, are moral functions, and they are rooted in our language. The words that carry these functions may change over time, but the functions persist, and if they do, it must be possible for most people to understand at any moment the words that are established in our language as terms of rebuke or praise. In this

[32] *Ibid.*, at 18.

exercise, of gauging ordinary usage – of recognizing insults, say, when we hear them – the judgments of truck drivers can be quite as reliable as the reactions of doctors and lawyers. But that moral function will always be contained in our language, because it is part of the constitution of our own natures, as moral beings. As Aristotle recognized, that animal with the gift of language bore a capacity to give reasons over matters and right and wrong, and something in his nature made him tend, irrepressibly, to the casting of moral judgments.

There was a flickering moment, in the early 1980s, when this awkwardness began to break in on the recognitions of Justice Byron White. The Court was faced with a case in which a group of Evangelical students was denied a place to meet and hold sessions of prayer on a campus of the University of Missouri (*Widmar v. Vincent* [1982]). The Court came to rescue of the "Cornerstone" group in this case, and protected the right of these students to meet on the campus. But the Court did not reach that judgment out of any particular respect for religion, or for the importance of religion in a republic. Rather, the Court arrived at its judgment merely as a further inference along the chain that began with *Cohen v. California*: It was inadmissible for a public university to discriminate against religious groups because it was illegitimate for anyone in authority to make discriminations based on the content of speech. Justice White had folded himself into the majority in *Cohen v. California*, but now it rather dawned on him, a trifle late, that the Court could not coherently build its jurisprudence on the notion that there was something radically subjective about speech. As White observed, the Court had evolved an elaborate jurisprudence as it sought to mark off the proper boundaries between religion and the state. And yet, all of that presupposed that it was possible to tell the difference between the "speech acts" that were religious or nonreligious. White pointed out in this vein that "as a speech act, apart from its content, a prayer is indistinguishable from a biology lesson." And with the same lens, a mass held at the university could be "indistinguishable from a class entitled, 'The History of the Catholic Church.' "[33] In this brief moment, White recognized that jurisprudence could not be constructed, at any point, on premises of relativism; but then he folded himself in once again with his colleagues,

---

[33] *Widmar v. Vincent*, 70 L Ed 2d 440, at 457 (1982).

continuing as best he could to alter here and there a fabric of law that was threaded through with faulty strands. By the time the Court reached the burning of crosses in the early 1990s, White found himself slightly incredulous, but incapable now of producing a dissenting opinion. For even he could not detach himself from the jurisprudence that he had helped to shape over 30 years. Conservatives, as well as liberals, were committed now to the notion that there was something about speech too subjective in character, too elusive in meaning, and beyond that, there were no standards of truth by which people in authority could distinguish any longer between the speech directed to ends that were legitimate or illegitimate.

But as White seemed to recognize, even people of ordinary wit suffer no philosophic strain in distinguishing between words that are meant as praise and words that are meant as attacks. And yet, thanks to Harlan and his colleagues in *Cohen v. California*, the law would be founded from that time forward on entirely different premises. The conviction would take hold, among conservative as well as liberal judges, that it was not legitimate or possible for the authorities to make discriminations based on the "content" of speech. The Supreme Court would strike down then any attempt to ban gestures of disrespect for the American flag, as with the burning or desecration of the flag. As Justice Brennan would explain, the Constitution made it untenable now for anyone in official authority to establish what may be orthodox or illegitimate to express through the treatment of a flag in symbolic expression.[34]

---

[34] If we were to hold that a State may forbid flag burning wherever it is likely to endanger the flag's symbolic role, but allow it wherever burning a flag promotes that role – as where, for example, a person ceremoniously burns a dirty flag – we would be saying that when it comes to impairing the flag's physical integrity, the flag itself may be used as a symbol – as a substitute for the written or spoken word or a "short cut from mind to mind" – only in one direction. We would be permitting a State to "prescribe what shall be orthodox" by saying that one may burn the flag to convey one's attitude toward it and its referents only if one does not endanger the flag's representation of nationhood and national unity.

We never before have held that the Government may ensure that a symbol be used to express only one view of that symbol or its referents. . . .

Texas v. Johnson, 491 U.S. 397, at 416–17 (1989). In the coming years, the liberal heirs of Brennan would bring the same conviction to the problem even as they carved out a massive exemption for this jurisprudence of the First Amendment: There would be no discriminations based on the content of the speech – unless the case involved protestors outside of abortion clinics. See *Madsen v. Women's Health Center, Inc.*, 512 U.S. 753 (1994), and *Hill v. Colorado*, 530 U.S. 703 (2000).

Some of us, still harboring the fragments of illusion, thought that the judges could not be fully serious, for what would they do when they encountered the case of burning crosses? The comedian Mark Russell once told the story of a family of Unitarians who moved into a Southern town, and in the middle of the night a group of bigots burned, on their lawn, a large question mark. Surely one could tell the difference, say, between a burning question mark and a burning cross. The former may be puzzling, but the latter has been invested with a rather definite meaning in our language and experience. Even one barely attentive to his times would understand that the presence of a burning cross, in the neighborhood, marked a problem or a crisis. And that man of ordinary wit would surely be able to tell the difference between a cross used for devotional purposes, in Christian services, and a cross used for the sake of terrorizing black people.

Yet, when a case of that kind made its way to the Supreme Court, the judges came together unanimously in striking down the attempt of the law to recognize those differences and forbid those forms of "expression" that constitute assaults. In *R.A.V. v. St. Paul* (1992),[35] the city of St. Paul had banned the burning of crosses, along with other forms of gestures and speech that were, in effect, performative acts of assault directed at groups defined by race, ethnicity, gender, and religion. It was a telling sign that the main opinion in the case was written by Justice Antonin Scalia, who had become the leading voice of conservative jurisprudence on the Court. Scalia registered an apt concern about speech that would be focused on political adversaries. If there were restrictions on assaulting speech, it was critical that the measures remain "neutral" in regard to their political tendency. For example, there could be laws barring political signs near polling places, but those laws could not be applied only to Republicans rather than Democrats. There could be a ban on "hateful" speech, but those laws could not be used in a manipulative way, to ban speech that was critical of gays, and yet not ban the kind of speech that smeared other people as "homophobes."

In all of this there was a point, and yet there was also a point gravely missed: There was in fact a species of defamation or assault, quite distinct and knowable, which acquired its viciousness as it diffused its

[35] *R.A.V. v. St. Paul*, 505 U.S. 377 (1992).

attacks on whole groups defined by race or ethnicity. The notion of group libel was taken quite seriously after the Second World War, as governments in Europe sought to foreclose the calumnies, the campaigns of vilification, which had been directed at Jews. In America, a comparable concern for the treatment of blacks, and the fomenting of racial riots, had found expression in the framing of comparable laws.[36] But Scalia thought there was a kind of symmetry in attacking say, Catholics as a group, and in attacking, in turn, the bigots who were "anti-Papist." He thought it revealed, quite sharply, the political tilt hidden in this legislation that "one could hold up a sign saying, for example, that all 'anti-Catholic bigots' are misbegotten; but not that all 'papists' are, for that would insult and provoke violence 'on the basis of religion.'"[37] Yet, if there was in fact a deep wrong in attacking people, not on account of their own acts, but on account of their race or religion, then there was no parity here. The person who objected to this kind of speech could not be seen simply as a different species of bigot, attacking another class of people (namely, those "spirited" people who burn crosses or attack others on the basis of their race or ethnicity). But in the meantime, Scalia and his colleagues seemed to confirm, ever more deeply, the moral skepticism that was engrafted onto the law by Justice Harlan in the Cohen case. The judges were unanimous now in holding that people in authority could not be trusted to make judgments about the content of speech, because there was no conviction, in the end, that there were grounds for judging the rightness or wrongness of the political ends that animated that speech.

And so, 30 years after *Cohen v. California* we find the melancholy fading of any differences on this matter between the conservative and liberal judges. It was no surprise then that conservative jurists, for the most part, were as dubious about natural law, or "moral truths," as the liberal judges and their allies in the academy, who taught the gospel of "postmodernism" and "multiculturalism." Clarence Thomas stood,

---

[36] The philosophic case, or the justification, for these kinds of laws I sought to make at length in my book, *The Philosopher in the City* (1981), *supra*, n. 26, chs. II–III. An earlier statement of the argument appeared under the title, "Civility and the Restriction of Speech," in Philip B. Kurland, ed. *The Supreme Court Review* 1974 (Chicago: University of Chicago Press, 1975), pp. 281–335.

[37] *Supra*, n. 35, at 391–2.

in this company, as a notable exception, or as a judge trying at least to recall the origins of the American law in "natural rights." But most of his colleagues in the courts reacted with a bemused tolerance, or with scornful dismissiveness, if anyone raised the notion of natural rights, or earnestly claimed to know of certain anchoring truths that were more than merely conventional.

All of that was taken as so much twaddle, or as a reflection of the innocence of an earlier age, when judges shared the "faith," then in fashion, that there were moral truths, or principles of right and wrong, that would be at all times the same. But that conviction was taken seriously only by a handful of judges, among the conservatives or the liberals. In that respect, as Henry James might have said, the jurisprudence of conservative and liberal judges offered "simply different chapters of the same general subject."

But without the moral premises of the founders, it is not at all clear as to what would form the ground of jurisprudence in this new age, delivered from those superstitions of the past. Was the substance of justice simply established through a flexing of power, as when a proposition was enacted into law by a majority, or simply proclaimed as "law" by people in authority? In our own day, it has become fashionable among commentators of the law to deride the notion of "substantive due process" as an oxymoron: If something is substantive, it cannot be merely procedural, or a matter of "process." But that awkward expression of "substantive due process" captures the understanding that ran to the root for the founders. Daniel Webster once traced matters back to that root, when he argued before the Supreme Court in the Dartmouth College case (1819). He encountered there the contention, often heard in our own day, that the "due course and process of law" is satisfied if property has been taken, say, through a deliberate act of a legislature, lawfully constituted to act. Webster then crystallized the problem in this way:

> By the law of the land is most clearly intended the general law; a law, which hears before it condemns; which proceeds upon inquiry, and renders judgment only after trial. The meaning is, that every citizen shall hold his life, liberty, property, and immunities, under the protection of the general rules which govern society. Every thing which may pass under the form of an enactment, is not, therefore, to be considered the law of the land. If this were so, acts of attainder, bills of pains and

penalties, acts of confiscation, acts reversing judgments, and acts directly transferring one man's estate to another, legislative judgments, decrees, and forfeitures, in all possible forms, would be the law of the land. Such a strange construction would render constitutional provisions of the highest importance completely inoperative and void. It would tend directly to establish the union of all powers in the legislature. There would be no general permanent law for courts to administer, or for men to live under. The administration of justice would be an empty form, an idle ceremony.[38]

In his notable lectures on jurisprudence in 1790, James Wilson could encompass the novel point that the American law began by actually incorporating a principle of revolution: It began with the recognition that there could be a wrongful law. Yet, that conclusion emerged only because Wilson, and the founders, began with a lively sense of natural rights. They were aware, that is, of substantive principles of justice that could be used then to judge the rightness or wrongness of any measure enacted in the positive law.[39]

For the jurists of our own time, this sentiment seems quite uplifting, laudable, even if they do not quite believe it. Liberal professors of law are especially willing to speak words of this kind as they encourage judges to engage their powers of office, in defending certain "rights" against the opinions of the public, reflected in legislatures. But that flexing of power could be justified only when the judges appealed to a standard of right and wrong apart from the votes of a majority. Liberal jurists and professors have been quite willing for judges to exercise that power when it comes to articulating certain rights to sexual "privacy," such as a "right to abortion" or a right to homosexuality. And yet, their ethic of liberation has proclaimed itself by declaring an emancipation from the constraints of moral truths. And so professors such as Ronald Dworkin or Laurence Tribe have been willing to have judges impose whole new ensembles of law, even when it means overriding moral sentiments held deeply among the

---

[38] *Dartmouth College v. Woodward*, 17 U.S. (4 Wheat.) 518 (1819), at 581–2.

[39] See Wilson's First Lecture on the Law, in *The Works of James Wilson*, ed. Robert Green McCloskey (Cambridge: Harvard University Press, 1967; originally published in 1804), v. I, p. 79. "A revolution principle," he said, "certainly is, and certainly should be taught as a principle for the constitution of the United States, and of every State in the Union."

public. Yet, at the same time, they have carefully avoided any claim that they are appealing to moral truths or natural law. And so, Professor Dworkin makes the most sweeping claim for an "empire" of law based on "principle." But the foundation for his judgments he finds in "a nation's political traditions and culture" – a formula that, in the nineteenth century, would have encompassed slavery in America. As for Professor Tribe, he has been quite emphatic in his judgments, but at the same time he has warned that, "even if we could settle on firm constitutional postulates, we would remain inescapably subjective" in the application of those postulates. In the end, as he says, he would fall back simply on convictions "powerfully held."[40] But of course, if it were a matter simply of posing the beliefs held firmly by judges, against the convictions held tenaciously by the public, it is not clear why the beliefs of judges, merely as *beliefs*, claimed a higher authority.

That none of this could supply the substance of a moral judgment, or a moral justification for any measure of law, should be clear even to youngsters who are beginners in the study of the law. But it can be plain to them only because they are, as reasoners, still anchored in the axioms that govern people of ordinary sense, rather than beings steeped in layers of "legal theory." That daunting spectacle, "legal theory," springs from the "science" of law that marked the advent of law schools. This "science" may take different paths, with different levels of refinement and perversity, but it will still be built upon the premises of legal positivism. Writers such as Dworkin and Tribe may strike off works that are discriminably their own, but they may be counted on, in one way or another, to adopt formulas that allow them to finesse the existence of moral truths. Their works will be layered with moral judgments, and they could be relied on to produce, through the clouds of heavy theory, the conclusions that just happen to coincide with the conclusions of liberal jurisprudence. But moral truths there must needs be – or propositions, we might say, that function, for Dworkin and Tribe, as moral truths. These estimable writers will supply an understanding of the things that are desirable, just, right; they will supply, indeed, the grounds that may entail

---

[40] See Laurence Tribe, *Constitutional Choices* (Cambridge: Harvard University Press, 1985), pp. 5, 6, 8.

practical judgments; and yet it will all be done while professing at every step that no moral judgments are being imposed on anyone. But with this kind of charade, our professors and judges drift ever further from the understanding of the founders, the only understanding that offers a coherent account of this regime of freedom and natural rights that the founders had established. The conceit of the new men in the law consists in this: They are evidently persuaded that the freedoms and the constitutional rights that they trumpet in this regime can really be detached from the moral foundations on which it was built and justified.

James Wilson insisted that the law in America would trace back simply to the understanding of "man," weighing his consent. And by "man," the founders would understand, with Aristotle, that primate who was distinctly suited to the polis, and the world of law, because he could "declare what is just and what is unjust." But even that elementary sense of things, and the implications tucked away in it, may be quite removed from the understandings held by our recent judges. The late Thurgood Marshall offers a sufficient, and preeminent, example. In the case of *Rhode Island v. Innis* (1980), a man was arrested for committing armed robbery with a sawed-off shotgun. On the way to the police station the officers in the car fell into a conversation about the missing shotgun. One officer remarked that there was a school for handicapped children in the area and "God forbid one of them might find a weapon with shells and they might hurt themselves." After several more minutes of this conversation, staged for the benefit of the man in custody, the suspect finally responded to the veiled appeal. He told the police he would lead them to the weapon. The police issued his "Miranda warning," he understood that he had a right to remain silent – and still he led the police to the gun. With the gun as evidence, the man was eventually convicted for kidnaping, robbery, and murder. But then, his lawyers appealed the conviction on the ground that he had been coerced or manipulated, even though he had never been beaten or intimidated into confessing. The Supreme Court upheld this conviction, but over the protest of Justice Marshall. Yet, what was the problem? Marshall complained that

> one can scarcely imagine a stronger appeal to the conscience of a suspect – any suspect – than the assertion that if the weapon is not found an innocent person will be hurt or killed. And not just any innocent person,

but an innocent child – a little girl – a helpless, handicapped little girl on her way to school.[41]

What could have been lower than that?: to appeal to the conscience of a defendant! In the world of law as it was envisaged by Thurgood Marshall, the human being who formed the object of jurisprudence was apparently not a being constituted in any significant way by a "moral" sense. He was not the kind of being who might feel guilt, or a need for confession or repentance. Nor could he have any plausible interest in avoiding harm to the innocent as a means of avoiding a deepening of his crime. The object of law or jurisprudence for Marshall was evidently Hobbesian man: a forked creature whose over-riding interest, whose chief animating motive, was self-preservation and the avoidance of pain. For a being constituted in that way it could never be "rational" to confess to wrongdoing and open himself to punishment. And so any appeal to his so-called conscience was an appeal for him to collaborate in his own punishment. Therefore it could be seen only as a form of manipulation; manipulation was a form of extracting evidence unfairly; and so the eliciting of evidence in this way had to be "unconstitutional."

In this manner, with the most unremarkable chain of steps, a genera-tion of jurists has incorporated premises that are at war with the moral grounds of anything that could call itself jurisprudence. And in a manner strange, yet equally unremarkable, even conservative jurists have absorbed the same premises from other angles. I mentioned previously an argument struck off even by some conservative judges, who expressed a sentiment heard commonly in their circles when they registered their dubiety about "natural law": The maxims of natural law, they thought, were so lofty and hazy that they had no objective standing, and they gave rise to persisting disagreements. As the argu-ment ran, there was no consensus on the principles of natural law, and therefore they could not supply the principles that judges could bring to bear in deciding cases.

But if there is never a consensus on matters of morality, then we must be driven back to the interests or the passions that we can count on all men possessing, quite detached from any moral sense. And that

[41] *Rhode Island v. Innis,* 446 U.S. 291, at 311 (1980).

interest will be, of course, that sovereign interest in self-preservation and the avoidance of pain. When the conservative jurists reject, out of hand, the prospect of knowing any "first principles" of a moral character, they too back into the notion of Hobbesian man. That calculating animal, detached from moral reflexes of any kind, becomes for the conservatives, no less than the liberals, the ground and the measure of our jurisprudence.

At the beginning of the law under the new Constitution, James Wilson could observe, in those lines quoted earlier, that the law in America would not begin with the notion of a sovereign issuing commands. It would begin "with another principle, very different in its nature and operations": "[L]aws derived from the pure source of equality and justice must be founded on the consent of those, whose obedience they require. The sovereign, when traced to his source, must be found in the *man*."[42] That notion of a natural "man" contained the moral world that separated the law in America from the things that came before; it would be the mark of the Novus Ordo Seclorum, a new order for the ages. The simple notion of a man extending or withholding consent incorporated the sense of human beings as "moral agents" or "creatures of reason," who could reason about the grounds of their well-being, and the things that were just or unjust. But now, as a result, quite precisely, of the doctrines put in place by judges over the past 40 years, that notion of a "man" has been dismantled, layer by layer. That original, jural man, contemplated in our law, has become, in a way, like the "Thin Man" in the famous story by Dashiell Hammett. He is fading away, becoming ever thinner, as the search for him continues. In the case of that jural "man," the man who formed, for Wilson and the founders, the very ground and object of our jurisprudence, the dismantling has proceeded through these stages:

First, there is the truncating of "man" from the man who is a moral being, as Thomas Reid said, by the "constitution" of his nature. By the insistence of the judges, conservative as well as liberal, the law must detach itself from any claims to know moral truths, even the minimal truths that would have to be understood by a man who claims the capacity to make moral judgments. The law must start, as Thurgood

---

[42] *Chisholm v. Georgia*, 2 Dallas 419, at 458 (1793).

Marshall suggested, by ruling out any definition of a man with distinctly moral reflexes. But that means, in turn, that it must rule out any recognition of a "moral law" beyond his own self-interest or self-preservation, a law that can guide his moral reasoning. To install the notion of a man constituted in that way is to take the first step in creating a new fiction: a law without moral judgments or moral purpose – a law, as Holmes said, from which words of moral significance have been banished altogether. The pretense here is that the law begins with the unwillingness to impose understandings of morality on its citizens. But that is a fiction, and a rather thin fiction at that, because the practitioners of this law are doing nothing less than imposing moral judgments. They are simply imposing moral judgments under a slogan of rejecting "judgmentalism." They do it, that is, for the purpose of rejecting the traditional morality, which had cast the most emphatic moral judgments in restricting sexual freedom. But that traditional morality did not act in the name of blind aversion. It cast prohibitions, and yet it did that out of a conception of the kind of framework that was more fitting and necessary to the moral significance of sexuality.

As the second step, the judges have installed a new license to take human life. They have installed that license under a new name and done something radically new in the western tradition: they have established a "right to abortion" utterly unqualified and unrestricted. That right, created entirely by judges, extends through the entire length of a pregnancy, and permits a woman to take the life of the child in the womb for virtually any reason, whether serious or casual. Whether the pregnancy threatens her life, or whether it threatens mainly her convenience or her plans for a career, it does not matter. There is no need even to offer reasons to justify the abortion; and of course, there are no arrangements set in place that would allow those reasons to be judged. But this matter has been freighted with significance since ancient times precisely because of the awareness that the lives extinguished in abortions are human lives. If they were not, the prospect of an "unwanted" pregnancy could hardly be very disturbing. It would require then expedients no more serious than the expedients necessary to deal, say, with an unwanted bird, or an unwanted orange.

With the advent of *Roe v. Wade*, the annual volume of abortions rose to about 1.5 million, and in recent years has tapered off slightly to about 1.3 million. In a conservative estimate, the years since *Roe v. Wade* have brought about 40 million abortions. But even a population morally anesthetized cannot settle in easily with the notion of killing human beings on that vast scale, and so the work of the judges, in creating this new license, had to beget even further works of imagination: People had to talk themselves into the notion that these beings, conceived by homo sapiens, carried in the wombs of women, were not really human beings – or at least not quite yet. This shift in labeling was not exactly easy to do if one had even a rudimentary knowledge of biology. And it was especially improbable in the light of what modern embryology was able to teach about the human embryo. But the powers of rationalization have been such that even people holding degrees from expensive colleges have been willing to affect, in public, that they have no firm knowledge of what is in a woman's womb. The founders had begun with the sense of something of moral importance attaching to human persons. And yet, for the sake of making us all more suggestible to a new right to abortion, the judges had to begin teaching a novel doctrine: that the taking of human life was not as portentous a thing as we used to think, because we are no longer as sure as we were in the past in our sense of what a human being is.

In the third step, that question of just what is a human being is converted into a matter now in dispute, and the presence of a dispute points to the power of someone in authority to resolve that dispute. The polity had begun with the sense of an association distinctly suited to that being of a certain nature, who was, Aristotle said, neither a beast nor a god. Indeed, we could have a polity, an association marked by law, only because there were beings of that nature. But now, in a reversal, it is *political power itself that will determine just who is a human being.* It is a decision to be made by people possessed of power, and that exercise of power is no longer to be tested by any standard outside itself. For apparently, there is no independent or objective measure of what constitutes a human being; a measure that would allow us to judge whether political power has been used here rightly or wrongly.

The momentum, then, that has brought forth this new right to abortion has forced an alteration in the very meaning of a "man." It has made it necessary to diminish the significance that attaches to the taking of a human life. It has compelled professionals in law and medicine to retreat to a position of agnosticism on the question of whether they can know the definition of a human being, and the source then of anything called "human" rights. That sense of what is a human being has been converted from an objective fact into a "political question," to be resolved by those with power.

Finally, to achieve the right end, that power had to be removed from the hands of citizens and lodged in the hands of judges. As it happened, the right to abortion could not be installed when the power to decide was exercised by citizens or voters, electing representatives or voting in referenda. In a string of referenda, preceding *Roe v. Wade*, the forces seeking a change in the laws were persistently losing at the polls. Except for New York, Hawaii, and California, the resistance in the country was remarkably steady.[43] The "abortion liberty" could be installed only by calling into play the power of the courts, to overturn the laws established by officials who were responsible to the public in elections. I should be quick to add that this is no "interpretation." It is the account offered by the proponents of "choice" themselves as they explained why they moved into the courts, and why even today they look mainly to the courts to preserve that right they helped to establish.

In the chapters that follow, I will take it as part of my task to show that these movements in the law have in fact taken place, as I have described them here. But the deeper burden of my argument is to draw out these further points of significance, which have been far from noticeable, and yet even more deeply shattering in their significance:

> As the judges have put in place the premises that are utterly necessary to secure the "right to abortion," they have had to bring about a thorough alteration in the understanding of the "human person." As they have done that, they have been compelled to dislodge the premises of the American founders, and install, in their place, premises that are actually incompatible with jurisprudence itself. They have created what might be called, quite literally, an "anti-jural jurisprudence."
>
> The judges have created a jurisprudence, that is, with the trappings of law, but without the moral substance. And in the same way, they have converted this regime into something else: a regime with all of the

---

[43] See Russell Hittinger, "Abortion Before Roe," *First Things* (October 1994), pp. 14–16.

surface features, or the outward forms, of a republic, but without the moral substance of a republic or regime of law. This was precisely the prospect that Lincoln had put before us in an earlier crisis: that as the republic began to absorb and defend the premises of slavery, it could have the forms of a republic, while the inner substance was removed. And as the people began to make themselves suggestible to the premises of slavery – as they came to incorporate these premises in their own understanding – they would, in that measure, cease to be a democratic people, even as they went through the outward forms of casting ballots and acting in the *style* of citizens in a democracy.

On that point, Professor Harry Jaffa has written most eloquently in his magisterial book on Lincoln, *Crisis of the House Divided*,[44] and of that, we will see more in a later chapter. I used to think that Jaffa, in his eloquence on this point, had been waxing metaphoric. I am now inclined to think that he was being quite literal. In the same way, I do not mean to be writing with a kind of literary flourish when I contend that we are in the midst now of a crisis running quite as deep as that earlier crisis, which stands out even more clearly for us today as a result of Harry Jaffa's genius at exposition. For in the crisis before us now, we have been asked once again to revise our deepest understandings on what constitutes a "human person." We have been asked to begin our law anew by beginning with a profound doubt that there is in fact a "nature" of human beings, which furnishes a ground of natural rights. And in the same cavalier sweep, we are asked to dismiss the ancient notion that something in that nature of human beings implies some rather clear moral judgments about the ways that are rightful and wrongful in the governing of human beings.

Once again, it needs to be said that those "ways" are not merely formal but substantive: The founders understood that certain forms of government were more fitting or legitimate for human beings. But Lincoln helped us understand that the teaching of the founders ran even more deeply: that there were certain things a democratic people could not be free to choose, for others or themselves, even if they were

---

[44] (New York: Doubleday, 1959); republished by the University of Chicago Press, 1973.

observing all of the forms of a democracy. We might say now, from that perspective, that they could not choose slavery or Nazism or genocide, and remain a democratic people. Our own people today may have an intuitive sense of why that is the case, without exactly being able to explain it. They may find it even more difficult to believe now that the same thing precisely could be said about the freedom to choose abortion. But if that is indeed the case – if my judgment here turns out to be warranted – then it would follow in the same measure that we are, right now, in a crisis quite as grave as that earlier crisis of our house divided. That we are not at the threshold of a civil war at this moment is hardly a test of the proposition I will be putting forth here. If the American people, in 1860, had made themselves so suggestible to slavery that they were no longer willing to resist it in principle, there would have been no war. But there would have been a deep alteration in the character of the American people. And there would have been a critical change in the nature of the democracy in America, even if the country lived happily in these years without being much aware that there was anything resembling a crisis. So much may be said, in turn, about our people, living affably through the economy of the 1990s and into the new millennium. Times may be good, the mood may be buoyant, but if I happen to be right in the argument I will be unfolding in the following chapters, there is a crisis nevertheless, a crisis every bit as grave, running to the core of the regime, and to the soul of our people.

Four

Abortion and the "Modest First Step"

A colleague of mine in History at Amherst recalled the day, as a young professor, that he walked into his first class, to begin his career as a teacher. He had been asked to teach a course on modern European history, beginning with the French Revolution. But as a literate young man, newly delivered from his graduate studies, he had an unnervingly precise sense of the vast gaps in his knowledge, as a man who would "profess" to teach the history of modern Europe. Nevertheless, there was the assignment. And, passing over other estimable candidates, knowing more or even less than he, the department had hired *him*. This was, then, his office, and for better or worse, the only thing he could do, as Henry James would say, was to grasp his warrant. As he later recalled, "I became a certified expert on modern European history at 9 A.M. on that Monday morning."

Something of the same sense must have broken in upon Senator Joseph Biden of Delaware after the Democrats regained the Senate in the elections of 1986. Senator Edward Kennedy had decided to forego the position he could claim as the Chairman of the Committee on the Judiciary. He had, in his sights, other projects that seemed to be more pressing in the Committee on Education and Labor (the problem of breaking the logjam that was stalling a bill on civil rights). Kennedy was content to retain his membership on the Committee on the Judiciary, while letting the chairmanship pass to the next ranking member, Senator Biden. By his own report, Biden had been a middling student, at best, at a less than middling law school. But now, in assuming the chairmanship of the Committee on the Judiciary, he was in the position of standing, as it were, as *first* among the judges of the judges: He would be the leading figure in a panel passing on the records, and the fitness, of people nominated for the federal bench. He would have to pronounce then on doctrines of jurisprudence and philosophy of which he had only the most distant acquaintance. He would be compelled to render commentaries on judges and lawyers with careers in the law, or with bodies of writing and scholarship that rather exceeded his own. In order to draw these nominees into a conversation, he would have to mention and discuss cases; he would have to sound as though he were familiar with cases, and whole branches of the law, that he could not honestly claim to know. In short, just like the new professor, he was obliged to start cramming and sound plausible. For here he was; it was his assignment, and so he had to enter the Committee room as the Certified Expert, brought forth by Democrats in the Senate, to express their outlook on matters jural.

That was the position he was in when Robert Bork was appointed to the Supreme Court in 1987, and it was a position that required more delicacy and feigning than even most senators could summon. Biden had expressed his dissatisfaction with nominees from the Reagan Administration who were too conservative for him and his party to brook. He had offered, in contrast, Robert Bork, as an evident scholar, who elicited respect quite apart from views that were markedly conservative by Biden's measures. But when Bork himself was actually appointed, there was an imminent danger for the Democrats that Bork would be the fifth vote in favor of overruling *Roe v. Wade* and putting the issue of abortion back in the hands of legislatures. Why that should have constituted a "problem" was itself a reflection of the changes that had taken place in liberal jurisprudence and the Democratic party. If Biden and his Democratic colleagues were right in their estimate that the American people had come to regard the "right to abortion" as a necessary, "constitutional" right; that life without this new right had become virtually unthinkable; then there could have been no problem in putting the issue back in the hands of political men and women. These people, like Senator Biden, were responsive to their constituents, and they would simply be in a position to enact into laws the measures that pleased their voters and secured this right to abortion.

That certainly would have been the approach more consonant with the jurisprudence of the New Deal and Justice Hugo Black: The

unelected judges were generally not to intrude themselves, to overturn the policies enacted by officers who were directly responsive to
the people in elections – unless there was a violation of some explicit
provision in the Constitution. Foremost among those provisions, for
Black, was the Bill of Rights. But there was nothing in the Constitution about such things as contraception or abortion. And so, in a signal
moment, Black did not think that there was anything in the Constitution that denied, to the legislature of Connecticut, the authority to
frame a policy that would restrict access to contraceptives.[1] Presumably, the same understanding would have made it quite as legitimate
for legislatures to do what they had done in this country up until 1973,
and protect the lives of unborn children.

Roe v. Wade and *Griswold v. Connecticut* had become the touchstone
for a new kind of liberal jurisprudence, as liberalism moved away from
the jurisprudence of the New Deal and into an entirely different register. With that new cast of the jural mind, Senator Biden could not
find anything congenial in the notion of returning the issue of abortion to the political arena. It was not a sufficient ground of appeal,
apparently, that the decisions, under those conditions, would be left
in the hands of himself and his colleagues – along, of course, with the
responsibility. For Biden, though, that kind of shift would also mark
the denigration of the right to abortion, as a lesser kind of right, a
right that could not be protected from shifting majorities in the political arena. But in that event, the Democratic party would have transformed itself into the party of the courts: It would take as its mission
the guarding, or the insulating, of the courts. And in turn, the courts
would go about the business of enacting the more advanced parts of
the liberal agenda, on matters such as "reproductive rights" or "gay
rights." Bill Clinton, in later years, would not seek to run for president by placing, at the center of his appeal, a campaign for gays in the
military. Nor would he trumpet abortion as a "public good," which
deserved to be promoted and sustained with public funding. Yet the
issue of gay rights suddenly soared into prominence in the first days
of his administration, and caused a rapid decline for Clinton in the
polls. Clinton would retreat from that position, but simply promote

---

[1] See again, Black's dissenting opinion in *Griswold v. Connecticut*, 381 U.S. 479 at
507–27 (1965).

the same ends with more circumspect and discreet means. Most discreet of all would be the instrument of simply appointing to the federal courts people who would then impose, in the name of the Constitution, the policies that the administration could not espouse in public or command the votes to enact.

All of this was quite in the air already in 1987, with the response to Robert Bork's nomination. A way had to be found then to oppose Bork, and after a testy set of confirmation hearings – attended by a public campaign quite novel and venomous, in the annals of confirmations for the Supreme Court – a way was indeed found, and Bork was denied confirmation.

Four years later, the problem was posed again, but with even more strain for Biden and company. With the retirement of Thurgood Marshall, President Bush nominated Judge Clarence Thomas for the Supreme Court. But Thomas was a black nominee not in the mold of Thurgood Marshall: He was hostile to notions of "racial entitlements" or hiring on the basis of race. He was averse to those schemes of racial preference, not because he was hostile to rights, but because he thought that there was a principle behind the Civil Rights Act of 1964, the same principle that lay behind the Civil War Amendments to the Constitution. That principle made it wrong to discriminate on the basis of race – made it wrong, that is, to assign benefits or disabilities on the basis of race, as though race "determined" the character of any person and established what that person deserved.[2] "As I would not be a *slave*," wrote Lincoln, "so I would not be a *master*."[3] Since he rejected slavery in principle, his rejection was utterly indifferent to the question of whether he stood on the advantaged, or the disadvantaged, side of that relation. Thomas was posing the same kind of question: whether there was indeed something in principle wrong with racial discrimination. When the matter was framed as a principle, the question would be asked, For whom is it wrong to discriminate on the basis of race? And the answer would come, in a moral voice: for anyone, for everyone. If it is wrong to let the awarding of a job pivot

---

[2] For a fuller statement of this problem, and the principle, see my *First Things* (Princeton: Princeton University Press, 1986), pp. 92–9.

[3] Lincoln, fragment, in *The Collected Works of Abraham Lincoln*, Roy P. Basler, ed. (New Brunswick, NJ: Rutgers University Press, 1953), v. II, p. 532.

on the basis of race, then it was quite as wrong to discriminate in favor of whites over blacks – or blacks over whites. Of course, the Fourteeenth Amendment could be read by some commentators to express a willingness simply to do more for black people, to make up for inequalities in income and social standing. From that perspective, the Fourteenth Amendment created rights distinctly for black people, and perhaps, then, solely for black people. But from an older under-standing, the Fourteenth Amendment had rather confirmed, for black people, the *natural rights* that blacks could claim, along with everyone else.

This understanding had not come out fully yet, in the writings of Clarence Thomas, as they would in later years, with the flow of his opinions from the Court. But there was a suspicion at the time that he was inclined in this direction – and that he too would be the fifth vote to overrule *Roe v. Wade*. For as it turned out, Thomas had been tutored on the writings of Lincoln, and the study of Lincoln had moved him to discover again, or discover anew, the doctrines of natural right.

Biden had become aware of this interest on the part of Thomas in natural right and natural law, and on the eve of the hearings on con-firmation, Biden (evidently with some help from members of his staff) delivered himself of a long article in the *Washington Post*, expressing his deep reservations about "natural law."[4] Picking up the cliches settled for many years in the law schools, Biden identified natural law with those reactionary judges of the 1930s, who resisted the New Deal, along with schemes of "social legislation" in the States. Those judges had to invoke principles of justice that could be posed against the votes of majorities, and so those principles had to sound like a species of natural law. The indictment then offered by Biden was that a judge who took natural law seriously would turn himself into an apostle of "laissez-faire" economics. He would be more inclined to

---

[4] See Biden's piece, on "Law and Natural Law," *Washington Post*, Outlook Section, September 8, 1991, pp. C1, C4. In the course of his article, Chairman Biden paid me the curious compliment of taking my own writings as an example of the kind of natural law he would seek to resist. But he fell into the awkwardness of misstating my own views – and offering a mistaken account of the cases he was citing. The late Meg Greenfield offered me the privilege of replying a day later, the day that the hearings opened over Clarence Thomas. See "Sen. Biden's Mistaken Account," *Washington Post*, September 10, 1991, p. A18.

"judicial activism" in striking down laws passed by legislatures to regulate the economy or bring about "social justice." And of course, it went without saying that a judge who took natural law seriously might go to the rescue of the unborn child and threaten that newly established right to abortion.

But even for a politician of Biden's flexibility, this outpouring of concern over "natural law" was an unmanageable stretch. For just four years earlier, during the hearings over Robert Bork, Biden's position had been *entirely the reverse*. In the case of Bork, the fifth vote to overturn *Roe v. Wade* would come from a man who was a confirmed "positivist." Bork's jurisprudence resembled that of Hugo Black, Franklin Roosevelt's first appointee to the Supreme Court: Unless the judges could invoke an explicit provision of the Constitution, they should hold back from blocking the judgments reached by legislators, or officers elected by the people. But now, against a legal positivism employed in that way, Biden was drawn to a notion of the "right to abortion" as a kind of natural right. And so it is quite striking – and hardly inadvertent – that when Biden opened the hearings, in 1987, over Robert Bork, he began by staking out a strong "natural rights" position:

> As a child of God, I believe my rights are not derived from the Constitution. My rights are not derived from any government. My rights are not derived from any majority. *My rights are because I exist.* They were given to me and each of my fellow citizens by our creator and they represent the essence of human dignity.[5]

The argument here was that we possessed rights quite apart from the rights that were "posited," or set down, in a statute or in the Constitution. Against those claims of "positive" law, there were rights that existed before the advent of any statutes or constitutions; "rights" that simply sprung from our natures as human beings. As Chairman Biden put it, those rights of a human being would come into existence as soon as that being comes to "exist." Cast in that form, the moral and juridical notion of rights would be anchored in an objective fact: the fact of human nature and the actual existence of a discrete, real person.

---

[5] *Hearings on the Nomination of Robert H. Bork to the Supreme Court of the United States,* Committee on the Judiciary, U.S. Senate, 100th Cong., 1st sess. (1987), pt. 1, p. 97.

But in that construction, Biden's understanding would seem to cover the child in the womb, as soon as that being comes to "exist." And yet, obviously, Biden could not have accepted that implication, for it would have extended the protections of natural law to the fetus, or the unborn child, and that understanding clearly would have impaired any claim of a "right to an abortion."

Biden might have averted that implication by holding that there was something more doubtful about the "facts" concerning the child in the womb: He might have professed to be agnostic on the question of whether there are indeed any facts we are obliged to respect, as "facts," to establish just when the child has come to "exist," and whether that being in the womb can be said yet to be human. A construction of that kind might have helped him reconcile his positions, and yet it would have marked a radical shift in the understanding of "natural rights." Senator Biden had declared, in explaining the logic of natural rights, that he had rights that did not depend on the will of any majority, rights that claimed their own, independent ground of truth. Presumably then, he would not have argued that human beings had a right not to be enslaved – and yet held, at the same time, that whether they were regarded, however, as human would depend on the opinions held by those around them. Of what sense would it be to claim that we have rights that do not depend on the sufferance of a majority, and then say that our very standing as humans – as rights-bearing beings – may itself depend on the opinions of the majority? Or even worse: Could it depend on the opinions of those, like the owners of slaves, who have a direct interest in denying these rights? In that case, how could the "existence," or the "human" standing of the child in the womb, be made any more dependent on the opinions or beliefs of others? And even more implausibly, how could that "existence" depend on the "opinion" of the person who may have an interest to be served by killing the child?

But a few years later, with the decision of the Court in *Planned Parenthood v. Casey*, in 1992, the "abortion liberty" seemed to be stamped now as quite secure, beyond any prospect of overturning. Presidents Reagan and Bush had managed to add, by that time, five new members to the Supreme Court; and yet, three of those judges went over to the "other side." In a notable, concurring opinion, Justices Sandra Day O'Connor, Anthony Kennedy, and David Souter argued that the right to abortion had been too long settled to be unsettled now. Over the 19 years since *Roe v. Wade*, people had come to absorb the lessons contained in this new law. They had incorporated the sense that there was a right to abortion as nothing less than a fundamental right, a right anchored in the Constitution, as firmly as if it had mentioned in the text. Some people had fallen then into a certain "reliance" on the prospect that this right would be available to them.[6]

The argument, cast in these terms, bore a critical resemblance to the argument offered to the Court in 1953–54 by John Davis, in defending the laws on racial segregation. They too had been long settled, for it was over 50 years since the Court, in *Plessy v. Ferguson*, had sustained a policy of segregation mandated by law. Davis argued that "somewhere, sometime to every principle comes a moment of repose when it has been so often announced, so confidently relied upon, so long continued, that it passes the limits of judicial discretion and disturbance."[7] People could have all kinds of reservations about the policy, and they could indeed be moved to change it out of a deep moral revulsion. But Davis thought it settled by now that nothing in the Constitution would forbid a legislature from establishing these arrangements of segregation. Once again, there was an understanding of precedents and law *quite detached from the moral content of the law*. And in that vein, the judges appointed by "pro-life" administrations could argue that they were obliged to recognize now this law settled over 19 years, even though they might not vote for such a law themselves.[8]

---

[6] As it was put in the plurality opinion, "for two decades of economic and social developments, people have organized intimate relationships and made choices that define their views of themselves and their places in society, in reliance on the availability of abortion in the event that contraception should fail." *Planned Parenthood v. Casey*, 505 U.S. 833 (1992), at 855–6.

[7] These remarks were made in the course of his oral presentation, in the reargument of the Brown case, and the comments came in an exchange with Justice Frankfurter. See *Landmark Briefs and Arguments of the Supreme Court of the United States*, Philip B. Kurland and Gerhard Casper, ed. (Arlington, VA: University Publications of America, 1975), v. 49, p. 490 (p. 42, in the transcript of the proceedings). For Davis's fuller argument on the case, see pp. 479–88.

[8] Or so it might have been said, at least, on the part of Justice Kennedy. Justice O'Connor, in her earlier incarnation, had served in the legislature of Arizona, where she was on the side of those seeking to remove, or scale back, the prohibitions on abortion. And Justice Souter had served earlier on the board of a hospital that had made a decision to perform abortions.

As the public awaited the decision in *Planned Parenthood v. Casey*, the Court seemed to be on the threshold of overturning *Roe v. Wade*. But the defection of the Reagan and Bush judges seemed to put the seal of permanence on *Roe*. And yet, not quite. A few years later, the public would be jolted anew over this question with the move to ban "partial-birth abortions." In that grisly procedure, an "abortion" is performed on a child, at the point of birth, with as much as two-thirds of the body outside the birth canal. As that bill became the subject of discussion and controversy, portions of the public would learn for the first time that, under the regime of *Roe v. Wade* and *Doe v. Bolton*, abortions could be performed for virtually any reason throughout the entire length of the pregnancy. As the argument bore on over partial-birth abortions, the surveys showed the support for abortion dropping once again, to levels known 20 years earlier, and the opposition to abortion once again rising.

And yet, with the blips up or down, the remarkable thing is that the distribution of opinion on this matter has varied only slightly over 25 years. But that stability, or that absence of dramatic breaks, is itself striking news, for it forms a notable contrast to the changes in opinion that were generated by *Brown v. Board of Education* in 1954. In the years following *Brown*, more and more of the public would come to absorb an understanding of the wrong of racial discrimination. But to the deep disappointment and surprise of the partisans of "abortion rights," the sentiments of the public did not show a comparable tendency to consolidate in support of that right to abortion. In May 1999, the Gallup organization published a survey, along with a comparison of the responses running back to 1975. In April of that year, 21 percent of the public affirmed the view that abortion should be "legal under any circumstances." Over the years, that figure has climbed as high as 34 percent, but it has usually hovered around a quarter (or 25 percent), and in May 1999, it was 27 percent. The modal response, remarkably stable, has centered on the judgment that abortion should be "legal only under certain circumstances." In April 1975, 54 percent of the respondents held to that view, which rather mirrored the state of the law in most places before *Roe v. Wade*. In May 1999, the sampling yielded a figure of 55 percent holding to that view. There had been a gentle decline over the years in the portion of the public that thought abortion should be "illegal under all circumstances." That figure had migrated from 22 percent to 16 percent. Still, the figures summed up to a story that does not quite accord with the sense of things portrayed in the media: More than 25 years after *Roe v. Wade* and *Doe v. Bolton*, only 27 percent of the public actually support the law created in those cases. About 70 percent of the public would reject that law, and hold that abortion should be legal only under certain circumstances. Or to put it another way, nearly three-quarters of the public think that abortions may rightly be restricted.[9]

What may be an even more remarkable piece of evidence came out of a survey of American women carried out in 1998 under the auspices of the Center for Gender Equality in New York, a group that strongly supports abortion rights. The survey was conducted by Princeton Research Associates, and the results were acknowledged by the sponsors as disappointing. For it appeared to them that American women were becoming more religious and conservative, and far more reserved about abortion. As much as 40 percent of the women thought that abortion should be allowed only in cases of rape or incest, or when the life of the mother was in danger. Thirteen percent thought abortions should not be permitted under *any* circumstances, while another 17 percent, not going as far as either of those other groups, thought that the restrictions on abortion should be far more severe. Again, about 70 percent of the women favored policies that would scale down dramatically the freedom to order abortions.[10]

But this remarkable constellation of opinion has gone hand in hand with results equally remarkable: The public, so deeply reserved about abortion, is even more reserved about enacting its opinions into public policy. Perhaps the public has absorbed the notion that it should not legislate its moral convictions; or perhaps the public has absorbed a certain unwillingness to overturn a precedent long settled. To put it another way, there might be a reluctance to "dispossess" other people of what they had come to regard as a "right." In the haze of these sentiments, the groups dedicated to "abortion rights" could continue to raise funds by sounding the alarm: The right to abortion never

[9] CNN/USA Today/Gallup poll: April 30–May 2, 1999.
[10] "The Impact of Religious Organizations on Gender Equality," (an evidently misnamed publication, which registered only shifts in opinions, not alterations in the actual state of equality), conducted for the Center for Gender Equality by Princeton Survey Research Associates, January 7, 1999.

seemed more secure, and yet for some reason it was always in imminent danger of being scaled back, chipped away, even repealed outright.

On the other side, the opposition could never let go, even with the demoralizing outcome in *Planned Parenthood v. Casey*, even when prominent conservative writers were willing to say, with sobriety, that this part of the "culture war" had been lost. And yet the reason that many people persisted, why they refused to let go, was precisely because of the analogy to slavery and that earlier crisis of the "house divided": Biden's argument over natural rights exposed all of its vacuities as soon as the question was raised as to how the issue of slavery – or any other matter of moral consequence – would be judged when it was inserted into the scheme of Biden's argument. And for some of us, the issue of abortion has taken the hold it has because we have seen it running to the same question of principle at the root: Once again, there is the powerful temptation to remove a whole class of human beings from the protections of the law through the simple device of classifying them as something less than human. With a shift in labels, someone becomes a "nigger" or a "darkie." But as Lincoln said, the question was whether "a negro is *not* or *is* a man. If he is *not* a man, why in that case, he is who *is* a man may, as a matter of self-government, do just as he pleases with him."[11]

Still, if the claim were that the black man was not in fact a "man," it was important to know just why not. What features did he lack? The question was freighted now with the awareness that we were not merely "describing," or explaining why a black man fell into one classification rather than another: Any feature brought forward to show why a black man was not a man would be bearing now a *moral* weight; it would establish why the rest of us would be *justified* in removing black people from the class of "men" protected by the law. As Lincoln set up the problem, he would offer a classic example of "principled reasoning." In my own writings on abortion, I've drawn on Lincoln's argument here as the model of moral reasoning in framing the problem and providing the very matrix for any deliberation on

---

[11] Speech in Peoria, Illinois (October 16, 1854) in *The Works of Abraham Lincoln*, Roy P. Basler, ed. (New Brunswick, NJ: Rutgers University Press, 1953), v. II, pp. 265–6 (emphases in the original).

this issue.[12] As it turns out, this was the form of argument that, in my own case, compelled me years ago to stop and pay attention – and to put aside the sentiments that could not withstand the tests of a more stringent, principled reasoning. The cast of that argument has been remarkable in moving people to get clear about the grounds of judgment and to settle, on those grounds, a notably different judgment. Lincoln's argument could be found in a fragment he had constructed for himself, in which he had imagined himself to be engaged in a conversation with an owner of slaves. He put the question of why one could be justified in making a slave of the black man, and he unfolded his reflection in this way:

> You say A. is white, and B. is black. It is color, then: the lighter having the right to enslave the darker? Take care. By this rule, you are to be slave to the first man you meet, with a fairer skin than your own.

> You do not mean *color* exactly? – You mean the whites are *intellectually* the superiors of the blacks, and therefore have the right to enslave them? Take care again. By this rule, you are to be slave to the first man you meet, with an intellect superior to your own.

> But, say you, it is a question of interest; and, if you can make it your *interest*, you have the right to enslave another. Very well. And if he can make it his interest, he has the right to enslave you.[13]

I would point out that nowhere in this chain of reasoning is there an appeal to faith or revelation. Aquinas once observed that the divine law we know through revelation, but the "natural law" we know through the reasoning that is accessible to human beings as human beings. Lincoln's argument could be understood across the divisions of religion or race or class – it could be understood by Catholics or Baptists, by geologists or carpenters or poker players. And one did not need a college education in order to grasp it. It could be understood then by ordinary people, using the wit of rational creatures, and in my experience no one, hearing the argument, has failed to grasp its import: There was nothing one could cite to disqualify the black man as a human being, and justify the enslavement of blacks, that would not apply to many whites as well.

[12] See my book, *First Things* (Princeton: Princeton University Press, 1986), pp. 362 ff.
[13] *The Works of Abraham Lincoln, supra*, n. 10, pp. 222–3.

Without the need for the slightest alteration, some of us have begun our own reflections on the problem of abortion by casting the argument in the same terms. And so we might put the question, "Why do you regard the child in the womb as anything less than a human being?" Is it because he cannot speak? Neither do deaf mutes. Is it because he seems to lack arms or legs? Well, other people have been born missing one or more of their limbs, or they have lost control over their limbs, and we have not thought that they have lost anything necessary to their standing, as human beings, to receive the protections of the law.

Anyone who enters this argument soon discovers that there is no tenable ground on which to claim that the child in the womb, the offspring of homo sapiens, can be anything less than a human being. But if that is the case, the argument then shifts to a second axis: It may still be justified, under certain circumstances, to take a human life (e.g., in self-defense). But the justifications we must bring forth now, for the taking of fetal life, must be quite as grave or compelling as the justifications we would demand in other instances for the taking of human life. As I have put it elsewhere, no one could doubt the strain that may be induced when a pregnancy presses the finances of a family, causes a woman to drop out of school, or becomes the source of a serious embarrassment. But the difficulty here is that we do not take it as a justification for homicide in other instances if an aged parent, say, may strain the finances or the psychological balance of a household. If people could be killed because they caused deep embarrassment, or suddenly became deeply unpopular, Mr. Clinton could have been in serious danger through several stages of his presidency – and in even more danger in the aftermath, when he left the White House in a blizzard of pardons.

This argument I have set forth and developed in its fuller length in other places, and I won't trespass on the time of my reader to stage the whole argument again here.[14] I would simply register the claim that the argument on abortion is grounded finally in principled rea-

---

[14] See *supra*, n. 12, chs. XVI–XVII, pp. 360–422. To paraphrase Montesquieu, in his preface to *The Spirit of the Laws*, I'm sure that the interest that has been drawn to this writing has been due more to the grandeur and importance of the subject than my own poor efforts. Still, as Montesquieu said, "I do not think I have been totally deficient in point of genius," and so with a certain manly confidence I would commend these writings, struck off at other times, to readers coming new to the subject.

soning, the kind of reasoning that could be understood on its own terms without any appeal to religious faith or personal beliefs. The moral case against abortion is treated frivolously, falsely, if it is treated, at the threshold, as a problem of legislating, for other people, on the basis of "religious beliefs" or merely "personal opinions." That argument is usually employed as a "stopper," to end arguments by forestalling them. After a certain number of years, that device has managed to work, especially as we find that the arguments over abortion may be quite disagreeable, and there seems to be more and more of an inclination to avoid talking about this vexing subject. And yet, that recoil of distaste obscures the fact, shown in the surveys of the public, that people remain perfectly capable of entering into conversations about the grounds on which abortions may be justified or unjustified. As the surveys have revealed, even people who describe themselves as "pro-choice" do not think that abortions should be permitted under all circumstances. In fact, the surveys have revealed a pattern holding steady over many years: Most people in the country think that human lives are destroyed in abortions – they affect no puzzlement, or agnosticism, about the species of that being in the womb. As noted previously, about a fifth or a quarter of the population have shown a willingness to permit abortions for any reason, without constraint. About a quarter to a third of the public has shown a disposition to regard abortions as wrong under all circumstances. Most people in the country think, then, that at least some abortions are wrong, or unjustified, and that they may be restrained by the law. And with that sense of things, they do not think that abortions should be performed for reasons that are less than weighty. Most people do not think that abortions should be performed as late as the third trimester of a pregnancy. In one Gallup survey, published in 1991, it was estimated that about 73 percent of the respondents (in a sample of more than 2,000 persons) would support a prohibition on abortion after the first three months of the pregnancy, except under conditions in which the life of the mother might be in danger.[15] Most people in the country

---

[15] See "Abortion and Moral Beliefs: A Survey of American Opinion," Washington, DC, February 28, 1991, p. 11. The study was conducted in the field by the Gallup organization, and commissioned by Americans United for Life, a pro-life group. But the survey was designed by Professors James Davis Hunter (University of Virginia), Carl Bowman (Bridgewater College), and Robert Wuthnow (Princeton).

do not think that abortions should be performed for the sake of convenience or to relieve the financial strain of the family. And they do not even think abortions should be performed for the sake of permitting a woman to finish school, or to avoid disruptions in her plans for a career.[16]

Mr. Roger Rosenblatt seemed to suffer a certain surprise, in addition, when he found that about 56 percent of the public in the surveys did not think that abortions should be performed because the child happened to be deaf or blind. A comparable number – about 53 percent – did not think abortions warranted in cases where the child was missing an arm or leg. Rosenblatt seemed especially puzzled that the public regarded these kinds of abortions as wrong, quite regardless of whether the abortion was performed early, in the first trimester, or later, in the third.[17] But perhaps the puzzlement might be dissolved with this construction: The respondents might have grasped the point in principle that they would not order the death of any other person simply because he was deaf or blind, or missing an arm or leg. If that was their understanding, the age of the victim would not have mattered in the slightest degree. And if people reasoned along the same lines in regard to the child in the womb, their aversion to abortion in these cases would have been, once again, quite indifferent to the age of the unborn child.

One savvy observer, who has followed these polls for a long while, summed the matter up in this way: About 60 percent of the public are opposed to about 90 percent of the abortions that are performed each year under the law put in place by *Roe v. Wade*.[18] And yet, the

---

[16] *Ibid.*, pp. 38–9.

[17] Roger Rosenblatt, *Life Itself: Abortion in the American Mind* (New York: Random House, 1992), pp. 186–8. There is one path of alternative reading: The survey asked whether the respondents "would definitely not consider an abortion" in certain circumstances. It is entirely possible that people who have come to view the matter as a "personal choice" would record their own aversion, while not yet being willing to restrict the freedom of other people to choose abortions for the reasons they themselves regard as unjustified. And yet, the tenor of the responses suggests that the respondents did not see the matter in that way. It rather appeared, from Rosenblatt's account, that the respondents were indeed expressing a judgment, on the things fitting for others as well as themselves.

[18] See also "Abortion and Moral Beliefs: A Survey of American Opinion," *supra*, n. 15, p. 5: "Americans generally disapprove of abortion in most circumstances under which it is currently performed."

surveys also reveal that, when respondents are asked about *Roe v. Wade*, a majority holds steady, from one season to the next, in supporting *Roe* and refusing to see it overruled. Those surveys naturally begot the question of how these different responses managed to hang together. I had my own surmise here, which I published in a piece in the *National Review* in 1988,[19] and which has since been confirmed. People may be opposed to most of the abortions performed under *Roe v. Wade*, and yet they support *Roe v. Wade*, and the conflicting strands might be reconciled in this straightforward way: Most people simply do not actually know what was *in Roe v. Wade*. A survey carried out by the Roper organization in the early 1990s finally confirmed the point: Only about one person in 10 could give even a faintly accurate account of the holding in *Roe*.[20] A professor at one of our most prestigious schools of law took an informal survey among her colleagues, and she found that, even among the professional students of the Court, only 5 of 25 could give an accurate account of that case.

Even professors of law are likely to have picked up the report, in the newspapers, that *Roe v. Wade* marked off pregnancy into trimesters; that it confirmed an unqualified right of a pregnant woman to order an abortion, for any reason, but only within the first trimester of a pregnancy. As the account ran, the state might have a more plausible and legitimate ground for protecting "potential life" as the pregnancy moves into its later stages and the fetus seems to look more and more like a baby. In a symposium at Loyola University Law School, in New Orleans, in the fall of 1997, Professor Robert George of Princeton was flabbergasted to hear another professor, the holder of a named chair at a nearby school of law, insist with the voice of authority that *Roe v. Wade* created a "right to abortion" only in the first trimester of the pregnancy. George was compelled to elicit testimony from other members of the audience acquainted with the law, to alert this august professor to what he had evidently missed: namely, that the trimester scheme in *Roe v. Wade* had been overridden, in effect, in the companion case of *Doe v. Bolton*. The Court, in *Bolton*, took account of that authority it had conceded to legislatures, to regulate or even prohibit abortions in the third trimester. But then the Court

[19] See "How to Roll Back *Roe*," *National Review* (October 28, 1988), pp. 30 ff.
[20] See *supra*, n. 15, pp. 13–14.

insisted that this authority of the State could nevertheless be overridden or trumped by a concern for the "health" of the pregnant woman. That notion of "health," however, would follow along the definition of health provided by the World Health Organization (WHO): it would encompass a concern for the "mental health" of the woman, along with her physical well-being.[21] But as Professor (and later, federal judge) John Noonan pointed out at the time, that meant that a woman had a right do order up an abortion if she thought she would genuinely suffer distress if she were denied one.[22]

We may have reached, in our day, a point of moral anesthesia, in which people order up abortions as readily as they order a "tummy tuck," or cosmetic surgery, without the least sense that they are doing anything of moral significance. And yet, it has not exactly been that way, even in our own time. Even when abortion has become routine, most people are aware of the fact that it is not a trivial surgery. The prospect of childbirth is irreducibly serious, and people usually have reasons when they seek to avoid the obligations that attend a pregnancy and a child. With serious reasons, or serious concerns, they could plausibly claim in any case to suffer strain – and risk serious depression – if they were denied this surgery. With this provision then for the "health" of the pregnant woman, the Court provided a device for dissolving even the most minimal restraints. Thereafter, there would be an effort to attach the same formula to any legislative measure that sought to impose restrictions on abortion. Even when the child was at the point of birth, with two-thirds of the body extruded from the birth canal, members of Congress sought to add an "exception" for the "health" of the mother.

The former dean of one of the most distinguished law schools in the country was struck in surprise and mild shock when I explained to him, at our dinner table, these precise ingredients marking the laws on abortion that the Supreme Court had wrought. For my friend, the dean, this subject did not come within his own field in the law. What he knew about the subject he knew as most educated people came to know it, by reading the *New York Times* or the *Washington Post*. And these journals, from the 1970s through the 1990s, had

---

[21] See *Doe v. Bolton*, 410 U.S. 179, especially 191–2.
[22] See John Noonan, *A Private Choice* (New York: The Free Press, 1979), pp. 10–12.

managed to filter, from their accounts, news that the public would find jolting.

But that is why some of us thought that we could bring about some striking effects with the most modest of measures; measures that would simply start a conversation, and do their principal work as "educational." They would have their effect mainly by imparting to the public some of the most elementary information about the current laws on abortion. But that was information the public was likely to receive as "news" of a rather disturbing kind. And thus was born the strategy of the "modest first step." The plan was to stake out, as a first step, the most modest position, which would break out to people that news they would find most surprising: that abortions could be performed in this country, not only in the first trimester, but throughout the entire length of the pregnancy – and even after the child emerged in birth.

The first statement of this strategy came in a statement I drafted for the then Vice President, George Bush, when he was running on his own for president and preparing for the presidential debates with Michael Dukakis. At the invitation of a friend deeply involved in the management of the campaign, I drafted a few things that could enter Mr. Bush's "preparation kit" as he readied himself for that encounter with the Democratic nominee. Years earlier, when I had consulted with the team of speech writers working for candidate Reagan, I used to say that I had written some of the best things Ronald Reagan never said. Here, too, I thought it rather doubtful that Mr. Bush would draw on what I had written, even though I had staked out, in this draft, the most modest measure that any candidate could propose. The draft had been written, in other words, to find the easiest way to talk about the matter of abortion. As it turned out, that indisposition on the part of George Bush to speak sentences on this matter became telling and decisive. Professor Robert George at Princeton put it well, and succinctly, when he remarked that the problem of George Bush for the pro-lifers was that "he was all action and no talk." As President, he would take the actions, and make the appointments, that sprung from a pro-life perspective, but at a critical moment, political movements require "talk." They require, that is, the kind of talk that frames the issue, imparts direction, and steadies followers who may need a certain firming up. Wanting that talk from a president, journalists may trip into flights of invention, as they actually have to make up a "story line" themselves and fall back upon their readiest cliches. As uncertainty lingers, followers too may begin to panic and fly off in the most implausible directions. The late Peter Braestrup pointed up once the most striking contrast in this respect in the performances of Lyndon Johnson and Richard Nixon. Johnson had known that the Tet Offensive was coming, early in 1968, but he had done nothing to prepare the public, or offer a construction of what was unfolding when that assault finally took place. As a result, reporters went off in several directions, drawing the direst implications from the fact that the Vietcong were able to stage an assault in the heart of Saigon so late in the war. In point of fact, the attack had failed. The Vietcong had been thoroughly routed – and even depleted in the effort. Yet, the experience was played by the press as an American defeat, a disaster of major proportions, a sign that the war absorbing so many men and resources, was probably unwinnable.[23]

But Braestrup offered, in striking contrast, the performance of Richard Nixon four years later, when the North Vietnamese and the Vietcong staged what became known as the "May offensive." This time, the president went on television as the offensive was beginning. Mr. Nixon gave an account of what was taking place – and the steps that the administration was taking, in turn, to deal with this initiative by the enemy. The initiative was beaten back, the strength of American arms was confirmed yet again – and no panic set in. The president had provided the story line; the journalists did not run through the countryside inventing their own. When the administration did not panic, when disaster did not ensue, the main story involved an account of an administration in charge of what it was doing, and of a government in South Vietnam secured by American support.

President Bush faced a moment of lesser drama, but comparable gravity, over the issue of abortion in 1989, and it must be said that he muffed it notably. In the spring of 1989, the Supreme Court decided the Webster case,[24] and with that decision, it virtually invited the political branches to begin legislating again on the matter of abortion. Chief Justice Rehnquist observed, in his opinion for the Court,

---

[23] See Braestrup's account in *Big Story* (Garden City, NY: Doubleday Anchor, 1978).
[24] *Webster v. Reproductive Health Services*, 492 U.S. 490 (1989).

that legislatures need not be confined to trimesters, or even to the test of "viability." He and his colleagues held out the possibility, in other words, that legislatures could begin to regulate abortions or protect what was curiously called "potential life," from the earliest moments, when it was known that this "life" was there. Reporters dashed out, almost instantly, to get the reactions of the president to this apparent breakthrough. They found the president on the golf course. So affected was he by the significance that freighted this moment – with the new possibilities suddenly opened for the saving of lives – that he was not quite inspired even to remove the wooden tee placed between his teeth. Speaking past the tee, he blurted out to the reporters something to the effect that there would be a statement on all of that later.

In the meantime, panic began to set in among the members of his own party. Some Republican congressmen, such as Jim Courter in New Jersey, had played themselves for years as "pro-lifers." Courter had made a minor career in lamenting the fact that the courts had removed from the hands of legislators the authority to pass laws protecting unborn children. But at the same time, the courts had nicely insulated the Jim Courters of the world from any responsibility to make decisions. Now, the Court seemed to sweep away that ban. From this point forward, Courter would be empowered actually to do something, in accord with the sentiments he had professed, to frame and pass legislation. And that prospect, suddenly made live, set off detonations. Some people in Courter's district were willing to live with him when he was simply posturing, but those who favored a right to abortion angrily wished to know at this moment whether Courter was serious about dispossessing them of what they had come to regard now as one of their fundamental rights.

For Courter, his district seemed to be exploding under him, and neither his party nor his president offered any direction. For years the Republicans had been complaining that the issue of abortion had been taken over by the courts. One would have thought that, when the Court made the first step in returning the issue to the political arena, the Republicans would have prepared themselves to have something to *say*. They might have been words to stake out some simple moves and prepare the ground for the first measures that might be put in place. They could have been words of assurance, words that dissolve a vague sense of apprehension. And the words spoken might have had that effect as they mapped out a few modest steps, which could readily command assent among people of moderation. Surely, it would have been possible to come forth with some minimal restrictions, say over abortions late in term, that could claim a wide consensus in the public. But in the presence of a political firestorm apparently building, people like Jim Courter did not feel they could offer measures, or reasons, overly refined. The result was that Courter panicked and did a 180-degree turn. Virtually overnight, he announced that he had experienced an epiphany. He realized how deeply some of his constituents really felt on this matter, and so he came to the judgment that the law should not intrude on these "private" decisions. He had become, in effect, "pro-choice" down the line.

These gymnastics, however, did no good for Courter. He gained a reputation instead as a man who not only "trimmed," but threw his principles overboard with the first signs of heavy weather. He failed in a run for governor of his state, and thereafter he would knock around in offices dealt him out of patronage, carrying with him the aura of a has-been in politics. But George Bush could have rescued the Courters of the world that day in 1989; he could have made them better than what they were. He could have avoided the panic in his own party, as other politicians were moved to abandon the pro-life position and become "pro-choice" overnight. The president could have arrested the panic by coming forth with a statement to steady everyone, define the moment, and mark off some steps that virtually every fair-minded person would have been able to accept. There was no want of drafts for speeches that would have worked at this moment, and one of them might have been the speech I had prepared for his debating kit, back in the campaign. That would have been the first statement for the strategy of "modest first steps" had it ever been made. If the strategy is ever employed, with effect, it might be said now that I was the author of some of the best things that George Bush had never said. In that early draft, we would have had Mr. Bush, or the president, saying something roughly along these lines:

"I know that this matter of abortion has been a straining issue, and the press often describes it as an 'emotional' and 'divisive' issue. But when people say it is emotional, they mean that it inspires strong feelings about the things that are right and wrong. That doesn't mean that we cannot reason about these things, as we have reasoned in the past about other issues of right and wrong that have stirred deep emotions in our people. We are, quite clearly, 'divided' on this question, as we have been divided on other questions in the past. And yet, the surveys reveal that we are not as divided as the many commentators suggest. In fact, there is a remarkable consensus on many points in the argument over abortion. Most people do not think that abortions should be available 'on demand,' for any reason at all, at every stage of a pregnancy. Even people who call themselves 'pro-choice' think that some abortions may be restricted, and some lives saved.

"Why not then begin to talk about this matter at the places where we readily agree, and why not begin to save even a handful of lives? The problem is that we have become unused to talking about this issue, and we have stopped talking about it in our public life because this matter has been ruled now for so long by the courts. It was removed from the hands of legislatures in the States, and when it was removed from the business of legislatures, it was removed from that arena in which ordinary men and women would talk about these matters, in ordinary language.

"This matter has been ruled so long now, and so exclusively, by the courts, that it would be necessary to have a conversation before we could set upon the task of legislating. Once that conversation begins, I think we would discover many more points of agreement than people suppose, and so I would even invite the 'other side' to decide where that conversation might begin. For after all, the people who favor 'choice' in abortion insist that abortion is not infanticide. They do not stand for the killing of children. But that implies that they are willing to protect the child at some point. *Let them simply tell us where, and we can begin there.* Might we suggest, in that vein, one of the most modest measures of all: Might we simply protect the life of the child who *survives* the abortion?

"There are only a handful of such cases each year, but it is not clear that we can protect the child even at this point. And yet, surely, no one would pretend to any doubts about the 'human' standing of the child at the point of birth. After all, the child is separated from the mother, the pregnancy is over, and the interests of the mother can be separated from those of the child. A child 'unwanted' could be placed now in the hands of people willing to nurture and protect it. And so, can we not begin at least at this point?: Can we not say that this child has a claim to the protection of the law, a claim that does not depend at all on the question of whether anyone happens to *want* her?"

"My own sense is that, if the conversation began, we would soon take other steps, to extend the protections of the law to the child in the womb. For almost no one in the country really doubts that the child in the womb is a human being, and certainly no one could point to any significant difference between the child one day after birth and the same child, in the womb, one day *before* birth. But then neither would the child be any less human thirty or sixty days earlier, and if we followed these steps I think we would find ourselves, as I say, extending the protections of the law to those innocent beings whose lives may be taken now even without the need to offer a justification.

"Of course, it is entirely possible that I will prove wrong in my estimates: It may be that we will *not* convince one another. Yet, that is what a conversation may mean: that we will carry this process forward, one modest step at a time, only as we succeeded in persuading each other, in every instance, that this is the right thing to do. And so why not? We may save, in the first instance, only a handful of lives. But why is that not worth doing? We have had 1.3 to 1.5 million abortions every year for sixteen years [in 1989]. What would be wrong in creating now the possibilities at least for saving even a handful of those lives? People could not think themselves dispossessed of any true rights; we could begin a conversation we have long needed; and we could do, overall, a vast good."

I do not pretend that I had written this draft in the accents of George Bush, but something like it could have been trimmed to his own speech. And while we cannot profess to know that the speech would have produced the effect we were seeking, I think it is fairly clear that a line of this kind, staked out at once by the president, could have saved the Jim Courters of the world. Courter could have taken his lead from the president, the leader of his party. Following that lead, he could have assured people that no one was going to be divested of whole bodies of rights. They would be invited, rather, to join him in taking the most modest steps – the first steps in using the law – and beginning a conversation. Was there really likely to be an uprising in his district if Courter had proposed now simply to protect a child born alive, a child who had *survived* an abortion?

What made that prospect more than a thought-experiment was *Floyd v. Anders*, a case that arose in a federal district court in South Carolina in 1977. A male child had survived an abortion, and a surgery, for 20 days after an abortion, and the question was posed as to whether there had been an obligation to preserve the life of that child. The answer, tendered by Judge Clement Haynsworth, was no: As Haynsworth "explained," the mother had decided on abortion, and therefore, "the fetus in this case was not a person whose life state law could protect."[25] Ordinarily, a child born alive is protected under the laws of a state, but now we had a new constitutional right, a right to abortion, and that new right worked its effects simply by shifting the labels: That child born alive was not a child, or a person, protected by the laws of homicide. That new being was merely a "fetus," marked for termination. In effect, the right to abortion was interpreted as the right to an "effective abortion" or a dead child.

Several years later, in *Planned Parenthood v. Ashcroft*, Justice Powell would take notice, in a footnote, of a doctor who had made, explicitly, this macabre argument that the right to an abortion is the right to an "effective" abortion. Powell pronounced that argument at the time as "remarkable."[26] From this observation, cast up in passing, a few pro-life lawyers have drawn the inference that the Court had rejected this claim, along with the whole corpus of premises that would stand behind it. And yet, from that comment, cast off in passing, in a footnote, we can draw no such inferences. To say that an argument is "remarkable" is not exactly the same as saying that it is *wrong*; and still less is it to explain wherein its wrongness lies. The brute fact is that the Court has never proclaimed this understanding to be wrong – and gone on to explain the ground of its wrongness. That omission cannot be charged merely to inadvertence: To explain why that claim is wrong – to explain why the child bears an intrinsic dignity – is to put in place the premises that would finally undercut, or dissolve, the "right to abortion" and all of the jurisprudence built upon that slogan.

But that is also what imparts such a larger significance to those steps, so apparently simple and so modestly drawn. There was no need here to dissemble: In writings over the next several years, I would

---

[25] *Floyd v. Anders*, 444 F. Supp. 535, at 539 (1977).
[26] See *Planned Parenthood v. Ashcroft*, 462 U.S. 476, at 485, n. 7.

acknowledge our expectation that, if these premises were put into place, the defense of abortion could essentially unravel.[27] And that is why those of us who took this line thought that the partisans of abortion would resist that first step, even though it meant a defense, in effect, of infanticide. Once the conversation was opened, once the public was aware that it was possible to begin speaking again about the conditions under which abortions were justified or unjustified, then the surveys gave reason to think that the sentiments of the public would drive matters quite quickly beyond those first, most modest steps.

But at the same time, our invitation to enter the conversation was earnest. For the public could indeed prove reluctant to extend the law, even where most people thought abortions were wrong. We might not have persuaded people to take many more steps beyond those first steps we had proposed. And yet, each step promised to save more lives. Each step would remind people that it was indeed possible to speak about the grounds on which abortions could be judged as justified or unjustified. The saving of even a handful of lives could be a sufficient satisfaction in itself. But beyond that, there was a good to be attained in principle simply by planting the notion that it was possible, once again, to have a conversation about the rights and wrongs of the matter, and to establish anew a point once taken as commonplace: namely, that this conversation, among ordinary folk, could find a reflection in the laws.

It did not take long, however, for the recognition to set in that it was no simple, or even practicable, task to impart speech to George Bush. And yet, it seemed to some of us that this plan should not be buried in the portfolio of George Bush's undelivered speeches. In the fall of 1988, during the presidential election year, I published a fuller account of the plan and its argument in the *National Review*.[28] And thereafter, as it was said in the Bible, I sought to teach these lessons going out and coming in; when I got up in the morning, and before I went to bed at night. To state the matter more soberly, I pressed this argument in a variety of settings, in articles and speeches, and most

[27] See "Anti-abortion but Politically Smart," *The Wall Street Journal* (March 25, 1995), editorial page.
[28] "How to Roll Back *Roe*," *National Review* (October 28, 1988), pp. 30 ff.; *supra*, n. 18.

importantly in a gathering of leaders from pro-life organizations that met quarterly in Washington, D.C. I was spending the academic year, 1991–92 in Washington, and in the spring of 1992 I had drawn a virtual mandate from this group to press the plan as a legislative proposal on Capitol Hill. Here I had the generous help of friends, such as Lincoln Oliphant and Clark Forsythe, in the drafting of the bill. Many other friends sought to open doors and set up meetings; and when the chance finally arose, several years later, to introduce that bill, Robert George from Princeton, and Michael Uhlmann from the Ethics & Public Policy Center, took turns at times in going door to door with me, in meetings with senators and congressmen and their staffs.

But from the first moments a resistance was encountered from the most unexpected source: the National Right to Life Committee in Washington. There had been movements, in the Democratic Congress, to pass a Freedom of Choice Act, a bill that would essentially codify *Roe v. Wade*, and weave the premises of that case more fully into the statutes of the federal government. That prospect deepened when Bill Clinton was elected president, and a pro-abortion party was in control of the executive and legislative branches. Over the next several years, Bill Clinton would waver on many things, but he made it clear, from his first moments in office, that his administration would regard abortion, not merely as a "regrettable choice," but as a positive good – as something to be promoted at every turn, even with the use of public funds. On the day of his inauguration, his first day as President, Clinton would sign orders to displace a series of executive orders from the Reagan and Bush administrations that had cast up inhibitions on abortions: There had been restraints on the performance of abortion in the military and diplomatic outposts of the country abroad. There had been the "Mexico City policy," putting the United States in opposition to any schemes, through the United Nations, to press poorer countries to accept policies of legalized abortion. There had been a ban on the "counseling" of abortion in facilities that received funding from the federal government. All of these things were now swept away in a stroke of the presidential pen.

With a Congress attached by the ties of party to an administration of this character, the pro-life lobbyists were put on their mettle. But they did not panic, and the absence of panic proved an aid to clearheadedness. For they retained a certain sobriety as they assessed the situation, and in their sober calculation, the votes were still not there. Even in a Democratic House, it was a close-run thing to pass a law that mirrored *Roe v. Wade*, a law that would permit abortion on demand throughout the entire length of the pregnancy. The seasoned pro-life lobbyists, who had "worked" Capitol Hill for years, were concerned now that our minimal bill, this most modest of first steps, would simply give cover to many congressmen wavering in the middle. The congressmen could vote for that "modest first step," and claim, on their record, a "pro-life" vote, to mollify many of their constituents on the pro-life side. But then they could "balance" that vote by voting, on the other side, to affirm abortion as a "woman's choice" and install the doctrine in *Roe* as the new matrix for the laws on abortion.

One leading figure at National Right to Life remarked that "even Nancy Johnson" could vote for that minimal bill and claim "pro-life" credentials. Nancy Johnson, Republican of Connecticut, was one of a cluster of Republicans always voting in favor of abortion. But other people, who had clocked many hours on Capitol Hill, were convinced that the Nancy Johnsons could never vote even for that "modest first step" – precisely because the import of that modest bill was so clear. Subsequent events would bear out that expectation in a manner that left even the experienced hands at National Right to Life rather astonished. For as modest as that bill was, the premises of the bill, planted in the law, would have to undermine the premises of any bill that refused to recognize the aborted child as a real entity, a real being, with standing to receive the protections of the law.

Or the bill would have been unsettling, that is, if people were affected by even a minimal sense of consistency and the canons of propositional logic. When it came to abortion, wide sections of the public had already shown a willingness to reach judgments without worrying overly much about the claims of consistency: How else to explain why large samples of the public, measured in surveys, regarded abortions as "wrong," as a kind of "murder," or unjustified killing – and yet were reluctant to have the laws forbid these killings, as they had been forbidden by the laws before 1973? The public, it was clear, could live with a large measure of inconsistency on this subject. In fact, it was hard to live with abortion at all without the willingness to suspend those vexing tests of principle: For why was it not the "woman's choice" to kill the newborn infant, whose presence could threaten to disrupt her life? Why was she obliged to give up that child for adoption, rather than discard it? Why would the law come down so heavily on the teenagers who would throw a baby in a dumpster on the evening of their prom in New Jersey? As one commentator observed, under the current laws on abortion they could have called in a doctor, without the need to inform their parents, and destroyed that child quite legally even at the point of birth, even as the child began to emerge.

And yet, the logic of the principle, the test of consistency, would never disappear or lose its hold, even for the defenders of "abortion rights." That signal fact was demonstrated time and again by their sensitivity to any measure that called into question the logic that supported the right to abortion. In 1999, Congressman Lindsey Graham of South Carolina introduced the "Unborn Victims of Violence Act," a bill that would extend the concerns of the federal law to the unborn child who might be killed in the course of a federal crime. Graham did not seek to extend the federal jurisdiction. His bill applied only to the kinds of crimes that were covered already by federal law. And so, for example, the federal law had been extended to cover the killings that took place in the course of drive-by shootings that grew out of the illicit dealing for drugs. The killing of bystanders was already covered by that federal law, and Graham proposed now to bring the unborn child into the class of bystanders, of innocent human beings killed in these assaults. The defenders of abortion understood at once that this bill struck at their deepest premises, for it considered an unborn child as a human being, a person with standing to receive the protections of the law. And yet, by the coin of that term "pro-choice," this bill might not have posed a problem: After all, the defenders of "choice" were committed to the notion that, if a woman "wanted" her child, that child was a real entity, who could be treated with pre-natal medicine and protected in the law. If a pregnant woman "wanting" her child was injured in an auto accident, and the baby had suffered injuries, the defenders of abortion had to support the right of that woman, or her child, to sue the negligent driver and secure damages for the injuries.

This sense of the matter was caught accurately, in the debate in the House by Representative Heather Wilson (R–NM). Mrs. Wilson had not aligned herself firmly with the pro-lifers in her own party, and so she could observe quite aptly that "One can be the most pro-choice person in this body and vote in favor of this bill with enthusiasm because it is not about the unwanted pregnancies; it is about the wanted ones." In response to the taunts emanating from the other side, Mrs. Wilson pointed out that she was cosponsoring the bills on domestic violence, "but it does not make sense to me to say that caring about the lost child somehow demeans that child's mother."[29]

Lindsey Graham's bill then was thoroughly consistent with the premises of "choice" in abortion. And yet, the proponents of abortion suffered no difficulty in recognizing that the premises of the bill really struck at their deepest premises, the premises that ran quite beyond the slogans about "choice." What the reactions would reveal was that, for the partisans of "choice," the child in the womb could be conceded no standing at all as a human, as the bearer of any rights, or the object of protection. As Graham's bill made its way to the floor of the House, the opposition adamantly refused to recognize that there was any victim of an assault apart from the woman who was pregnant. In *U.S. v. Robbins*, decided in the court of military appeals in March 1999, an enlisted man in the air force had beaten his wife and killed the child she was carrying in her womb, the child they had already named Jasmine. The military prosecutors came down hard on the assault inflicted on Mrs. Robbins. But they did not think they had the authority to prosecute separately for the killing of baby Jasmine. That was the omission, the gap in the law, that Congressman Graham's bill was meant to supply. But as the Democrats resisted Graham's bill, they professed to see no injury beyond the beating suffered by Mrs. Robbins.[30] They could not make themselves acknowledge that, quite discriminable from the assault on Mrs. Robbins, was an assault that proved lethal for another small being. That someone *actually died* was a matter that had to be screened out, denied any recognition as a fact, if the "pro-choice" position could sustain itself.

The opposition on the floor was led by Representative Zoe Lofgren of California, who complained that Graham's bill

---

[29] *Congressional Record* (September 30, 1999), p. H9050.
[30] See the comments cast up during the debate on the floor of the House – especially the remarks of Representatives Jerrold Nadler (NY), Nita Lowey (NY), and Rosa De Lauro (CI); *Congressional Record* (September 30, 1999), pp. H9049, H9050–1.

recognizes a member of the species Homo sapiens at all stages of development as a victim of crime, from conception to birth. This affords even an embryo legal rights equal to and separate from those of the woman.

Her corrective was an amendment that "recognizes the pregnant woman as the primary victim of a crime." But a "primary" victim implies at least a "secondary" victim; and yet, Lofgren's amendment recognized no such victim. It recognized only "assaultive conduct against a pregnant woman." Once again, the ideological screen came down: The only thing recognized was an assault on a woman, and that theme ran as a thread through the attacks mounted by the Democratic women in the House. Representative Nita Lowey (D–NY) complained, with some vitriol, that Graham's bill had "taken an important principle, the constitutional right of a woman to have control over her own pregnancy, and hijacked it."[31] The principle had solely to do with a woman's control of a pregnancy; it offered no recognition of another life, the target of assaults, or the distinct subject of prenatal surgery.

The resisters were compelled then to strike the most improbable postures. But those logical gymnastics were utterly necessary if they were to fend off any erosion, any chipping away, of that right to abortion. What the encounter confirmed, though, again was that, for the defenders of abortion, *these logical connections counted*. Yet, not only did they count; they were apparently regarded as decisive, for even the most modest steps had to be resisted if they bore anything in principle that endangered the rationale for abortion.

Hence, there was ample reason to think that our proposal, the most modest first step of all, could not be accepted without resistance. But in the press of the moment, with the concern over the Freedom of Choice Act, there was a willingness to defer to those experienced lobbyists on Capitol Hill, who made their living every day by gauging the inclinations, and moves, of congressmen. We held back then discreetly, in those days in 1993, out of a concern for the larger cause. And as the lobbyists had expected, the partisans of abortion, fired by the sense of possibility, suddenly discovered the limits of their reach. They could not in fact enact that bill, even in the heady first year of the Clinton Administration. With the elections of 1994, the prospects for the

---

[31] *Ibid.*, at H9050.

Freedom of Choice Act came to a conclusive end. For the Republicans swept into control of Congress for the first time in 42 years, and the party that came into office was very much a pro-life party in its main cast. Only two pro-life incumbents lost their seats, and those were Democrats replaced by pro-life Republicans. In no instance was a pro-life incumbent unseated by a pro-choice candidate. On the other hand, many pro-choice candidates went down to defeat.[32] With Mr. Clinton still holding the powers of the executive, there were of course the most severe limits on what a pro-life majority in Congress could accomplish. But with the Republicans in a position now to introduce bills, order up hearings, and bring bills to the floor, there seemed to be new possibilities opened for initiatives in legislation. The natural question was, What would the first step be, in unfolding a series, or sequence, of moves?

By April 1995, in the first spring of the Republican Congress, there was a proposal ripening, a measure that seemed to draw a wide interest among pro-life congressmen. This was the bill taking, as the center of its focus, the procedure that would come to be known as "partial-birth abortions." The idea for the bill had apparently sprung from the offices of National Right to Life, when the staff had come upon a remarkably candid account of this procedure on the part of one of its inventors, Dr. Martin Haskell. The technical name for the procedure was Dilatation and Extraction (D & X). The name was readily confused with so-called "D & E" abortions (Dilatation and Evacuation), but the distinction helped to mark off more precisely the nature of the D & X. The D & E involved the removal of the child in pieces. D & Xs were meant as an improvement over D & Es for late abortions (around 20 to 26 weeks); and the D & E, in turn, had been heralded as a procedure notably safer than the alternative methods of injecting saline or using prostaglandins. With these latter procedures, there would be contractions, along with amplified, lingering pain. With a D

---

[32] In Georgia, for example, Bob Barr was elected for the first time as a pro-life Republican, defeating an incumbent, Buddy Darden, who was pro-choice or pro-abortion. In the races for the Senate, candidates such as Spence Abraham in Michigan, Bill Frist in Tennessee, Rick Santorum in Pennsylvania, and Mike DeWine in Ohio, displaced or defeated pro-choice Democrats. As the figures were tallied by National Right to Life, the net gain of pro-life members in the Congress came to 40 in the House and six in the Senate.

& E, the child would be dismembered, and there would be a need to deal with the problem of crushing the head, for the head often proved the most difficult to remove. Beyond that, there was the occasional need for the surgeon to return to the uterine cavity, to deal, as the saying went, with "matter" imperfectly removed.

Against the background of this experience, D & X offered a dramatic difference. It would remove the child in one piece – or sort of. There was still that matter of the head, and this is where the D & X would make its distinctive contribution. This is also where the public was given the most direct account of the procedure in a paper done in 1992 by Dr. Haskell. The doctor brought to his description the experience of performing over 700 of these procedures. But his account was a model of artless candor, and the staff at National Right to Life found that they could hardly do better than to let Dr. Haskell speak for himself, in describing the surgery he was now commending to the public:

> With the lower extremity [of the fetus] in the vagina the surgeon uses his fingers to deliver the opposite lower extremity, then the torso, the shoulders and the upper extremities.
>
> The skull lodges at the internal cervical os. Usually there is not enough dilation for it to pass through. The fetus is oriented dorsum or spine up.
>
> At this point, the right-handed surgeon slides the fingers of the left hand along the back of the fetus and 'hooks' the shoulders of the fetus with the index and ring fingers . . . Next he slides the tip of the middle finger along the spine towards the skull while applying traction to the shoulders and lower extremities. The middle finger lifts and pushes the anterior cervical lip out of the way.
>
> While maintaining this tension, lifting the cervix and applying traction to the shoulders with the fingers of the left hand, the surgeon takes a pair of blunt curved Metzenbaum scissors in the right hand. He carefully advances the tip, curved down, along the spine and under this middle finger until he feels it contact the base of the skull under the tip of his middle finger.
>
> [T]he surgeon then forces the scissors into the base of the skull or into the *foramen magnum*. Having safely entered the skull, he spreads the scissors to enlarge the opening.
>
> The surgeon removes the scissors and introduces a suction catheter into this hole and evacuates the skull contents. With the catheter still in place, he applies traction to the fetus, removing it completely from the patient.

In short, the brains are literally sucked out of the child. But the cool detachment in the writing actually belies the experience in these surgeries. The same researchers who commended these procedures to the public had found this persisting theme: The D & X shifted the burdens and trauma from the pregnant women to the doctors and nurses. As for the practitioners, they found their justification, as two of them said, in "a strong sense of social conscience focused on the health and desires of the women." They relied, that is, on the doctrine of "women's rights," or the "right to an abortion" to steel themselves, and to screen from view the things that should have been instantly evident to the senses.

The willingness to discuss this gruesome procedure as though it were a trivial or routine matter was itself already the reflection of a moral sensibility quite anesthetized – a sensibility that was clearly distant now from the sense that there was anything the least problematic, morally, in what was taking place. The procedure and the presentation provided, then, a matter that deserved to be placed before the public, with the procedure made the object of legislation. The staff at National Right to Life seized the moment to make this move, but they counted on the expectation that most people in the country had not been morally anesthetized in the same way as Dr. Haskell. The political move made sense only on the assumption that, for most people in the country, the screen of ideology had not come down; that most people would encounter, with eyes unclouded, the description of Haskell's novel procedure. When they did, they would see what it described – a child at the point of birth having its skull crushed. It was assumed, also, that most people would recoil from what was shown to them: They would not be taken in by the thin pretext that this was an abortion, and not an act of infanticide, because the head of the child had not yet emerged from the birth canal! And indeed, that expectation would be largely borne out. As the issue of "partial-birth abortion" was put before the public in surveys, the main effect was a recoil on the part of the public – and even more than that: the numbers on abortion, drifting upward for a while, began steadily to move downward again, in the support registered for abortion.

The National Right to Life Committee had resisted that earlier measure, that most modest of first steps; and yet it had now found a measure nearly equivalent. That earlier proposal had been brought forth for the sake of planting premises and having an "educational" effect. And now, National Right to Life was using the bill on partial-birth abortion to produce the same effect: As the bill lingered in the business of the public, the news was gradually brought home to more and more people that abortions could be performed right up through the time of birth.

By the end of that first year of the Republican Congress, the sentiment in support of banning this procedure had spread widely and affected many Democrats as well. On November 1, 1995, the bill banning partial-birth abortion passed the House by a vote of 288 to 139, a margin wide enough to override the veto expected from President Clinton. (The measure had revealed the split among Democrats on this issue, but even so, the vote revealed parties that were strikingly different in their dominant tendencies. The Republicans voted for the bill at a level of 215 to 15, and the Democrats largely against, at a vote of 73 to 123.) On December 7, the bill would pass the Senate, but with a vote of 54 to 44.[33] Once again, the bill could not have been enacted without Democratic votes, but in this case the managers were nine votes short of what they needed to override a veto.

After some back and forth over the different versions of the bill in the Senate and the House, the House passed the bill with some clarifying amendments on March 26, 1996, with substantially the same vote (286 to 129). The veto came about two weeks later, on April 10. The pro-choice, or pro-abortion, interest was the one interest Bill Clinton had never compromised in a career affected by compromises on virtually everything else. The ideological core of the Democratic party had come to regard this issue as the touchstone for those moral and religious differences that defined the "culture war" – and the main mission now of the liberal party in American politics. As Mr. Clinton stood his ground firmly, he bound to himself ever more securely the support of the radical feminists and the hard Left, in New York and California, that more and more defined the core of activists in the party. That binding effect would yield the most spectacular effects in 1998, when Clinton was seriously threatened with impeachment, and his conduct had made it necessary even for Democrats in Congress to

---

[33] Again, the differences between the parties were revealing: Republicans voted for the bill at a level of 45–8; Democrats voted against by a score of 9–36.

offer schemes of "censure." But no matter what distaste they affected in public, no matter how much they made it clear that they disapproved of the president's antics, they had the deepest stake by now in a president who had proved so steadfast in defending the interest they had come to regard as the most precious of all. They could not readily abandon a president willing to stand up, even on the issue of partial-birth abortion, and say the things their position required him to say, at that moment, if he would preserve the right to abortion unimpaired, unconditional, and thoroughly unqualified.[34]

For Mr. Clinton could do that only by screening out, ruthlessly, the facts that made even members of his own party recoil. He was compelled to pretend – as the defense of unrestricted abortion compelled him to pretend – that there was no one in the picture who counted apart from a pregnant woman and an abortionist. In the world and words of Bill Clinton, there was no head being punctured, no brains sucked out, no head collapsed. There was not even a being, or a small child, present, who was suffering an assault and death. As Chico Marx once famously asked, "Are you going to believe me – or your own eyes?" The true measure of Clinton's fidelity was that he was willing to deny earnestly the things that were plainly in sight for anyone with eyes to see. And that fidelity had to earn for him, in the election, a loyalty equally unimpaired. One female reporter remarked, at the height of the controversy over sex with an intern, that she herself would willingly give oral sex to Clinton just to show her gratitude for his defense of abortion rights.

The veto by Bill Clinton represented then no idle striking of poses. It was a stance that brought a vast political return, and the effect was enhanced as Clinton, with that veto, bought time. As months turned into years, and Clinton's veto held, Clinton's trademark audacity became catching. His allies, even those with a more cultivated sense of shame, began to speak the same words, and affect the same blinders, if they were to stave off again the bill on partial-birth abortions.

When Clinton was reelected to a second term, over the feckless Bob Dole, there seemed little prospect that the bill could be enacted and signed into law – unless those nine votes could be gained in the Senate.

---

[34] On this point, see Robert George "The Clinton Puzzle: Why Do Liberals Love Him So?" *Wall Street Journal* (October 6, 2000).

Of course, anything worth doing was worth doing yet again: To rein-troduce the bill in Congress, to air the issue once again, offered the chance to erode even further the willingness of the public to support a right to abortion that was never qualified, never subject to restraints under any condition. Even if the managers fell short, they were con-fident that the "educational" value of the bill remained quite potent. It could be used with a still considerable effect in the upcoming elec-tions to the Congress in 1998.

But in the meantime, something happened on the way to the con-gressional elections. While the issue was stalled at the national level, bills on partial abortion, in one form or another, were introduced and passed in several states, including Michigan, Illinois, and Nebraska. By the spring of 1998 bills had been passed, or brought to the threshold of passage, in about 20 states. Every initiative within the States brought the chance to air the issue once again, to break out, to the public, things that would come as unsettling news. In that sense the campaigns in the separate states fed into the same cause. They were shaping the same sentiment of the public that the supporters of the bill would draw upon as they sought to build support for a federal bill.

And yet, something intervened to throw things off stride – and make matters, for the pro-lifers, considerably worse. By the spring of 1998, a series of decisions began to appear in the federal courts, as federal judges began to enjoin, or even strike down, the bills on partial-birth abortion in the States. As we shall see, the grounds on which the judges blocked those bills were rather implausible, and at times quite contradictory. The judges reached for all varieties of improbable rea-soning, and it was clear that the judges were not overly particular or fastidious about the reasons they were content to set down on paper. Indeed, the point coming through this series of decisions was that the reasons really did not matter. Reasons used in one state could be at odds with reasons used in another, but the major point, coming through the decisions, was univocal: The political class in charge of the courts was making brutally clear that it was having none of this. The judges would not permit even the most modest of first steps in the restriction of abortion, out of a concern, no doubt, that those steps would soon be followed by others, until at last the right to abor-tion could come directly, and seriously, into question.

The performance of the judges was audacious to the point of cynicism, and yet these moves seemed to go unnoticed in Congress, because political Washington was suddenly taken up with a scandal so exciting the media, so absorbing the public attention, that it blocked the view of everything else. Toward the end of January 1998, the Lewinsky affair broke. The first news began to appear on the escapades of President Clinton with Ms. Monica Lewinsky, who had served as an intern in the White House. With the Lewinsky matter heading the news every night, it was hard to notice the concert of judges, in the federal courts, blocking with the most contrived reasons these measures they were determined to quash. It was not surprising that members of Congress, and even the pro-life lobbyists, did not notice what was building before them. Some of them did notice, but they did not think it would finally matter: The string of decisions was becoming quite uniform – only the laws in Virginia and Wisconsin would be sustained by federal courts, and even then it took a kind of continuing vigil on the part of judges such as Michael Lutting in the Fourth Circuit (in Virginia) to keep other judges from getting around their orders and scuttling the new law.[35]

Still, the pro-life lobbyists were convinced that the matter was going up to the Supreme Court, and they were convinced that they would win with this issue, even with the Court that produced *Planned Parenthood v. Casey*. For even while that Court had affirmed *Roe v. Wade*, it had sustained almost all of the regulations in Pennsylvania that cast up slight barriers, or inhibitions, on abortions. In fact, Justices O'Connor, Kennedy, and Souter had been willing to overturn one earlier decision that had struck down the requirement of a waiting period of 24 hours. As the judges took these small steps, they argued for a larger measure of authority for the States, in these regulations, to consider the interests of the unborn child, and not merely the health of the mother.[36] There were ample reasons, then, to think that even this

---

[35] See Judge Luttig's precise – and luminous – opinion for the Court of Appeals in Virginia, in *Richmond Medical Center for Women v. Gilmore*, 144 F. 3d 326 (June 30, 1998).

[36] See *Planned Parenthood v. Casey, supra*, n. 5, at 873, 882–3. For example: "We . . . see no reason why the State may not require doctors to inform a woman seeking an abortion of the availability of materials relating to the consequences to the fetus, even when those consequences have no direct relation to her health. . . . We would

Supreme Court would agree that the right to abortion had to find its limit when the process of birthing had begun.

The pro-life complex in Congress – the congressmen, their staffs, and the pro-life lobbyists – were determined then to hold steadily with the plan they had set for themselves. They would continue to work for the bill on partial-birth abortion, even though there was little prospect that it would be passed just yet over the veto of President Clinton. That constancy could be a supreme asset in politics; but in this case, it distracted the pro-lifers from seeing what was unfolding before their eyes. By the summer, Judge Payne in Virginia, taking note of the trend of decisions, struck down the law on partial-birth abortions in that state. The pattern of judgments, accumulating in the lower federal courts, evidently struck Payne as ringingly apt or congenial, for they now described, for him, an "overwhelming and persuasive quantum of authority."[37] If that sense of the matter took hold, the Supreme Court would be reviewing a series of decisions revealing a rather lopsided and emphatic judgment. To use an old expression of Felix Frankfurter's, those decisions, uniform in their meaning, would arrive at the Supreme Court with a certain "momentum of respect." The convergence of the decisions in the lower courts, the weight of their agreement, could well tip the Court in their favor. By the fall of 1999, the matter entered a new phase of decisiveness, and the answer would not be long in coming. For in October, the federal court of appeals for the Seventh Circuit, sustained the laws on partial-birth abortion in Wisconsin and Nebraska.[38] Those laws had been struck down in the lower courts, as they had been struck down almost everywhere else. But a decision that sustained the law on

think it constitutional for the State to require that in order for there to be informed consent to a kidney transplant operation the recipient must be supplied with information about risks to the donor as well as risks to himself or herself. . . . We conclude . . . that informed choice need not be defined in such narrow terms that all considerations of the effect of the fetus are made irrelevant." *Ibid.*, at 883. See also my piece, "A Season for the Chameleons: Abortion, the Supreme Court, and Justice Kennedy," *Crisis* (April 2000) pp. 10–16.

[37] *Richmond Medical Center for Women v. Gilmore*, 11 F. Supp. 2d 795, at 818 (June 25, 1998). He was later overridden by a three-judge panel of the Court of Appeals, with Judge Luttig writing for the court. See 183 F. 3d 303 (July 29, 1998).

[38] For an account of Judge Easterbrook's rather cagey argument – and Judge Posner's dissent – see my piece, "There is Nothing Vague About Partial-Birth Abortion," *Wall Street Journal* (November 1, 1999), p. A54.

its merits now created a conflict among the circuits of the federal courts. There would be more pressure on the Supreme Court then to resolve the issue, and in January 2000 the Court agreed to hear the case on appeal.

By June 2000, there would be a decision. Of course, the Court might still not resolve the issue: There were several ways in which the Court could send the cases back down to the lower courts on various technical issues. In that way, the Court could keep the process churning, while avoiding the need to reach any decisive judgment one way or the other. Still, what was hovering now as a prospect was the chance to get a test, in the Court, on the strategy of the "modest first step." The Court had created the right to an abortion – would it now be willing to say explicitly that there must be a limit to this liberty, as to all other liberties? But this was not the best way in which to present the "first step," and those of us who had framed this approach did not have the same confidence now, in 1999, that we would have had ten years earlier, if the matter had been presented to the Court. For the framers of the bill on partial-birth abortion had not taken care to fill in the simple point that was at the center of that earlier and most modest measure of all, to protect the survivors of abortion: They had never established the premise that the child at the point of birth, the child targeted for abortion, was an entity with real standing in the law, a being whose injuries somehow counted.

With that critical point left unmade, there was a far larger cloud of uncertainty enveloping this issue of partial-birth abortion as it made its way now to the Supreme Court. As for the pro-life groups, they seemed to be engaging in a kind of sleepwalking, serenely unmoved by the spate of decisions that were accumulating in the federal courts through the spring and summer, spilling over into the fall of 1998. To be fair, they were not inattentive. They were alert to every decision going against them in the courts. But they did not have a sense quite yet of what they could do, in coping with the problem, other than continue along the path they had marked off for themselves, in passing that bill on partial-birth abortions. What they did not seem to notice was that matters were moving into an alarming phase, with something distinctly new. As the judges summoned the nerve to defend abortions even at the point of birth, they began to defend abortion with a language far less affected by a sense of inhibition, reluctance, or regret.

In the sweep of their convictions, they began to put in place premises that made the case for abortion even more radically than they had made it in the past. And indeed, they were moved to install now premises that were at war with jurisprudence itself.

Five

Antijural Jurisprudence

Henry James said of one of his characters that he was the victim of perplexities from which a single spark of direct perception might have spared him. If we were to credit their own words, we would have to suppose that a cluster of federal judges, men and women who had been schooled at the priciest academies in the land, really could not fathom what was meant by a "partial-birth" abortion. For in one decision after another, beginning in the summer of 1997, and picking up momentum, in a building series of decisions by the spring of 1998, the judges were confronting bills on partial-birth abortion in the States, and striking down every one of them on the claim that the statutes were afflicted with a fatal "vagueness." In the legends of the law a "vague statute" might be something on the order of an ordinance that barred any "fooling around in the park." It would be vague in the sense that it was tellingly imprecise about the conduct it meant to forbid, and so even the ordinary person, strolling in the park, might not have a fair warning of the kind of conduct that might be punishable. Under those conditions, a person of ordinary prudence might take care to steer a wider course away from the range of conduct that could run afoul of the law. And therein the vague statute would do its further mischief: It would create an incentive for people to avoid even behavior quite innocent, the kind of behavior that the law would not have a chance of forbidding if the law had to address the matter directly, and in terms quite explicit justify its statute.

If there had been something "vague" about the definition of "partial-birth" abortions, surgeons in the business of abortion would have run the risk of being deterred from performing abortions that remained quite legitimate in the eyes of the law. But because the law on partial-birth abortions dealt with only the smallest fraction of abortions performed in the country, that problem promised to be virtually negligible. Even so, it was predictable that a crew of doctors, allied with Planned Parenthood, would come into court instantly to challenge a new law on abortion. And in challenging the law, the doctors would claim, as the ground of their complaint, bewilderment. They had to affect a certain incomprehension as to what was meant by a "partial-birth abortion," and they had to profess that they could discern only with haziness the lines that separated partial-birth abortions from other kinds of abortions. But that was precisely what they were willing, in these cases, to do. And in crediting these claims – in showing a willingness actually to act upon them – judges had to be willing to break from the conventions that defined quite sharply in the past the "ethic" of judges in a democracy. They also had to overthrow that sense of the worldliness and skepticism that marked the temper of a judge: After all, when citizens come into court, clamoring for an injunction, claiming that they are imperiled by the laws, the "sober" judge known to legend and song would typically ask just what reason the complainant had to think that he was the object of prosecution. Had he been arrested or warned? Had he received a citation, or for that matter, any other sign to indicate that he was an object of interest to the authorities?

But apart from the urbanity that seemed to come along with the post of judge, the restraint of judges was bound up with the morality of a democratic regime. Judges were supposed to be confined to cases and controversies, to instances in which the law was actually being enforced on particular persons. Instances of that kind might reveal implications of the law that had not been foreseen by the framers of the bill when the matter had been cast, as legislation, in terms that were impersonal and abstract. If the judges were willing to pass judgment on a statute, without the occasion of a case, then the judges would be put on the same plane as legislators: Lacking any record of a case, they would simply be pronouncing on the legislation. They would have to vote finally on their sense of whether the legislation, in the abstract, was desirable or constitutional. But in fact they would be legislators on a more exalted plane, for their own votes, striking down a statute, would be sufficient to override the votes of those other public officials, who had voted the bill into law. And yet, unlike those other legislators, these legislators in robes, exercising a trumping power, were not elected to office. They would not have to suffer the torments of running for reelection.

This kind of power, exercised by unelected judges, had been understood from the beginning as a power that was deeply problematic in a republic, in a government that rested on the consent of the governed. The sense of propriety, arising from the character of the regime, was that judges in a democracy should be obliged then to work under a distinct discipline that would confine their judgments and the reach of their power. They would hold back their hands, they would not plunge into an issue, until they were presented with an actual case in controversy. And while they held back their hands, power would remain in hands other than their own; the hands of people who were elected to office. But that was precisely the understanding that judges subverted if they were willing to strike down statutes without the confining conditions of a real case, involving real persons in danger of real prosecutions. And yet, those were the constraints that the judges showed themselves all too willing now to throw off or treat with a remarkable nonchalance in the string of cases on partial-birth abortion. In the cavalier sweep of their judgments, they would not stop even to offer a justification for this extraordinary unconcern for the restraints on their office. They would busy themselves, rather, in the effort to assemble justifications, and everything would begin with the fiction that they found something hopelessly vague in the definition of a "partial-birth abortion."

And so the federal court of appeals in the Sixth Circuit professed to find something too hazy, too hard to grasp, in the definition of a D & X abortion (Dilatation and Extraction), the definition that was supplied by the legislature of Ohio:

> The termination of a human pregnancy by purposely inserting a suction device into the skull of a fetus to remove the brain. "Dilation and extraction" procedure does not include the suction curettage procedure of abortion or the suction aspiration procedure of abortion.

Even a cursory reading would suggest that this language was evidently meant to concentrate the bill on the kind of abortion that was performed at the point of birth, not on the abortions performed by cutting up the child or vacuuming out its parts. Later on in the opinion, Judge Barbara Kennedy described the D & X procedure, with lines that might have been taken from Dr. Martin Haskell, the man who had given the world this novel procedure:

> ... Finally, the physician removes the scissors, inserts a suction catheter into the hole, and removes the skull contents. The head will then compress, enabling the physician to remove the fetus completely from the woman.[1]

Now, where is the vagueness in any of this? Of course, the judges did not exactly mean that the statute was unintelligible. What they really meant was that the statute still could not establish a clear barrier between the abortions that were permitted and the abortions that were forbidden. As Judge Kennedy pleaded, the D & X abortion might not always be so easy to distinguish from the D & E (Dilatation and Evacuation) abortion, where the child (or rather "fetus") is being cut up. For in that procedure, too, the surgeon may have to use clamps to compress the head. And in some cases, as she pointed out, "some physicians compress the head by using suction to remove the intracranial contents" (i.e., brains).[2]

The problem of "vagueness," then, was not in the language, or in the clarity of the statute. It lay rather in the claim that there was no clear way of distinguishing the killing done on the child near birth with the killing routinely done in other abortions, even grislier. But one of the clearest things that had to be known about the drafting and the politics of the bills on partial-birth abortion was that these bills had sprung from the strategy of the "modest first step." The framers of the bills were working with the plan of engaging the issue of abortion on the terrain of the hardest cases for the partisans of abortion, the abortions that took place at the point of birth. The framers had made it their object, that is, to concentrate on the abortions at the end of a full pregnancy, at the point where anyone of common sense would see a "birth," marked by the emergence of a baby, not a "fetus." The drafters were trying to avoid any attempt to confound

---

[1] *Women's Medical Professional Corp. v. Voinovich*, 130 F. 3d 187, at 199 (1997).
[2] *Ibid.*, at 198.

what they were doing with the regulation of abortion. They were trying to deal with abortion at a point where even the most adamant defender of abortion could not look at the emerging infant and describe it as anything other than a child. The legislators went out of their way then to insist that they were not presuming to reach that vast mass of abortions now permitted under the law. They were concentrating, as they made clear, on this one type of abortion, with the baby turned around, so that the feet emerged first instead of the head, and with the abortion performed when only the head of the child remained in the birth canal. An awareness, then, of the political strategy behind the bill, and the intention reflected rather precisely in the drafting, should have been quite enough to indicate that no one performing ordinary abortions, uncovered in the bill, would have been picked out as a test case and made the object of a prosecution.

In effect, Judge Richard Bilby in Arizona acknowledged these points when he noted that the framers of the bill in that state had meant to "erect a firm barrier against infanticide" (*Planned Parenthood v. Woods*).[3] The remarkable thing in these cases – made all the more remarkable precisely because it has not been remarked upon – is that judges such as Bilby have gone on, in language suitably muffled, to argue that the legislators may not do this anymore: They may not erect a barrier, indecorously firm, against infanticide if that legal proscription would have the effect of inhibiting abortions anywhere else in the stages of pregnancy. And yet, why should it? Why should the law have this chilling or inhibiting effect, apart from anything it might do to awaken the practitioners to the fact that they are, after all, dismembering human beings? Apart from that, however, there could be a chilling effect from the law only if there was a serious prospect that the legislators, or the administrators of the law, meant to use this statute in an uncontained way, to prosecute surgeons who were performing other kinds of abortions. But that is exactly what is tested through the requirement of a case in controversy: We wait to see exactly how this statute is being applied in practice.

Instead, the judges were willing to plunge in at once to enjoin the enforcement of these laws before they had any evidence about the character of that enforcement. The judges seemed to be acting then

---

[3] 982 F. Supp. 1369 U.S. (1997), U.S. District Court for Arizona.

as another political chamber, to which a faction may appeal when it has lost in the other political chambers of the legislature and the executive. In breaking in this way from the traditional constraints, the judges had to accept a "facial challenge" to these laws that ran beyond the rules that must usually inform facial challenges. The Supreme Court restated the logic of the matter in 1987, in *United States v. Salerno*:[4]

> [A] facial challenge to a legislative Act [said the Court] is, of course, the most difficult challenge to mount successfully, since the challenger must establish that no set of circumstances exists under which the Act would be valid. The fact that [an Act] might operate unconstitutionally under some conceivable set of circumstances is insufficient to render it wholly invalid, since we have not recognized an "overbreadth" doctrine outside the limited context of the First Amendment.[5]

But when it came to the matter of abortion, the operating rule of the judges now seemed to be just the reverse: A law restricting abortion was *presumed to be unconstitutional* if there was any conceivable set of circumstances in which it *might* be applied in an unconstitutional way. This was not a change that the judges were inclined to install in general, or in principle; it was a rule apparently carved out to apply, as part of a special regime, only for this enclave of the law dealing with abortion. Judge Kennedy in the court of appeals in Ohio explained that this was not something struck off by the inventiveness of her colleagues. But rather, as she contended, this understanding was installed by the Supreme Court in *Planned Parenthood v. Casey*[6] in 1992. The Court, in that case, held that a law on abortion could be held unconstitutional on its face if "in a large fraction of the cases in which [the law] is relevant, it will operate as a substantial obstacle to a woman's choice to undergo an abortion."[7] From this perspective, it does not matter at all that the cases be few, or the numbers insignificant, when set against the vast scale of things. The question is whether the law works a substantial inhibition or restriction. And yet that is, after all, the purpose of a law – not to offer an exhortation, but to forbid and restrain something wrongful. For the person restrained, that law must always be "relevant," and the inhibition "substantial."

---

[4] 481 U.S. 739. [5] *Ibid.*, at 745. [6] 505 U.S. 833. [7] *Ibid.*, at 895.

In other words any law in the field of abortion, any law that imposes a serious restriction on the freedom to choose or perform abortions, no matter how circumscribed and modest, must be open at any time to a facial challenge precisely because it does restrict this freedom, which is apparently given the standing now of a "first freedom."

Judge Kennedy's point seemed to be confirmed when the Supreme Court refused, in the spring of 1998, to take *certiorari* in reviewing that judgment of Judge Kennedy and her colleagues in the Sixth Circuit. In refusing to review the judgment, the Court left unchallenged this reading offered by Judge Kennedy about the new rules over facial challenges and abortion, the new rules that were put in place by *Planned Parenthood v. Casey*. Justice Thomas registered his own protest here, joined by Justice Scalia and Chief Justice Rehnquist. For these justices, there was a need to settle this matter and decide whether the traditional rules, restated in *Salerno*, had been superseded now, and replaced by a new regime, created in *Planned Parenthood v. Casey*.[8]

But until that sense of things is dislodged, the right to abortion has been made the object of a special protection by the federal judges, using a new regime of rules, tailored solely to the needs of that "abortion liberty." Yet, more than that: The judges had now prepared the ground for striking down a *federal* law on partial-birth abortion if it were passed again in a subsequent Congress and enacted over the veto of the president. For the courts had now set in place layers of argument to establish that a law addressing partial-birth abortions would be unconstitutional. The same doctors and clinics who claim to be threatened or "chilled" by the laws passed, say, in Illinois and Michigan, would presumably claim to be quite as chilled and threatened by any comparable law passed at the national level. The same plaintiffs, then, would go into courts again – the same courts presided over by the same, friendly federal judges – and they would no doubt produce the same result.

This new, advanced state of things, attained by the judges, could be sustained mainly by the willingness of the judges to employ the levers of the law, and their lawyers' wit, to tie up any legislation that seeks to impose even the mildest restraints on abortion. That wit seems to become ever more necessary when the judges, in the sweep of their

---

[8] See *Voinovich v. Women's Medical Professional Corp.*, 149 L Ed 2d 496 (March 1998).

advocacy, find themselves asserting, with conviction, arguments that stand in conflict with one another. And so, on the one hand, it became critical to the argument of "vagueness" that the doctors could not tell the difference between partial-birth abortions, proscribed by the law, and the abortions that they performed. But on the other hand, it was part of Judge Payne's insistence, in the district court in Virginia, that this procedure of the D & X was notably safer for the pregnant woman than other kinds of abortion so late in the pregnancy. By removing the fetus substantially intact, the surgery would avoid the risks of laceration and infection that are present when the fetus is being dismembered in the womb and parts are floating about in the birth canal. To bar the D & X, then, said Judge Payne, was to bar a procedure that was distinctly safer to the mother. That ban could not be compatible then with any law that gave a decisive weight to the interests and health of the pregnant woman.[9] But if this procedure were distinctly, and knowably, safer, then the procedure itself must be *knowable* – and *distinct*.

Judge Michael Luttig would later point out, in the court of appeals in Virginia, that the American Medical Association (AMA) had opposed this procedure on partial-birth abortion, and when it weighed in on the issue, the association did not seem to have any trouble in identifying, with exactness, the procedure it was condemning. "The procedure called 'partial birth abortion,'" said the AMA, "is medically known as intact dilation and extraction."[10] As Judge Luttig noted, that procedure was defined by four features: (1) the deliberate dilatation of the cervix, usually over a sequence of days; (2) the conversion of the fetus to a footling breech; (3) the extraction of the body except for the head; and (4) the "partial evacuation of the intracranial contents of a living fetus to effect vaginal delivery of a dead but otherwise intact fetus."[11] It was plain that the statute was never meant to cover abortions by suction curettage or by dilatation and evacuation. Contrary to the imaginings of Judge Payne, the law could not really encompass a procedure in which an umbilical cord, or any part of a

---

[9] See *Richmond Medical Center v. Gilmore* 11 F. Supp. 2d 795, at 808 (June 1998).
[10] Cited by Judge Michael Luttig in *Richmond Medical Center v. Gilmore*, 144 F. 3d 326, U.S Court of Appeals, Fourth Circuit (June 30, 1998), at 327.
[11] *Ibid.*, at 328.

fetus, happened to be dragged through the birth canal on the way out. The fetus may be killed, may be dismembered, but as Luttig sought to explain, these abortions are not performed with the intention of bringing a fetus "through the vagina for the purpose of killing it there, but only to complete the removal" of a fetus, or its parts, after the killing has taken place.[12] Among people of ordinary wit, that distinction should be crystal clear. It seems to have required a post-graduate training in law in order to become incapable of grasping what seems clear enough to people of ordinary sense.

Throughout the controversy over partial-birth abortion, the media had shown the most curious inclination to steer around some of the oldest rules of journalism. It has been standard advice, given to every cub reporter, to incorporate in the opening paragraph the "what" of the story: in this case, "what" *was* the procedure thought to be so repellent that it was being forbidden? Instead of conveying those basic points, the media usually told listeners and readers first that the procedure is highly "rare," performed late in pregnancy. These circumlocutions were evidently designed to avoid playing into the hands of the pro-life groups, by reporting, to the audience, news that was likely to prove rather unsettling to the public. And yet, by guarding themselves politically in that way, the reporters and commentators were also faulting on the minimal responsibility of the journalist. For they could not impart an intelligible sense of the purpose of the bill if they would not render a minimally honest account of the state of affairs that the bill sought to forbid.

To be told that the procedure was "rare" was not to be told anything of substance; and yet even there, the media declined to draw out the implications of that rather prosaic point: If the procedure is rare, it must be quite distinct; but if it is rare, how do we know that it is so safe?: How could there have been enough cases to support a claim of statistical significance? Judge Payne, in Virginia, acknowledged the point made by one expert witness for the defense (Dr. Boehm), that "there have never been any studies comparing the trauma caused to a woman's cervix, uterus, or other vital organs depending on the different procedures used."[13] The claim that the procedure was safer than others could not be an empirical claim, resting on evidence collected

[12] *Ibid.*, at 329. [13] Payne, *supra*, n. 9, p. 825.

in a systematic way. The judge thought it was reasonable however to conjecture that "there is less risk of leaving fetal tissue behind or of sharp fetal fragments puncturing the uterus [in this kind of abortion], and thus it 'might be safer for the woman.'"[14] The AMA had testified, in Congress, that there were virtually no conditions under which this surgery advanced the health of the woman in any physical sense. Payne's speculation might prove accurate in any instance, but it was not based on any procedures that satisfied the properties of an "experiment." It was a species of conceptual reasoning, which might have been right or wrong, but it *depended critically on the assumption that this class of abortions was quite distinct conceptually from the variety of other abortions.* And yet, once that predicate was in place, Judge Payne would have dissolved the very ground of his argument. For he would have undercut, decisively, the claim that the statute was vague in its object, hazy in what it proscribed, and the source then of serious threats to surgeons, who might find themselves performing one of these surgeries without quite knowing it.

If Judge Payne had been right, that the distinctions among these surgeries were defectively "vague," then Dr. Philip Stubblefield in Boston would have been in serious jeopardy, for charges of fraud. Stubblefield had been the Chairman of Obstetrics and Gynecology at the Boston University School of Medicine, and he testified on the side of the plaintiff before the federal court in Nebraska. In defending the procedure, Stubblefield told the court that the D & X procedure was so familiar, so precise in its definition and its surgical advantages, that he was adding a section on this operation to the chapter he regularly contributes to the reference known as *Dr. Nichols's Testbook of Gynecologic Surgery.* He also planned to teach the procedure at his teaching hospital.[15] But Dr. Stubblefield would surely be guilty of a certain confidence game if he offered to teach, for remuneration, a medical procedure that could not be distinguished from other kinds of procedures.

When these strands of reasoning are collected from the opinions, it becomes clear that reason is not exactly their defining feature or their

---

[14] *Ibid.*
[15] See *Carhart v. Stenberg*, U.S. District Court in Nebraska (July 2, 1998), 11 F. Supp. 2d 1099, at 1111–12.

animating force. What comes through, rather, is a certain steadfastness on the part of judges, a willingness to persist even with arguments that – to take a line from George Eliot – are "not strenuously correct." What we sense in these cases is the steeliness of the judges, their remarkable obduracy in standing their ground, as a measure of their determination simply to prevail. "Do I contradict myself? Well, then, so be it; I am a man, or a judge, of many parts." And this too is not new under the sun; this too we have seen before. Yet, not quite. Something is, perforce, different; something was compelled to be different as a consequence of that original strategy that brought forth the bill on partial-birth abortion, the strategy of taking modest first steps, and beginning at the simplest level. The object was to begin at the point of birth, where even the partisans of abortion could not claim, with a straight face, that they had doubts about the species, or the human standing, of that small being who was killed. The defenders of abortion seemed to be skillful in staging the public argument by putting the focus on those "hard cases" of rape and incest. And yet, those kinds of cases represented only about half of 1 percent of the abortions performed in any year. But the scheme of modest first steps would have the effect of shifting the burden and making the debate take place on the terrain of the hardest cases for the partisans of abortion – not rape and incest, but the abortions that took place at the point of birth. Still, the judges flicked away any embarrassment and held their ground. But in preserving their commitment to abortion unimpaired, unqualified, they were compelled to say things that judges, or cultivated men, could not have said in public in another age.

And so, in Nebraska, federal judge Kopf, in the district court, insisted that if the drafters of the law had meant to ban only D & X abortions, they had done a clumsy job, because, as Kopf put it, the doctors who perform abortions "routinely 'deliberately and intentionally' deliver 'vaginally' a 'substantial portion' of a living fetus in order to kill it when performing a D & E."[16] In other words: Dismemberment "R" Us. That is what we *do*; that is what this surgery, and the life of the clinic, has as its object.

In case anyone happened to miss the implications of the dialogue, Judge Kopf pointed out that the surgeon, in his ordinary work here, "deliberately intends to shear the 'partially-delivered' intact limb from

---

[16] *Ibid.*, at 1128.

the fetal body."[17] I realize that I may betray here a certain nostalgia for the 1940s and 1950s, and it may be that I look upon that era of my boyhood with a tint rosier than the character of our people really warranted. But my own serious hunch is that any jurist – or any person, for that matter – would have been embarrassed, or at least affected with a certain sheepishness, if he had to explain in public that we must protect the freedom of professionals and honest workmen, whose work happens to involve the dismembering of live, innocent human beings, and especially babies. That was not something, in an earlier day, that would have been looked on as ordinary "work." Nor was it likely to be seen as work affected with a deep constitutional protection because it was somehow bound up with a "constitutional right."

The most "modest first step" of all was the proposal simply to preserve the life of the child who *survived* the abortion. As simple as it was, that proposal had a political bite, because the proponents of abortion could not admit even the smallest step that acknowledged the human standing of the child. But of course, in the strictest sense, there was no incompatibility between that measure and the "right to abortion" that was articulated in *Roe v. Wade.* If we take the claim made familiar in its abstract language, purged of any moral significance, the right to abortion was the right to "terminate a pregnancy." It was the right of a woman to be separated from a pregnancy, or child, she did not "want." But neither of those "rights" strictly entails a right to destroy a child when the pregnancy can be ended without the death of the child. Still, it should be plain that, if that distinction could be made, it would argue decisively against abortion even at earlier stages in the pregnancy: After all, with the advance of incubators and artificial lungs, it has become possible to sustain premature babies at 20 to 24 weeks of gestational age, and that figure promises to be pushed back even further. In that event, it would become reasonable to ask a pregnant woman simply to carry the newly conceived child for a few months more, when the woman may not even be "showing" and the child can be saved.

But then again, if the law could do that, why could it not command a pregnant woman to preserve the pregnancy just a bit longer, for every additional week or month enlarges the possibility of preserving

---

[17] *Ibid.*, at 1130.

the life of the child. And yet, a law that could talk itself into that posture might as well talk itself into the understanding that existed even before *Roe v. Wade*: Why not give the child the best chance of living, by carrying her through to birth, and then giving the child up for adoption? We are reminded that a pregnancy never obliged a woman to accept the responsibility for raising a child she did not want. The woman was free to separate herself from the child, but not on conditions that would have resulted in the death of an innocent being. In that sense, the law was informed, in relation to pregnancy, by the same premises that operated everywhere else: A landlord who could remove an intruder, or even a burglar, from his home with means that were less than lethal, could be obliged to avoid using lethal means. With the same axioms in play, it seemed to be understood in the past that the remedy for an unwanted pregnancy was an adoption, not a lethal surgery carried out on an innocent being. If the mother was faced, in the pregnancy, with a crisis, the child was an unwitting agent in her problems. For the child exercised no volition; it did nothing, knowingly, to bring about the "problem." And certainly the child bore no fault. The common sense of the law was to attend to the interests of the mother, but on terms that would deliver the child into the hands of people who were committed to its protection and nurturance.

But as the law has been turned, decisively, from those paths and rationales, it has become plain that the "right to abortion" is fueled in part by a passion that could be expressed in this way: "I cannot give away what is my own, or what I can see, clearly, as a child. If I could give up a child of my own, I could as readily carry the pregnancy to term, and give up the child for adoption." In cold, hard fact, it is easier to kill this thing, not yet seen as a child, than to give away what is seen clearly as a child of "one's own." With these moves, we are but one step away from the conclusion that Judge Haynsworth drew in *Floyd v. Anders* in 1977, without being so impolitic as to make it unnervingly explicit: namely, that the right to an abortion must entail the right to an effective abortion, or a dead child. As I noted earlier, even some pro-life lawyers were willing to tell themselves that the Supreme Court had rejected this view, though the Court has never done any such thing. But the recent wave of decisions on partial-birth abortion should have had the effect of jolting these lawyers from their beamish slumber. For the judges in the lower federal courts were compelled now to defend abortion at the point where there was no chance to feign skepticism about the human standing of the offspring. They would encounter abortion at the point where it was indistinguishable from infanticide. What must be said here, in the most sobering account, is that the judges, in these cases, have stepped up to the issue of infanticide – and they have not shrunk from it.

To be sure, they have not quite endorsed it in a full-throated way or proclaimed infanticide as a positive good. Yet they have made it clear, in a chilling way, that they will not be put off, or distracted, from the defense of abortion, even in the cases where abortion merges with outright infanticide. And so, in the case in Arizona, Judge Richard Bilby noted that the framers of the bill had been willing to leave untouched, unthreatened with restraint, the vast volume of abortions. The drafters had been determined to proscribe only this small, confined class of abortions, in which the killing was especially gruesome. Still, this attempt to cast up a barrier against infanticide could not be accepted casually if it had the effect of inhibiting other abortions, which remain legitimate in the eyes of the law.

Several months earlier, Judge Kopf had found a fatal defect in the law on partial-birth abortions in Nebraska: As Kopf observed, that law made no provisions for the health of the mother. The framers of the law did not evidently think that such provisions were necessary, because the procedures of D & X abortions had nothing to recommend them in serving the health of the mother. The only exception might be some notion of "mental" health so expanded as to lose any confining definition: for example, that a woman might suffer acute distress, or mental anguish, if she were barred from having one of these surgeries. But even if there were some risk to the health of the mother, the framers could have been forgiven for wondering just what danger any mother would have to face before she would find an apt remedy in crushing the skull of her unborn child and suctioning out his brains. The defenders of the law were disposed then to argue that the issue of harm was largely beside the point – and indeed that even *Roe v. Wade* and *Planned Parenthood v. Casey* were beside the point – because, as they put it, "the Supreme Court has never recognized a constitutional right to kill a partially born human being."[18] Their

[18] *Carhart v. Stenberg*, 972 F. Supp. 507 (D. Neb. 1997), at 529.

insistence, in other words, was that the right to abortion cannot entail the right to kill the child, the child at the point of birth, or the child in the midst of birth. It must be regarded then as quite telling that the court, faced with the assertion of this principle, treated it as a matter of no consequence. If the defenders were right, then that simple line should have been dispositive: there has never been a "constitutional right to kill a partially born human being." That line should have said enough to ward off the objections of the court and supply a sufficient explanation of why a legislature would protect the life of a child at birth. But in turning that argument aside, in treating it as a matter of no consequence, the judge was in effect revealing something that even pro-life lawyers had sought to deny to themselves: Judge Haynsworth's notorious dictum in *Floyd v. Anders*, that the child who survived an abortion was not a child protected by the laws, was not only quite conceivable; it was in fact the decisive, or operative premise, that was being installed now by the judges.[19]

That premise could be installed more easily if one simply pretended that there was no baby there to be killed, no victim whose presence could complicate the case. That is not entirely easy to do with a baby so visibly present. But then again, it was remarkable as to what might be done if a conceptual screen could be brought down, and the baby blocked from view, not by actually barring people from looking, but simply by changing the words and inducing people not to look. Reduced to its elements, this is the work of the conjurer. He can stand before people, and distract them from seeing what is before them by moving, with the subtlest gestures, to draw away their gaze. That turned out to be the nature of Bill Clinton's art when he vetoed the federal bill on partial-birth abortions. But the best clue to the play of mind at work here comes from *Huckleberry Finn*. Huck had contrived a story and told Aunt Sally that his boat was delayed because "we

---

[19] The reader may consider whether the same operative premise is not also at work in the opinion handed down by Judge Charles Kocoras in February, striking down the law on partial-birth abortions in Illinois:

> In those rare instances when the fetus is still "alive," cutting the cord may cause its death within six to ten minutes. In completing the delivery during this time period, the physician may have 'partially vaginally delivered' a living fetus. . . . In addition, in cases where a woman spontaneously aborts, it may be in her best interests for the physician to complete the abortion. *Hope Clinic v. Ryan* [N. Dist., Illinois], 995 F. Supp. 847, at 855 (February 1998).

blowed out a cylinder-head." Aunt Sally reacted: "Good gracious! anybody hurt?" "No'm. Killed a nigger." "Well, it's lucky; because sometimes people do get hurt."

For certain people, at a certain time, blacks simply did not register as real "people," whose injuries somehow *counted*. In a remarkably similar way, Bill Clinton could look out on the experience of partial-birth abortion, and never apparently see a child, whose skull was being crushed, and whose head was being collapsed as the contents of the skull were being suctioned out. That child made no impression of Clinton's visual or perceptual screen, because the injuries suffered by this small being simply could not be allowed to count. Both the victims and the injuries had to be filtered out by the theory that came along with "abortion rights." For that notion of rights could not be sustained while there was any recognition of a separate human being suffering injuries that were lethal.

What prescribed this altered vision was clear enough politically; but it required separate arts of illusion to bring off this trick. Mr. Clinton flexed the arts of the illusionist through the device of coming before reporters at a press conference and putting his accent on the threat to the "health" of a pregnant woman. He began by announcing that he would have joined the move to protect a fetus from this gruesome procedure but for his concern for the health of the pregnant woman as the preeminent or sovereign interest, the interest that trumps all others.[20] For the sake of amplifying his point Mr. Clinton brought in a few women who professed to have had a partial-birth abortion. One case involved a fetus ensnarled in the umbilical cord, others involved complications late in pregnancy, but none of them posed a threat of death or even of long-term physical impairment to the mother. In fact, as critics quickly pointed out, it was not even clear that the procedures performed in all of these instances really met the description of a partial-birth abortion. And true to the testimony of the AMA, it was not clear as to why the health of the mother would have been enhanced in any of these cases by a partial-birth abortion. Mr. Clinton could count on the fact that most of the press and public would not linger long enough to strip away the layers of deception. But when the layers of these accounts were peeled back, they seemed to reveal

[20] See the *New York Times*, April 11, 1996, p. 1.

simply women who would suffer a certain distress if they were not permitted finally to dispose of their unborn children (or their fetuses) and their pregnancies.

All of these points were drawn out in the case of Eileen Sullivan, who was among the women presented by President Clinton as exemplars of his cause. Over the next several months, Sullivan would be converted into a kind of poster child for the cause of resisting the bill on partial-birth abortions. She would appear with Mr. Clinton, and she would be brought out in press conferences by the National Organization of Women. She would also be recruited to testify in Congress, in March 1997, when the judiciary committees of the two houses held joint hearings on partial-birth abortion. Ms. Sullivan seemed also to have a certain political value, because she presented herself as springing from a "rather large Irish Catholic family," with a mother working as "an adoption placement worker with Catholic Social Services." According to Ms. Sullivan's testimony,

> Our baby's brain was improperly formed and pressured by a back-up of fluid; his head was enlarged; the palate was cleft; the heart was both malformed and failing; the liver was malfunctioning; the feet were clubbed; and there was a dangerously low amount of amniotic fluid.[21]

As Ms. Sullivan summed up the prognosis, "the anomalies were incompatible with life." But left unexplained was the question of why any of these maladies pointed to a partial-birth abortion. Why was the condition of the child treated, or even eased, by crushing his head? Apparently, the decision was not meant to minister to the interests of the child; it was done rather to "help improve our chances of future pregnancy." But this procedure also ran the risk of producing an incompetent cervix as a result of the need to enlarge the cervix for this procedure, and the experience produced, in the case of one woman, five miscarriages. Why did Ms. Sullivan and her doctors suppose that it was an appropriate therapy here?

To fill in that explanation was not something Ms. Sullivan regarded as part of her mission. But she would take it as a grave offense when

---

[21] See "Partial-Birth Abortion: The Truth," Joint Hearings before the Senate Committee on the Judiciary and the Subcommittee on the Constitution of the House Committee on the Judiciary; 105th Cong., 1st sess., March 11, 1997, p. 125.

anyone was indecorous enough to press the question. One person gently raising that question was Dr. Curtis Cook, a specialist in maternal-fetal medicine at Michigan State University. Dr. Cook appeared on the same panel with Ms. Sullivan and another woman, Maureen Britell, who had elected to have a partial-birth abortion. He sympathized with the women, but he pointed out that neither in the case of Ms. Britell nor of Ms. Sullivan would a partial-birth abortion have been "necessary." With Ms. Britell, the situation of "a cord preventing a baby from delivering is something that we run into quite commonly and frequently have to either reduce the cord or even cut the cord in order to successfully deliver the baby." He went on to say that "we don't kill the baby in doing that. We deliver the baby quickly after cutting the cord." The procedure of partial-birth abortion was apparently the "least invasive" for Ms. Britell. But that is to say, it was a procedure designed for *her* interest, not that of her child.[22]

Before Dr. Cook could turn to her own case, Ms. Sullivan intervened, heatedly. "I have a problem," she said, with Dr. Cook "responding to it almost at all in your professional capacity," since the doctor did not know her. After all, he had never examined her or her records. Dr. Cook responded that he would be "more than willing to review any medical records people wanted to make available." But that very offer was treated, by Ms. Sullivan, as an egregious offense, a presumptuous willingness to inquire into records that Ms. Sullivan regarded as personal. "No, no, no," she said, "I will not release my medical records." Sensing a moment to be exploited, even at the risk of coherence, Representative John Conyers of Michigan intervened to reproach the doctor: "[I]t is a little bit unseemly that a medical doctor would be engaged in this kind of confrontation with witnesses . . . I know you don't conduct your professional life like this, but it is a bit of a stretch for you to listen to some witnesses . . . and then explain to them that their doctors had different things that weren't brought to their attention."[23]

Congressman Conyers has managed a successful career in Congress without pretending to be a logician. But here he surely exceeded himself with something that had to be unseemly for a legislator engaged in a legislative hearing. Left in the shelter of her personal life, no one would have had any reason to raise questions about the ground

[22] *Ibid.*, p. 132.   [23] *Ibid.*, p. 135.

of Ms. Sullivan's judgment. Yet, Conyers seemed to forget the cardinal point that Ms. Sullivan had presented herself as a witness, bearing "testimony" for a legislative hearing. She presented herself, that is, as a person whose experience would bear directly on the predicate of the legislation, and establish the falsity of that predicate. Under those conditions, it was not only legitimate, but even obligatory, for her to submit to a review of the alleged "facts" on which she offered that account of her experience. Without that evidence, why would she be credited in any way as a bearer of testimony relevant to the bill before the committee? Imagine that the Congress was at work on a bill to forbid the fraud of self-advertised alchemists, claiming to turn tin into gold. Imagine further that a woman flies in from Los Angeles to report that the law is misconceived, for it is indeed possible to turn tin into gold, for after all, she reports, she has "done it." The Congressmen ask to see her records, and let a detached observer with competence review them. But she retorts, in high dudgeon, that this is a "personal" experience, and that she regards it as an invasion of her privacy to have those records reviewed. Her testimony is to be credited on the strength mainly of the fact that *she offered it*. And it would be churlish beyond description for anyone to demand of her now that she also establish the truth of her claims.

Dr. Cook, without being censorious, was being perfectly correct. As for Mr. Clinton, it was clear that, even with his agile mind, he did not show the least interest in probing very far beneath the surface in inquiring just how, exactly, a partial-birth abortion might have served the health of the pregnant woman. But he knew enough at least to know that, in his accent on "health," he was covering over a deception bordering on outright fraud: When he insisted that he would have been willing to sign this bill if there had only been a provision for the "health" of the mother, he must have known that he was lying outright. For Clinton trod on this ground very carefully, with the steps of someone who had been precisely briefed. And so he was likely to know, better than most lawyers, that, under *Roe v. Wade* and *Doe v. Bolton*, the "health" of the pregnant woman encompasses "mental health." Any doctor could testify that his patient would suffer distress if she were denied an abortion, and that was sufficient to satisfy the formula of "mental health." In the case of partial-birth abortion, any doctor could report that this procedure was the least traumatic for his patient, in removing the unwanted fetus late in term. To insist on the exception for "health" was to suggest a willingness to bar these abortions, while in fact being willing to bar nothing.

But this willingness to cover over the subtler parts of the law, not widely known, was as nothing compared with the willingness to stand up in public and lie directly about the things that were plainly in the bill. For contrary to Mr. Clinton's statement on the veto, the bill had in fact made provision for the life and health of the mother. The AMA had testified that the procedure of partial-birth abortion could not be ordered up plausibly by any interest in advancing the health of the pregnant woman. Still, the framers of the bill anticipated the rhetoric that would be used against them, and so they leaned over further in the bill to offer "exceptions" to protect the life of the mother. Those precautions might not have been required; still, it was provided that the bill would not apply if a partial-birth abortion would ever be "necessary to save the life of a mother because her life is endangered by a physical disorder, physical injury, or physical illness." That formula left out, of course, the case of the woman whose life would be threatened because she might be moved, in distress, to take her own life if she were denied the right to have an abortion. That version of saving "life" or "relieving distress" could not be credited in this bill, as it could not be credited, coherently, in any other bill.

But far more interesting than the deception, or the arts that sustained it, was the understanding that had to lie behind the whole performance. For if one took seriously the concern for the "health" of the mother, would one not be led then to pose some questions rather concrete and precise: for example, what exactly was the degree of danger, or the impairment, to the health of the mother, and what was a tolerable cost for coping with that risk? If one were aware, at the same time, that there was another being present – an entirely innocent being, whose skull was about to be crushed – the calculations over "health" would have to be altered in a jarring way. The question would then be posed, more naturally – and more sharply: what interest in "health" could plausibly justify a pregnant woman in having the head of her child punctured and the brains sucked out? Would it be bursitis? Chronic problems with the kidneys? The prospect of long-term depression? Or would we require nothing less than life-threatening dangers? But that provision was already incorporated in the bill. To raise seriously the question of health is to raise these kinds of questions. Yet, the comparisons cannot be made without inviting embarrassment. More than that, they cannot be made without drawing attention to the fact that there is, after all, another being present, feeling pain and sustaining an assault. What was remarkable about Mr. Clinton's performance was that there wasn't the slightest concession to the fact that there was indeed anyone else present aside from the pregnant woman. There was, apparently, no one else in this picture, whose "health" or safety could possibly matter.

But in the most curious way, Mr. Clinton's performance brought the matter full circle, for it brought the problem back to that most modest first step of all, the first step that the National Right to Life Committee had disdained. The pro-life lobbyists had thought it far too simple, far too modest, to begin merely by seeking to preserve the life of the child who had survived the abortion. Yet, that simplest of all steps had the advantage at least of installing these critical premises:

> that the child emerging from the abortion is a real entity, with stand-
> ing to receive the protections of the law;
> that her injuries count in the eyes of the law;
> and that the claim of the child to the protection of the law cannot pivot
> on the question of whether anyone happens to *want* her.

The pro-life lobbyists thought that they would overleap these sim-plest of steps – so simple, in fact, that they hardly seemed worth putting in place. But if they had been put in, Bill Clinton could not have been in the position of pretending that there was no child present. With the bill on the survivors of abortion, the interests of the mother would have been detached entirely from the interests of the child. In dealing with that bill, President Clinton would have been compelled to address the situation of a child, born alive, a child who could be preserved and nurtured now without injury to the mother, or detriment to her interests.

It seems highly unlikely that Bill Clinton, focused entirely on the child, would have sought to explain to the nation why it was neces-sary to turn away from saving a live child, whose presence threatened no one. Lest we be accused of becoming beamish ourselves, I would not dismiss entirely the possibility that, if Bill Clinton had talked himself into the public rationale for taking that first step, he might have taken a long stride toward a willingness to accept the next step, and finally signed a bill on partial-birth abortion. After all, the bill on the survivors of abortion would mark the limits of abortion in drawing a line at infanticide. The bill on partial-birth abortion would then offer the first chance of barring the killing of the child with a so-called abortion at the point of birth. Of course, the partisans of abortion might insist that infanticide emerges only when the child is separated from the mother. But this thin pretext may become even thinner and less tenable once even the defenders of abortion have acknowledged that the child at the point of birth can be protected by the law.

As summer gave way to fall in 1998, the decisions on partial-birth abortion began accumulating in the federal courts, and as they did, they threw into the face of the National Right to Life Committee the results that flowed from the reluctance to fill in that first and simplest step. For if the Congress had moved earlier to fill in that first step, it was hard to imagine how the judges would have challenged the measures to protect a child born alive. In that event, the judges would have signed on, confirmed, ratified, the premises that supplied the ground for the bill on partial-birth abortions. When that statute arrived then in the courts, the judges would have affirmed, by that point, the premises that made the new bill quite plausible. But with those premises not filled in, the bills on partial-birth abortion in the States were vulnerable to quibbles, or challenges, that were not without point. And so, for example, right after the congressional elections in November 1998, a string of decisions in federal courts struck down the bills on partial-birth abortion in Wisconsin, Kentucky, Arkansas, and Florida. The case of Wisconsin was particularly instructive, because the bill was overturned in the Court of Appeals for the Seventh Circuit, in an opinion written by the redoubtable Richard Posner.

Posner had shot into prominence early, in the school of "law and economics," when he was a professor of law at the University of Chicago. He was appointed to the federal bench early in the Reagan Administration, and there he continued his style as a prodigy. But brilliance seeks out further levels of novelty and surprise, and to the astonishment of his old allies, Posner's turnings led him into a strange alliance with the Left on the campuses. For he began to place himself, in the academy, with the party of deconstruction and postmodernism. And now, with his opinion in *Planned Parenthood v. Doyle*, he gave to the concert of the judges a "postmodernist" twist: "Partial-birth abortion is a gruesome procedure," he remarked. "But all abortion procedures, and indeed a vast number of surgical procedures unrelated to the reproductive process, including forms of cosmetic surgery that strike many people as frivolous, are bloody and horrible."[24] In the style of postmodernism, the abortion was removed from the domain of truth to the domain of appearance: Some people were revolted by abortions, some were revolted by face lifts and nose-bobs. All of these procedures are bloody, they remove tissues, they make people queasy – and some of them simply involve the dismembering of a live, innocent human being. But in this way, the killing of a child (or a "fetus") is placed on the same plane as a nose-bob.

The AMA had tendered the opinion to Congress that, in every occasion in which the procedure of partial-birth abortion was used, there were other procedures available, likely to be far safer to the pregnant woman. But as Posner noted, that did not dislodge the question of whether it was *conceivable* that under some circumstances, this procedure might yet be safer for the mother, since it did not leave any fetal parts behind in the womb, where they could cause infection. Once that premise was installed, the pregnant woman would be conceded a dominant right to seek her own self-preservation, and make her own estimates of the level of risks she was willing to accept.

Yet, with that kind of move, the question was transformed in a way that, even now, is only dimly appreciated. Posner had become famous as a proponent of "law and economics," in a style that swept away moral questions and replaced them with the calculations of utility, reduced to precise, empirical measures. But Posner now recast the problem: there would be no attempt to gauge in exacting terms the relative harms threatened to the pregnant woman or the child. These calculations would all be superseded now, or transcended, by the force simply of axioms – most notably, the axioms that recognize, in the pregnant woman, the only bearer of rights, the only person whose interests counted. Posner absorbed those premises as his own, and so

---

[24] 162 F. 3d 463, U.S. Court of Appeals, Seventh Circuit (November 3, 1998), at 470.

he could point out that under the law created by the courts, the State of Wisconsin could claim here "no interest in fetal life." In fact, the state had claimed only the authority to regulate a certain kind of procedure. As Posner argued then, "the statute cannot discourage abortions – cannot save any fetuses – but can merely shift their locus from the birth canal to the uterus." He could ask then quite plausibly just why the state could claim an interest in making that shift.[25]

And indeed, why *would* it have had an interest in such a shift? The style may not exactly be fetching, but Posner had touched the core of the logical problem in the bills on partial-birth abortion. The framers, for all of their wit, had never bothered to fill in the key premise, that the child is a real entity, with standing to receive the protections of the law. Posner's opinion should have brought home this point quite forcibly to the pro-life lobbyists: Without that anchoring premise – that the child is a real entity, who can be protected – the issue will always be tilted in favor of the woman who would order up one of these grisly procedures.[26]

But even apart from Richard Posner, the same lessons were being brought back from the wars of litigation by lawyers who were defending the bills on partial-birth abortion. What was remarkable was that another kind of filtering seem to be setting in place on the pro-life side as the people who had a stake in the bills on partial-birth abortion could not seem to grasp the import of the news brought back from the courts by lawyers such as Nick Nikas in Arizona. Or rather, they could hear the accounts, but they could not quite see the mosaic, or the design, that those accounts were forming. I encountered Nikas at a meeting of lawyers and legislators in Chicago in August 1998, and

---

[25] *Ibid*. For my own commentary, see "Courts Strike Down Laws Against Partial-Birth Abortion," *Wall Street Journal* (December 7, 1998).

[26] Posner played out the same argument just a year later, but with an unmistakable edge of anger, mingled with contempt for his colleagues, as he found himself on the losing side, with his earlier opinion, in effect, overridden. But in a revealing, and startling, passage, Posner expressed a deep concern for the health of the abortionists, while the fetuses were screened entirely from view. Those "physicians," he said, "already are frequent subjects of picketing and other harassment and occasionally of physical assaults." As for the one whose assault is the object of the surgery, well "from the standpoint of the fetus . . . it makes no difference whether, when the skull is crushed, the fetus is entirely within the uterus or if its feet are outside the uterus." See *Hope Clinic v. Ryan* 195 F. 3d 857, at 879 (October 1999).

I tried to suggest in a column in *Crisis* magazine that the pieces in the account could be assembled to reveal an intelligible lesson.

In the litigation in Arizona, federal Judge Richard Bilby had come at least to the critical recognition that the framers of the statute had sought to "erect a firm barrier against infanticide." But that elementary truth had not come trippingly from the word processor or the lips of Judge Bilby. He was compelled to cast the issue in that form because Nick Nikas had framed the issue in that way as he defended the statute in Arizona. For Nikas had the wit to see that the bill on partial-birth abortion accomplished its purpose as it focused the issue at the point of birth. With that focus, the bill could mark the limits to abortion by casting up the barrier against abortion at the point where abortion was even more plainly, and undeniably, infanticide. In drawing the issue in those terms, Nikas moved the judges to say, at last, what had been left implicit all along: namely, that the right to abortion could be secured only if there were a willingness, finally, to throw over any lingering "prejudice" against infanticide.

Nikas had shown the best instincts of a lawyer, in moving to the point where the statute was most defensible. But he was apparently unaware that, in his casting of the argument, he was moving outside the rationale of the bill offered by the National Right to Life Committee. He was describing the path of a rather different argument, leading back to something older and even more familiar. The question might be put indirectly in this way, to reveal what was disclosed in the puzzle: What would have been described, or reconstructed, once we had moved through the set of three arguments that Nikas had presented in Arizona, and then later, in sharpened form, in Nebraska? Consider the ingredients.

First, Nikas found that the case had to be focused on abortions *at the point of birth*. The proponents of the bill on partial-birth abortion had thought that the bill offered this edge of cleverness: that it would bring the restrictions on abortion into the second trimester of the pregnancy. But that became, in fact, a lever that the judges could use against the bill. That very possibility, of moving into the second trimester, confirmed for the judges that this bill could not be contained. The bill professed to speak of the time of birth, but if its logic flowed over into the second trimester, the bill could bar doctors from doing abortions that were still quite legitimate under the rulings of the courts.

Second, Nikas argued that *Roe v. Wade* involves, at most, the right to "terminate" a pregnancy, not the right to kill a child. The pregnancy must come to an end at the time that the "birthing process" begins. At that point, it must be legitimate to protect the child. In other words, the right to an abortion cannot entail the right to a dead child. Judge Bilby responded that this was very clever, but perhaps too clever, and above his pay level: The Supreme Court might come to ratify an argument of that kind, but for him, as a federal judge in the hinterland, there was still an abortion going on, and this looked to be just another way to restrict the right to do abortions.

Third, Nikas discovered that there was a problem in handling the expert testimony even with the experts on his side: The question would be posed as to whether it was *conceivable*, possible, that there were circumstances under which the procedure of partial-birth abortion could in fact be the safest procedure for a patient. For after all, the baby would be removed here without leaving fetal parts behind, in the body of the mother. Nikas's experts, honest people that they were, would of course acknowledge that to be the case. But that acknowledgement of a bare possibility then set up the conclusion: for those patients, for whom this could be the safest procedure, the denial of the surgery constituted an "undue burden."[27]

---

[27] The language of "undue burden" came from Justice Sandra Day O'Connor in *Planned Parenthood v. Casey*, 505 U.S. 833, at 876–88, where the standard is set forth, and then applied to the provisions of the legislation in the balance of the opinion, through page 901. In the course of the argument, the plurality opinion noted, at different points, the regulations that would not constitute an "undue burden." And so, for example, a waiting period of 24 hours was not thought to put any serious obstacle before the woman exercising her "choice" on abortion. Nor was there an undue burden when the state imposed a requirement of "informed consent" – even when the requirement was not aimed so much at the health of the mother, but at the end of awakening in the pregnant woman a concern for her unborn child. Years later, in *Stenberg v. Carhart*, in 2000, Justice Kennedy would profess his shock at Justice O'Connor for abandoning these parts of the plurality opinion in *Casey*. What seemed to be swept away, years later, were passages of this kind, delivered by the judges in the plurality:

> We conclude . . . that informed choice need not be defined in such narrow terms that all considerations of the effect on the fetus are made irrelevant. As we have made clear, we . . . permit a State to further its legitimate goal of protecting the life of the unborn by enacting legislation aimed at ensuring a decision that is mature and informed, even when in so doing the State expresses a preference for childbirth over abortion. In short, requiring that the woman be informed of the availability of information relating to fetal development and the assistance available should she decide

Let me add up the points that emerged: The argument, even for the bill on partial-birth abortions, needs to be cast at the time of birth; it needs to be cast as an argument against infanticide. It has to convey the point that the right to an abortion is not the right to a dead child; and yet, that argument is defeated finally because the law would still be dealing with an abortion, where the issue can be raised about the safety of the mother, or her dangers of infection. Does the conclusion not become clear? The claim to protect the child must be concentrated at the point where there is no longer an entanglement with the interests of the mother. And what is the closest point near abortion not entangled with those interests? What is the earliest point at which the law can tenably reach right now to protect the child? And the answer, I think, would have to be: the point, <u>after</u> an abortion, where a child may survive.[28]

But with those questions, and the answers they bring forth, we are brought back to that most "modest first step" of all: the bill to protect the child who survives the abortion. That seemingly modest step would establish at the same time that the Congress may indeed lay hands on this subject, that it may act to protect the child who has been involved in an abortion.

The burden of my argument here has been that a decisive turn was taken, finally, with this train of decisions on partial-birth abortion in the federal courts. There had been suspicions, for years, of a certain drift among the judges away from the principles, or the moral premises, of the American Founders. But the cases on partial-birth abortion required judges to reveal more fully what had been lurking there all along. And what comes out now, I would argue, are premises that are utterly at war with the premises of the founders, the logic of the Constitution – and in fact with the premises of jurisprudence itself. Those points may seem, on the surface, overly drawn, but I think they may come out more clearly as sober truths when the principles revealed in these cases are posed against the understandings of the founders.

---

to carry the pregnancy to full term is a reasonable measure to ensure an informed choice, one which might cause the woman to choose childbirth over abortion. This requirement cannot be considered a substantial obstacle to obtaining an abortion, and, it follows, there is no undue burden (*Casey*, at 883).

[28] For the review of Nikas's argument, and the lessons it brought forth, see my piece, "Backing into Old Truths," *Crisis* (October 1998), pp. 10–11.

I invoked earlier the writings of James Wilson of Philadelphia, who was one of only six men who had been both a signer of the Declaration of Independence and a member of the Constitutional Convention in 1787. He was also a member of the first Supreme Court, appointed by George Washington, and in the presence of the President and Vice President, he took up his chair of jurisprudence at the University of Pennsylvania, in Philadelphia, in 1790. In these opening lectures on jurisprudence, Wilson took matters to the root: The very purpose of the government was not to create new rights, but to secure and enlarge the rights we already possessed by nature.[29] But if we are the bearers of natural rights, the question might be posed, When did we come into possession of those rights? The answer, tendered by Wilson, followed a direct path: Natural rights spring from the nature of human beings; they are not conferred simply by positive law. Therefore, those natural rights had to come into existence for us when any of us simply began to be:

> In the contemplation of law, [wrote Wilson] life begins when the infant is first able to stir in the womb. By the law, life is protected not only from immediate destruction, but from every degree of actual violence, and, in some cases, from every degree of danger.[30]

Wilson recalled the practice, running back to ancient Greece, of exposing newborn infants, or confirming to their fathers the power of life or death. But the common law, he said, marked off a radically different tradition: "With consistency, beautiful and undeviating, human life, from its commencement to its close, is protected by the common law."[31]

Just a few years later, in the case of *Chisholm v. Georgia* (1793), Wilson would take the occasion, at a kind of beginning of the American law, to return to the root of the law in the principles of general jurisprudence. This was the case in which Wilson pointed out that the law in America would be placed on a different foundation from that of the law in England. I would recall that passage yet again, because it bore out the understanding of this project of government

---

[29] James Wilson, "Of the Natural Rights of Individuals," in *The Works of James Wilson* (Cambridge: Harvard University Press, 1967; originally published in 1804), II, pp. 585, 591.
[30] *Ibid.*, p. 597.   [31] *Ibid.*

as a project committed, in its telos, or its governing purpose, to the protection of natural rights. The law in England, made familiar by Blackstone, began with the notion of a sovereign issuing commands. But the law in America, said Wilson, would begin "with another principle, very different in its nature and operations":

> [L]aws derived from the pure source of equality and justice must be founded on the consent of those, whose obedience they require. The sovereign, when traced to his source, must be found in the *man*.[32]

These passages, brought back again, mark a notable shift in the jural mind from Wilson, on the one hand, to Payne, Bilby, Kopf, and Posner, on the other. It used to be understood that the protection of life, or a protection from the unjustified taking of life, stood at the center of the commitments of the law. The right not to suffer an unjustified assault on one's life stood as a natural right, a right that began as soon as we ourselves began to be. But if the rejection of homicide stood as the first, or the central, commitment of the law, that commitment had to begin with an understanding of the being who is the subject, or object, of this protection by the law. The notion of government by consent implies an understanding of the kind of creature who alone is capable of weighing the things that are good and bad, and tendering his consent. It surely could not be squared with such an understanding of the polity and the law that we could evade the defining commitments of the polity, or ignore the objects of protection, through the simple device of changing labels: "That is not a human being, but a 'gvork.' It is not a 'snark' but a 'bojum.' That is not a human or a person protected by the law; it is merely, as Judge Haynsworth said, a 'fetus,' marked for 'termination.'" This is not merely a shift in labels; it is a decision, freighted with moral significance, to remove a whole class of beings from the class of beings who have a claim to the protection of the law. That kind of shift cannot be carried through on the strength of mere assertion. Nor may it be merely stipulated, as a gesture of the positive law, by people who simply have the authority to issue commands. That kind of a shift must bear the heaviest burdens of justification.

---

[32] 2 Dallas 419, at 458 (1793), italics in original.

And yet, Judge Bilby and his colleagues would instruct their audiences now that infanticide is no longer, as we used to say, such a big deal. But that can be the case only if homicide has ceased to be such a big deal. With small steps, without even quite noticing, people may make their way gradually to conclusions that would have startled them in the past. In this case, they do it, not by affirming murder as a way of life, but simply by talking themselves into the notion that there is something now, in our day, far less portentous about the taking of a human life. And perhaps that is the case because we no longer attach the same reverence that Wilson attached to the notion of a "man." Why we no longer summon that reverence is a matter I shall return to later; but by this point, the evidence virtually abounds that we do not. That biped who conjugates verbs may give us the genius of the Internet, and yet his presence, in large numbers on this planet, is not regarded as a growing asset of talent and moral promise, but as a blight and a threat. Whatever can be said about that biped, as a figure of mysterious origin who excites our wonder, he clearly does not elicit, among the educated, a sense of reverence – the sense of reverence that made it, for Wilson and his generation, a deep crime to take the life of the child in the womb. There would seem to be, then, a subtle but emphatic break with the understanding of the founders, for evidently we can no longer take the notion of "man" as the very core, or ground, of our jurisprudence.

But if "man" is no longer, the ground of our jurisprudence, it may be because:

(a) we are no longer as clear, or as certain as we used to be, as to what constitutes "nature" and human beings. Or,

(b) even if we thought we understood what a human being is, we are inclined to regard our judgment here as a matter of opinion or convention – or even as a certain tribal preference for our own species.

And so we may be content to leave to the decision of the community, or the political process, the authority to determine just who is a human being. But that is to say,

(c) we must assume that there is no intrinsic meaning or dignity that attaches to the notion of a human being. Whether there is such a meaning will depend entirely on whether we, as a community, will attribute it. If we do, the taking of life will be significant, even portentous; if not, it will be one of those lesser things, more readily borne.

As we follow out this line of reasoning, emanating from judges, we are led, surely and without the least strain, to this conclusion: The judgment on just who counts as a human being is a judgment entirely of the positive law. We depend, that is, on the positive law to settle the matter because we see no other source of understanding, no other ground of judgment, apart from the opinions dominant in the community, the opinions that will find their reflection, finally, in the judgments pronounced by those in authority. That kind of assertion would have been regarded once as at least startling, and very likely heretical in a republic. For we can assert, in this way, the decisive place of political authority only if we think there is no standard of moral judgment apart from authority, and no standard that can guide authority apart from the "opinions" that are dominant in any place. Of course, there is nothing shocking in that account from the perspective of those, now prominent in the academy, who deny at the root that there is any such thing as human "nature," or moral truths grounded in that nature. But if there is no human nature, there can surely be no intrinsic dignity in human beings, the source in turn of rights of an intrinsic dignity, which do not depend, for their truth or their rightness, on the positive law.

In that case, as I will argue more fully later, even the "right to abortion" would be purged of its substance as a right. For that right, too, could be nothing more than the creation of the positive law. And if it can be created through the positive law, as a reflection of "opinion," it may be scaled back, or even repealed through the positive law, when it no longer accords with the opinions or the preferences of a majority. The point is that once we begin to follow the premises, and the paths of reason, marked off by the judges as they seek to resist even the most minimal restrictions on abortion, those paths lead back, inescapably, to the pure logic of the positive law: brute positive law, a positive law whose exercise cannot be tested any longer by any standards of right and wrong, *by any principles of judgment, outside itself.* Under these conditions, the exercise of power would indeed become the source of its own justification.

The steps in this reasoning may not seem, at any point, very startling. What is portentous in them may be obscured at any moment by the benefits they profess to bring in vindicating the "rights" of people to keep ordering, or performing, partial-birth abortions. But when we follow out the paths of the reasoning, or trace them back to their root premises, we will have discovered that there has been nothing short of a transformation of our jurisprudence, an alteration in the character of the thing. The best analogy for what is taking place here may be drawn from that discovery that Justice Scalia happened upon in a moment of epiphany in an otherwise quite prosaic case: the discovery of rights so exquisite and pure that they worked virtually *to extinguish themselves.*

The occasion for the discovery came in a series of cases involving claims of symbolic speech. In one notable case, a group claiming to represent the homeless pitched tents in LaFayette Park, adjacent to the White House. To any onlooker, the spectacle might have appeared rather plainly as a disarrangement of the park, and one that had to affect security for the president. But as the argument ran, the demonstrators were "expressing," in that act, a concern for the homeless, and so their expression should be taken as a First Amendment right that overrides other concerns of the law.[33] The same kind of argument was played out somewhat later in the case of "topless dancing" in Indianapolis.[34] As Scalia addressed the arguments in these cases, he pointed out that every bodily gesture could be translated or converted into an act of "expression":

> [V]irtually every law restricts conduct, and virtually *any* prohibited conduct can be performed for an expressive purpose – if only expressive of the fact that the actor disagrees with the prohibition.[35]

A willingness to drive through traffic lights blazing red may be taken as a gesture of opposition to lights that are overly long, or even to the restraints that impede the liberty to travel.[36] If we assign to rights of

---

[33] See *Clark v. Community for Creative Non-Violence*, 468 U.S. 288 (1984). Scalia's critical comments on the claims of expression here were expressed during an earlier phase in this litigation, when Scalia was sitting as a judge in the federal court of appeals in the District of Columbia. See *Community for Creative Non-Violence v. Watt*, 703 F. 2d 586 (1983), especially Scalia's dissent, 622 ff., and the dissent he joined, 608 ff.

[34] See again, *Barnes v. Glen Theatre*, 115 L Ed 2d 504 (1991), especially pp. 518–520.

[35] *Ibid.*, at 518.

[36] In the earlier stages of the litigation over tents outside the White House, Judge Wilkey offered, in dissent, the example of tourists staging a comparable act of symbolic speech: "Rather than pay for a hotel, they apply for a permit to camp on the Mall 'to dramatize and protest against the high cost of hotels.' " See *Community for Creative Non-Violence v. Watt, supra*, n. 33, at 620.

the First Amendment a first standing, a preeminent place, within the scheme of the Constitution, then we may assign a certain trumping power to these claims of rights. But in that event, the people who mass on the town common to protest, or to speak against their government, may be overborne by another crowd of partisans, quite as passionate in their determination to press their views and silence the demonstrators. The crowd that now summons an overpowering force is itself engaged in an act of expression. If that expression is to be honored, not repressed, then it has the effect of quashing into insignificance the first act of expression, on the part of the demonstrators. To put it another way, an attempt on the part of the authorities to protect the rights of the first set of demonstrators may itself be offset, and overcome, by other acts of expression by the second set of demonstrators. In that way, the fundamental right to speak becomes *a right that cannot practicably be vindicated*. In our willingness to assert rights to a degree of unparalleled refinement, to contrive rights so pure that they never yield to restraints or offsetting duties, we back into a set of rights so exquisite that they finally have the quality of extinguishing themselves.

I would suggest that the judges have created something comparable now in the recent train of decisions on partial-birth abortion. It is not that the judges have been spirited in their willingness to challenge legislatures, for that is implicit in their office and function, and if the task of judging is done at all, it should be done in a vigorous, spirited way. What is striking now about the performance of the judges, and the mark of a new stage in our jurisprudence, is that the judges have been compelled to offer a defense of abortion that is explicit, unshaded, unaffected by apologies or qualifications. As they have done that, they have put in place premises that are ultimately at odds with the grounds of their own authority, for they are at odds with the premises of jurisprudence itself. The law is no longer committed, as part of its central mission, to the protection of human life, for it is no longer clear that there is a "nature" that marks the things that are distinctly human and supplies the ground of "natural rights." Aristotle recognized that political life began with the understanding of that creature who was suited distinctively *by nature* for the polis. But what was once the predicate of political life, and a government by consent, has been converted into a question. Men and women in judicial office now profess to regard the question of "What is a human being" as an inscrutable, religious matter. The question then of "what beings are protected by the law now as human beings" is a question that must turn entirely on the positive law, for there are apparently no objective standards that yield an answer objectively true. It is no longer taken for granted, as an axiom of the law, that there really are human beings, with a distinct nature as moral agents, which fits them distinctly for law and political life. The question, "What is a human life?" becomes a question for political authority, and the question will have to be answered then without the consultation of any standards of moral judgment outside of the opinions held by those who exercise power.

James Wilson observed that the American law began by incorporating the revolutionary premise that there could be an illegitimate law: That was the case only because the American law began by rejecting positivism as the source of law, and recognizing an independent standard of right and wrong outside the positive law. To displace or extinguish that sense of things is to remove what Wilson and the founders thought was distinct to the American law. But American law was making more explicit here the premises, or the moral understandings, that were necessary to law in the strictest sense: a measure could be enacted with all of the formal trappings of legality, and yet be utterly wanting in the substance of justice and lawfulness. The overturning of those premises would count as nothing less than the eradication of law at its moral root. And yet, that act of overturning is precisely what the judges have now carried through, without the least sense that anything momentous had taken place.

But why should all of this appear so unthinkable to us, as though we had never seen anything like it before? As we shall recall in the next chapter, we had the example, in the nineteenth century, of senators of the United States who defended slavery in principle and rejected the principles that underlay a government by consent. Which is to say, they rejected the very premises of the regime in which they stood as high officers of state. Why should it seem so startling then, or implausible, that judges, those other officers of state, could drift into fallacies of a similar nature? There is nothing in the least unprecedented about it: Men and women could fill the offices of judges in a constitutional order, while rejecting the moral premises that stand at the root of jurisprudence itself.

For the new jurisprudence reaches its completion by detaching itself from every premise necessary to the notion of lawfulness. It rejects the logic of natural rights; it denies that any of us has rights of intrinsic dignity because it denies that there is any such intrinsic dignity attaching to any human being, as the subject and object of the law. Since it denies that human beings have a standing or existence in nature that must be respected by the law, it denies, at the same time, that human beings have any jural standing apart from the positive law. When we look, then, for the presence of "law," we find mainly the trappings of office: we have men and women in robes sitting in offices of dignity; we have elaborate procedures and forms, and schools to instruct people in the forms. But we have now, with full solemnity, the forms without the substance of law. A mature profession has a title for every occasion, and we might say then that the judges have given us a full-blown, articulated jurisprudence, but a jurisprudence without its substance. We have attained in fact the state of Antijural Jurisprudence.

Six

Prudent Warnings and Imprudent Reactions:

"Judicial Usurpation" and the Unraveling of Rights[1]

When we grasp the principles disclosed in the recent decisions of the courts on partial-birth abortion, we see at work furnishings of mind, among the judges, strikingly different from the furnishings of mind that were evident in the jurists of the founding generation. As I have suggested, these changes have been long in the making, and yet, when they finally break in upon us in their import, they can be startling nevertheless. Someone might aptly ask, if all of this is so radical and even treasonous – rejecting of the very premises of the American regime – why has it not been especially noticeable? But in all of this, there is nothing novel: The point has been aptly made that the moral life often consists in discovering the further implications of our own principles. The changes in American law have been in the making since the end of the nineteenth century, and they have accelerated since our jurisprudence moved into a new liberal phase with *Griswold v. Connecticut* (on contraception) and *Roe v. Wade* (on abortion). But over the last 20 years, in a series of decisions, the courts have been compelled to make ever more explicit the new understandings on which their new jurisprudence must come to rest. As that

---

[1] It would not detract, I think, from this chapter, but perhaps underline its seriousness in another way, to note that this chapter had its origins in remarks I was invited to offer, along with my friends in the Symposium of First Things, at the School of Law at Loyola University in New Orleans in October 1997. We were invited there by the dean of the law school, John Makdisi, who offered us the chance to engage with certain critics of our position, and in turn to restate, and sharpen, our arguments.

remarkable man of all seasons, John Paul II, has put it, they are understandings that come to a focus on the nature of "the human person." They are understandings about nature, and about life – its beginnings, and its ends.

The ancient question is whether human beings possess a distinct moral nature, which discloses in turn its telos, in distinctly moral ends, and a rather emphatic understanding about the terms of principle on which that human life must be led. To venture into those questions at all is the venture into the question about the terms on which new life is generated. It must make, after all, the most profound difference as to whether humans are spawned in random matings, or whether they are brought into the world within a framework of lawfulness and commitment, the framework we have come to know as "marriage." The liberal project has made its claim to audacity in its claim to bring about something new, something strikingly at odds with "traditional morality," and the conventions of law that sustained that morality.

But teachings so long planted, in the biblical tradition, and the tradition of classical philosophy, could not be inverted overnight without shocking the population at large. As Plato recognized, the multitude may not be capable of philosophy, but people at large are conservative in their reflexes, and if certain ways of life are grounded in the nature of human beings, the aversions, the public recoil, are likely to be felt right away. The warning bells are especially likely to be set off when people in authority decide to promulgate, on their own, useful innovations in morality for the improvement of the common folk. It is hardly astonishing that these changes could not be accomplished through the forms of republican government, in modes of decision that depended on "the consent of the governed." With the exception of New York, California, and Hawaii, the people at large remained deeply resistant to changes in the laws, long in place, to protect even nascent life in the womb.[2] The strategy of moving finally to the courts, or taking the courts as the principal arenas of political change, reflected the sober awareness that the cause of abortion could not be achieved through referenda or the politics of a democracy. It could be achieved only by appealing to those men and women (largely men) of a certain class, who exercised authority as judges. In surveys of opinion,

---

[2] Russell Hittinger, "Abortion Before Roe," *First Things* (October 1994), pp. 14–16.

the support for abortion has always run stronger among men than women.[3] As John Noonan has pointed out, the support for abortion has always found its strongest constituency among upper-class white Protestant males, and the people whose plans of life would always be more threatened by an inconvenient pregnancy with a woman from an inconvenient class.[4] And as Bernard Nathanson has recorded, it was one of the strokes of political genius in our time, the achievement of those men who founded the National Abortion Rights Action League, that they could frame this issue, so critical to their own interests, as "a woman's issue, a woman's right, a woman's choice."[5] Part of the political savvy, of course, was to read the political landscape, and that landscape was so patently discouraging that the scheme for advancing "abortion rights" would have to be pursued through the courts.

As a result of *Brown v. Board of Education*, in 1954, the federal courts gained a new legitimacy for an activist posture in striking down old laws, or overriding even older conventions that had the force of law. Without the experience of segregation, it is hard to imagine the course that the Supreme Court would begin to mark off as it moved to issues once thought to be too charged politically for the courts to enter. As judges ordered the reapportionment of legislatures, the redesign of school districts, and the allocation of public housing, the move into questions like abortion seemed to fit into the larger framework of judicial activism. But there is where the conservative imagination rather failed and gave a certain cover to this extension of judicial authority. The conservatives, mired in their own positivism, would not complain about the moral substance of these decisions, but mainly about the "activism" of the judges. The judges, it appeared, had strayed from the forms that confined them to a more limited and constrained exercise of power. That was no doubt the case – as indeed

---

[3] This point was confirmed rather clearly in one of the classic studies of public opinion on this subject, designed and reported by a scholar who, herself, happened to be "pro-choice." See Judith Blake, "The Supreme Court's Abortion Decisions and Public Opinion," *Population and Development Review*, 3, nos. 1–2 (March and June 1977), pp. 45–62; reprinted in *Human Life Review* (Winter 1978), pp. 64–81. See also James Davison Hunter, *Before the Shooting Begins* (New York: The Free Press, 1994), pp. 90–1.

[4] See John Noonan, *A Private Choice* (New York: The Free Press, 1979), pp. 49–51.

[5] Bernard Nathanson, *Aborting America* (New York: Doubleday, 1979), pp. 47–66, especially 52–3.

I have suggested here, in noting the drift of the judges from the conventions that traditionally disciplined and constrained their power with requirements of "standing" to sue. But the notion of "activism" discloses nothing of the ends to which that activism is directed. If judges of a later day honor the precedents set by activist judges, they simply confirm the victory of those who were incontinent in their use of power. The remedy for activism may have to be found in a willingness to overturn wrongful judgments, improvident precedents. But that course of remedies may readily strike observers as rather "activist." Or it would strike an observer in that way if he abstracted from the moral substance of the decision and noted only the willingness of the judges to break from the past.

As the federal courts extended their reach, even in the days of Nixon and Warren Burger, the conservative critics obscured the problem as they complained merely about activism. In November 1996, that estimable journal, *First Things*, staged a Symposium on Judicial Usurpation and "The End of Democracy?" The writers assembled in that project offered a precise account of a trend of decisions that went beyond mere activism. Step by step, the federal courts had shown a willingness to challenge, at their root, the laws that restrained the taking of human life at the beginning (with abortion) and at the end (with euthanasia and assisted suicide). With the same sweep, the judges were willing to think anew, and map anew, the begetting of human life, in mechanical fertilization or the storing of embryos. But then again, the courts became willing to pronounce anew on the meaning of sexuality as they took the first steps in altering the understanding of marriage. What the judges were doing, virtually on their own, was remodeling the very matrix of the laws on birth, death, sexuality, and marriage. As the participants in the symposium sought to warn, this was not simply a record of activism. It was a record that reached into the deepest premises of our law and the meaning of "the human person."

In that symposium in *First Things*, I offered one of the essays, along with my colleagues and friends, Robert George, Russell Hittinger, Robert Bork, Richard Neuhaus, and Chuck Colson. To our surprise, that symposium set off tremors in the land, as we began to raise doubts running to the very legitimacy of the regime; the regime that had now been altered, in its character and principles, by the ascendance of the judges. But in all of this, there was no counsel to overthrow an elected government in the United States. We were rather taken aback that our critics, including several of our own friends, did not give us credit for understanding the canons of prudence. We did not think that we were calling for the overthrow of an elected government when we cast up warnings: We were trying to show that certain critical thresholds of principle had been crossed, without much awareness, among the judges or the political class, that there had taken place anything much worth noticing. As we dealt with the criticism, or the heated reactions, it became clearer to us that the critics did not take seriously the notion that a regime could be changed decisively in its essential character, while the forms of political life seemed to remain undisturbed. But that is to say, the critics did not take seriously that prospect put forth so compellingly by Lincoln in his "House Divided" speech in June 1858: that indeed the moral substance of a democracy may be removed, while the outward forms remained the same.[6]

In his magisterial book on the Lincoln-Douglas debates, *Crisis of the House Divided*, Harry Jaffa sought to condense Lincoln's understanding here in this way: that "a free people cannot disagree on the relative merits of freedom and despotism without ceasing, to the extent of the difference, to be a free people."[7] In a related passage, Jaffa remarked, again construing Lincoln, that "if the majority favors despotism, it is no longer a free people, whether the form of the government has already changed or not."[8] I used to think that Jaffa, in these passages, was waxing metaphoric. But over the past few years, as this argument has deepened over judicial usurpation and the symposium in *First Things*, it has appeared to me that Jaffa and Lincoln should be taken here quite literally. Jaffa's teacher (and mine), the late Leo Strauss, once remarked that he had "understood Spinoza too literally because I did not read him literally enough."[9] In

---

6 See the Speech at Springfield, Illinois (June 16, 1858), in *The Collected Works of Abraham Lincoln*, Roy P. Basler, ed. (New Brunswick, NJ: Rutgers University Press, 1953), v. II, pp. 461–9.

7 Harry V. Jaffa, *Crisis of the House Divided* (New York: Doubleday, 1959) p. 336; republished by the University of Chicago Press, 1973.

8 *Ibid.*, p. 334.

9 Strauss, *Spinoza's Critique of Religion* (New York: Schocken Books, 1965; originally published in 1930), p. 31.

a similar way, I might say now of Lincoln, and the most elegant expounder of his thought, that I did not understand quite how deeply their arguments ran, because I did not understand them literally enough.

A congressman, getting ensnarled in his own syntax, declared, "A friend of the farmer . . . one of whom I am which." I would say: a participant in that symposium in *First Things*, one of whom I am which.[10] But even I was startled by the resonance that the symposium managed to generate in the land – and I was even more astonished by the adverse reactions of some of our friends, from people, you might say, within our family.[11] The symposium was arranged for the purpose of sounding a warning, and we certainly produced our effect if some people were in turn alarmed by the alarm we had sounded. Burke once remarked that the seasoned political man, "who could read the political sky will see a hurricane in a cloud no bigger than a hand at the very edge of the horizon, and will run into the first harbor."[12] "Head for a harbor," said one of our friends, "not start a revolution" – not urge people to the threshold of insurrection.

But we had sought, in several ways, to direct people away from a course of lawlessness, and of our own prudence I'll have more to say in a moment. Yet, I was struck in contrast with the notable want of prudence shown by our erstwhile allies: Their reactions seemed to me out of scale, for they seemed to be taking far more offense at us than at the offenses that we had sought in detail to describe.[13] They professed to share our judgments in the main about the wrongs pro-

---

[10] Again, see "The End of Democracy?," *First Things* (November 1996), pp. 18–42.

[11] See, most notably, the Symposium in *Commentary*; the letters, the exchanges, and resignations, published in *First Things* (January 1997), especially pp. 2–3 (Gertrude Himmelfarb and Walter Berns). Some of these pieces were assembled, in a representative collection, by Thomas Spence – see Mitchell Muncy, ed., *The End of Democracy?* (Dallas: Spence Publishing Co., 1997). The editors arranged a sequel in which some of the original participants, joined by other supporters, restated and sharpened their arguments. See *The End of Democracy? II: A Crisis of Legitimacy*, M. Muncy, ed. (Spence, 1999).

[12] Edmund Burke, "Thoughts on the Cause of the Present Discontents [1770] in Burke, *Selected Writings and Speeches*, Peter J. Stanlis, ed. (Anchor Books, 1963), at 123.

[13] See the Symposium, "On the Future of Conservatism," *Commentary* (February 1997), pp. 14–43.

duced by the judges, but they gave us ample reason to doubt that agreement. It might be said more accurately that they reached the same conclusion about the wrongness of certain decisions produced by the courts, but it became clearer now that they did not share the understandings that lay behind our judgments. At several levels, they did not understand the deep wrong of these cases as we understood them, and therefore they could not see, in the same way, that these cases were describing a genuine "crisis in the regime."

For our own part, we never thought that we were repudiating the American regime. Quite the reverse: We were seeking to vindicate the principles of the regime, to restore them in the face of a political class that was artfully replacing that regime with something else. Our friends seemed to take as gravely serious the threat that we writers were posing, and yet they could not take with the same seriousness the warning set forth by Lincoln: namely, that a regime quite republican in its outward forms could be converted, in its substance, into something else, something radically different. Which is to say, our friends were curiously failing to take seriously the classic understanding that even decent regimes may fall into a certain corruption, even while they retain their outward forms. We were told that because certain "crazies" in the 1960s railed against America and declared a crisis in the regime, that there could not be, in America, a crisis in the regime. Or that anyone who cast up a warning had to be touched with the same frenzy, bereft of judgment. In mapping out the problem, I would start with the simplest things, with a sense of our current situation, and I mean here a sober estimate, not a flexing of interpretive genius. My friend Mary Ann Glendon tells me that she steals from me, and I'm going to reciprocate by stealing from her – from a story she has used deftly, in recalling that scene from the film, Young Dr. Frankenstein, with Gene Wilder. Dr. Frankenstein was led into his Schloss, his castle, by Igor the hunchback, played by Marty Feldman. The young doctor Frankenstein gently touches Igor's back, and says, "I may be able to help you with that hump." And Marty Feldman says, "What hump?"

Mary Ann Glendon then observed, with Tocqueville, that

> Tyranny need not announce itself with guns and trumpets. It may come
> softly – so softly that we will barely notice when we become one of those

countries where there are no citizens but only subjects. So softly that if a well meaning foreigner should suggest, 'Perhaps you could do something about your oppression,' we might look up, puzzled, and ask, 'What oppression?'[14]

Flashback, for a moment, to an evening, in Washington, D.C., in 1986, the day after the Supreme Court refused to strike down the laws on sodomy in the States.[15] The Court left that judgment then in the hands of legislatures. At a party in town, a old friend, a seasoned lawyer in Washington, asked me, "Do you really want *politicians* making decisions on matters of this kind?" And I said, Consider what you are saying: that as people were drawn to office through the process of elections, they were rendered less fit to address questions of justice or matters of moral consequence. It was the most damning thing to be said about a democratic regime. It was also clear that my friend was part of a growing class of people who would readily prefer to be ruled, on the matters of the highest consequence, by people in judicial office – by a corps of people who do not have to suffer the rigors of running for election. Those judges would be drawn, of course, from the best law schools, rather like the school that my friend had attended. The judges were as likely to be people drawn from the same circles; in short, they would be people rather like my friend.

This is not a fiction, or a fable of the future; I take this to be a mark of our current situation, and the understanding of a good hunk of the people who form our political class. Indeed, without this understanding it would be hard to account for the intensity that was focused on defeating the nominations of Robert Bork and Clarence Thomas. Those nominations became freighted with a larger significance because either man was understood to be, potentially, the fifth vote in favor of overruling *Roe v. Wade*.[16] But for both men, overruling *Roe v. Wade* meant returning the question of abortion to the political arena of legislatures in the States. Both Bork and Thomas have been far from the point of finding, in the Constitution, the ground for protecting unborn children against the decisions of legislators who would with-

[14] Mary Ann Glendon, Comment in Antonin Scalia, *A Matter of Interpretation: Federal Courts and the Law* (Princeton: Princeton University Press, 1997), pp. 95–114, at pp. 113–14.
[15] See *Bowers v. Hardwick*, 478 U.S. 186 (1986).
[16] 410 U.S. 113 (1973).

draw the protections of the law. But if there was really a constituency now behind the "right to abortion," if that right commanded the depth of support that Joseph Biden and Edward Kennedy claimed for it, then there should have been no threat presented by Bork and Thomas. The issue of abortion would merely have been taken out of the cloistered arena of the courts and returned to the domain of a public politics. And there the public sentiment might have insisted on retaining the right to abortion – if that sentiment was as unequivocal, as unshaded with exceptions, as the law created by the Supreme Court.

But of course it was not, as Biden and Kennedy must have known. They had ample evidence to suspect that the public could not be depended on to install again a regimen of abortion in which abortions would be permitted for any and all reasons, throughout the entire length of the pregnancy. That kind of arrangement, produced by the courts, could be sustained only by the courts. What has to be under-stood about the Democratic party in recent years is that, in the after-math of *Roe v. Wade*, the party had become, in effect, the party of the courts. The party would take it as one of its central missions to pro-tect the authority and insulation of the courts – and the courts in turn could be counted on to enact certain parts of the agenda of the Democratic Left that the party could not declare in public or make the ground of a public campaign. Most of the Democrats would vote, in 1996, for the Defense of Marriage Act;[17] and Mr. Clinton, in the dead of night, would quietly sign the bill. But Mr. Clinton would continue to appoint to the bench the kinds of judges who could be counted on, in the long run, to expand the reach of "gay rights," or to find grounds for striking down laws that did not accord a legiti-mate standing to "same-sex" marriage.

I take it, then, not as a speculation, or a bit of science fiction, that we have an important part of the political class that is quite willing to remove certain matters of moral consequence from the sphere of popular government, or common deliberation. And it is willing to do that, because it has powerful reason to expect that the country is willing to be ruled on these matters by a corps of lawyers, rather like themselves, who will reflect in their rulings the liberal ethic that now prevails in the law schools and the universities.

[17] See 28 U.S.C. Sec. 1738 (c) (West Supp. 1997).

In my own contribution to the Symposium[18] I had written on the case of *Romer v. Evans*[19] and gay rights, and the way in which the sentiments articulated by the Court were making their way from legal institutions into private settings. In a gesture of steely contempt, barely concealed, the Court declared that a tradition of Jewish and Christian teaching on sexuality and homosexuality could be dismissed, as Justice Kennedy said, as nothing more than an "animus." It was an aversion that could claim for itself no reasoned grounds of support.[20] Once the Court has declared, from the highest levels, that moral reservations about homosexuality reduce to nothing more than a blind, unreasoned prejudice, it becomes all the easier for professional associations of all kinds – bar associations, associations of law schools, universities – to incorporate in their procedures an avowal that there should be no discrimination on the basis of "sexual orientation."[21] And so, in one major law firm in New York, a senior partner, a serious Catholic, had opposed in public certain regulations on so-called "sexual orientation." This senior lawyer was suddenly, discreetly, dropped from the recruitment committee of his firm. For his presence on a committee engaged in hiring would invite the charge that the

---

[18] "A Culture Corrupted," *First Things* (November 1996), pp. 33 ff.

[19] 517 U.S. 620 (1996).

[20] Of Amendment II, in Colorado, Justice Kennedy could proclaim, without a trace of hesitation, that "its sheer breadth is so discontinuous with the reasons offered for it that the amendment seems inexplicable by anything but animus toward the class it affects; it lacks a rational relationship to legitimate state interests" (*Ibid.*, at 632).

[21] Justice Scalia, who seems to be tuned in quite precisely and realistically to the ways of the world, anticipated these moves already in his dissenting opinion in Romer:

> When the Court takes sides in the culture wars, it tends to be with the knights rather than the villeins – and more specifically with the Templars, reflecting the views and values of the lawyer class from which the Court's Members are drawn. How that class feels about homosexuality will be evident to anyone who wishes to interview job applicants at virtually any of the Nation's law schools. The interviewer may refuse to offer a job because the applicant is a Republican; because he is an adulterer; because he went to the wrong prep school or belongs to the wrong country club; because he eats snails; because he is a womanizer; because she wears real-animal fur; or even because he hates the Chicago Cubs. But if the interviewer should wish not to be an associate or partner of an applicant because he disapproves of the applicant's homosexuality, then he will have violated the pledge which the Association of American Law Schools requires all its member schools to exact from job interviewers: "assurance of the employer's willingness" to hire homosexuals. (Bylaws of the Association of American Law Schools, Inc. § 6-4(b); Executive Committee Regulations of the Association of American Law Schools § 6.19, in 1995 Handbook, Association of American Law Schools. *Ibid.*, at 652–3.)

process of hiring was biased at the outset by the presence of a man who bore what the Supreme Court itself has pronounced an "animus." But that problem would be the same if this senior partner merely exercised his franchise as a partner to vote on the tenure, or retention, of young associates. That is to say, his very presence in the firm begins to constitute the immanent ground of a grievance, and of litigation. Law firms are nothing if not sensitive to incentives, and they will quickly come under an incentive to forestall the problem at the threshold through the simple expedient of not hiring people who are – shall we say? – "overly religious." In this way, a new orthodoxy makes its way outward: it moves from public laws to rules governing private firms, corporations, and universities, until it begins to affect the things that people will find it safe to say to one another even in private settings. As the late Leo Strauss taught years ago, the notion of the "political regime" extends beyond the formal institutions of government to the ethic that pervades the way of life of a community.[22] What we are seeing, in the movement on gay rights, is a movement that is promising to alter the political regime itself.

But that movement can be seen even more fully, even more deeply, on the issue that almost all of us, gathered in *First Things*, regarded as the central, or architectonic, question right now in our politics, the question of abortion. In my business, as we used to say, I see a lot of the public, and my travels bring me into touch with audiences that have not been uniformly sympathetic on the matter of abortion, to put it mildly. I have usually broached the problem to them by noting, right away, that in the absence of any extended argument, I would not expect them to share my position on abortion. But I ask them simply to flex their imaginations in this way for the sake of understanding their fellow citizens who cannot regard this issue as anything less than overriding: Imagine that some people look out on the scene, and they think that abortion involves the taking of human life. They also understand that they are not indulging fancies about leprechauns or centaurs; they know they can also summon a substantial body of evidence from embryology to

[22] See Leo Strauss, *Natural Right and History* (Chicago: University of Chicago Press, 1953), pp. 135–6, and *passim*.

confirm that this is not some odd, religious opinion on their part. These convictions are not at all then like emphatic views on the Hale-Bopp comet. In that event, if these people have reason to think that human lives are taken in these surgeries, they look out and see that 1.3 million lives are being taken each year – as though the government had withdrawn the protections of law from a whole class of human beings in this country. What would we have thought, after all, if 1.3 million members of a minority could be lynched without restraint, and without the need even to render a justification? Again, I don't ask people to share this judgment, but to encompass merely this recognition: If other people did look out at the country and saw these things taking place, where would you expect them to rank this concern within the overall inventory of things political? Would it rank just below the concern for interest rates or unemployment? Once we understand what people see, how could we react with outrage or bafflement if we find that these people cannot see that issue as anything other than central – that they cannot see it merely as peripheral?

Some of our friends reproached us for making the issue of abortion a kind of litmus test of the regime. Their complaint then was that we were, on balance, making too much of abortion. But we had to wonder if they, on balance, were making too little of it, and whether the issue did not come down to this: that in their heart of hearts, some of our friends really were not possessed by a lively sense that there were real human beings getting killed in these surgeries. Yet, if it turned out that we were the ones who were seeing more accurately, that sense of things would have to add force to the claim that our law and politics had entered a new phase, marking nothing less than a crisis in the regime.

Our understanding of the crisis was arranged, one might say, in tiers, but what was curious is that our friends did not recognize, in the first instance, just where we were holding back and showing forbearance. In our indictments of the regime in its current state we hardly said anything more severe than could have been said of the regime in the middle of the nineteenth century, the republic that made its accommodation with slavery. The presence of slavery marked a corruption or a flaw running deep, to the very root of a polity founded on the principle that human beings deserved to be ruled only with their consent. And yet, as Lincoln understood, the opponents of slavery could not have been justified in taking up arms to overthrow an elected government that sustained slavery. They could not have done that without violating the very principle they were seeking to vindicate, for they would have put themselves in the position then of ruling people without their consent. But the same problem in principle would have to constrain us today. As long as elections are open, and we are free to persuade our fellow citizens, we could not be warranted in using force outside the law. Some of us have been careful also to be guided by the teaching in Plato's *Crito*, a work that offers some powerful instruction in prudence for holding back and respecting the law, even when we are utterly persuaded that the cause of justice lies on our side.[23]

But on their own part, our friends should have been alert to the fact that the same constraints would have come into play even if we had a democratic government that was presiding over an Auschwitz and shipping people to killing centers. And yet, what if someone asked us, under these conditions, "Would it be wrong to rescue the innocent victims, who are about to be killed unjustly?" Could we honestly tell them that it would be wrong, even when it means running counter to the law?

The same problem in principle must come into play, even in a muted form, with the matter of abortion. It bears recalling here that many of our friends among the critics would not really contest us on the question of abortion taking human lives. On that point, they would concede our premise. But in that event, what could they honestly say to the person who now asks, "Would it be wrong, or unjustified, to rescue the innocent human beings who are being killed in these surgeries?" Our friends do not seem to recognize, in Lincoln's words, just how much we have had to bite our lips and "crucify [our] feelings"[24] for the sake of urging people to obey the law in these instances. When people ask us earnestly – as I have been asked, in interviews on

---

[23] For my own treatment of this problem, see my book, *First Things* (Princeton: Princeton University Press, 1986), pp. 224–7.

[24] Letter to Joshua Speed (August 24, 1855), in *The Collected Works of Abraham Lincoln*, Roy P. Basler, ed. (New Brunswick, NJ: Rutgers University Press, 1953), v. II, pp. 320–3, at 320. "It is hardly fair for you to assume, that I have no interest in a thing which has, and continually exercises, the power of making me miserable. You ought rather to appreciate how much the great body of the Northern people do crucify their feelings, in order to maintain their loyalty to the constitution and the Union."

radio – about the rescue of the innocent, we turn away from offering encouragement. Without surrendering the argument, we try, decorously, to change the subject, or we simply counsel them to obey the law. I fear, though, that for many of our friends, Lincoln's words could be adapted again: Nothing may satisfy them until we cease calling abortion wrong, and begin calling it right.[25] Nothing else may ease their minds or quiet their angers.

Given what was at stake, it seemed to me that our severe critics among our friends were themselves showing the most pronounced want of prudence, for their reactions were out of scale, and they were lingering on the surface of things without tracing matters, in a serious way, to the core in principle. And by that I do not mean simply that they had not thought through the matter of abortion, but that they had not treated with a sufficient seriousness the notion of a genuine crisis in the regime. As I suggested earlier, they did not seem to take seriously the depth of the issue that Lincoln framed for us in the crisis of the "house divided." The telling emblem of that crisis, the little example that told all, was the case Lincoln would cite of Senator Pettit of Indiana. Pettit had made quite a stylish point in insisting that the self-evident truth proclaimed in the Declaration of Independence – that "all men are created equal" – was nothing less than a "self-evident lie."[26] As Lincoln understood, of course, the American republic did not begin with the Constitution, but with the Declaration of Independence, and that "proposition," as he put it, on which the nation was founded and dedicated. But evidently, there were portions of the American political class that were no longer committed to that proposition. They would vote to sustain a regimen of slavery, and they would acquiesce in every alteration of the laws, every abridgement of constitutional freedom, that was necessary to preserve those arrangements of slavery. In other words, men who filled the office of senator might nevertheless be *acting on premises that were incompatible, at the root, with the premises that underlay their offices.* For the office of senator held its meaning or coherence only as it was part of a

---

[25] See Lincoln, Speech at Cooper Union (February 27, 1860), in *Ibid.*, v. III, pp. 522–50, at 547–8.

[26] See *ibid.* (Debate with Stephen Douglas at Alton, Illinois, October 15, 1858), at 301–2.

republic, or a government based on the consent of the governed. But the moral commitment to a government by consent sprung from that moral axiom, that "all men are created equal," that human beings did not deserve to be governed in the way that men governed horses and cows. The Senate found its place within a certain regime. Senator Pettit was an officer of high standing, he held an office within an institution defined by that regime. But he rejected the very premises that underlay the regime in which he held his office. He established in his own case a lesson that cannot be dismissed: that it was possible for people to hold high office within a political regime, and yet be entirely disloyal, in the sense of rejecting the deepest premises of that regime. And if that much could be said about senators, it could be said about judges, and any people who form the political class in our own day.

In classic terms, this was a case of the "corruption" of the political order, and as the ancients understood, this kind of corruption had to be an immanent possibility even in the best of regimes. Why should we suppose, then, that this country should be exempt from these dangers, inherent in political life? The American regime was, without question, a republic and a constitutional order. But within the framework of that regime, the need to keep reinforcing the system of slavery was imparting to the law an authoritarian character. Slave codes, sentinels, passports, curfews – the system of slavery was made all the more explicit as slavery moved from the plantation into the cities. Frederick Law Olmsted, visiting the South, remarked that he had seen "more direct expression of tyranny in a single day and night in Charleston, than in Naples in a week."[27] And in this way, a government that remained outwardly a republic could be transmuted into something strikingly different in its substance.

Even now it is not appreciated as to just how penetrating was Lincoln's argument here, or just how sobering was the lesson he was trying to convey. Some of us have argued for years that Lincoln's arguments on slavery, and the crisis of the republic at the time, were the closest analogies to the questions we were facing with abortion and our recent crisis. But for some of us it has become ever clearer that Lincoln's argument was not merely analogous: He was dealing

---

[27] Quoted in Richard Wade, *Slavery in the Cities* (New York: Oxford University Press, 1964), p. 98.

with the same problem, or to put it another way, our problem today radiates from the same questions in principle, which is why that problem of abortion has held such a grip on us.

In his debates with Stephen Douglas, Lincoln sought to warn off those Republicans and Free-Soilers who were drawn to Douglas and his scheme of "popular sovereignty" in the territories of the United States. That scheme was offered for its pragmatic appeal, as it promised to deliver some territories to the side of freedom, while it preserved the civic peace. Douglas's plan would have preserved the peace by striking a posture of neutrality in regard to slavery. As Douglas said in that famous phrase, "I don't care" whether slavery is voted up or down; that moral question would be left for the people of a territory, or a state, to decide for themselves. But as Lincoln would point out, there was nothing neutral in the "don't care" policy. As Lincoln put it in the debate in Quincy, Illinois:

> [W]hen Judge Douglas says he 'don't care whether slavery is voted up or down,' . . . he cannot thus argue logically if he sees anything wrong in it; . . . He cannot say that he would as soon see a wrong voted up as voted down. When Judge Douglas says that whoever, or whatever community, wants slaves, they have a right to have them, he is perfectly logical if there is nothing wrong in the institution; but if you admit that it is wrong, he cannot logically say that anybody has a right to do a wrong.[28]

Aquinas and John Stuart Mill had reminded us that, when we say something is wrong – that it is wrong, say, for parents to torture their children – we mean that it is wrong for everyone, for anyone; that anyone may rightly be restrained from torturing infants, that anyone may rightly be punished for performing that act. If someone told us then that he would leave parents to their own judgment on these matters, that he "doesn't care" whether they torture their children or not, he has not taken a position of neutrality. He has decided, in effect, that the torturing of infants stands in the class of those things "not wrong."

Lincoln's charge against Douglas was that the very object of his policy was to break down the sense, in a democratic people, that there was something "wrong" in slavery. His device was to treat the matter

---

[28] *The Collected Works of Abraham Lincoln, supra,* n. 24, v. III, pp. 256–7.

persistently, in Lincoln's words, as a "morally indifferent thing." And so Douglas would say that certain states, in their economy, feature oysters, certain of them feature cranberries, and others use slaves. As Lincoln pointed out, Douglas grouped slaves with cranberries and oysters, morally indifferent things. Or he encouraged us "to speak of negroes as we do of our horses and cattle."[29] But if the American people backed themselves into that state of mind, their indifference to slavery in the territories would readily spill over into the states as well. If they came to think that the ownership of human beings was a legitimate form of property, they would have to agree more readily that citizens of the United States should not be dispossessed of their ownership of this property in slaves when they entered a territory of the United States. But in that event, why should they be deprived of that legitimate property when they entered another state? The "privileges and immunities" of citizens of the United States describes a body of rights that may be portable for citizens as they travel from one state to another. Why will it not be discovered that this right to own slaves is part of that body of rights, carried from one place to another, and protected then in the States as well? And why should other citizens object to any of these claims? Why, indeed – if they have talked themselves into the notion that they may be quite indifferent on the question of whether one human being may rule another without his consent?

I would bring back, then, those two passages drawn from Harry Jaffa, trying to explain Lincoln, and I would make those passages the ground of further reflection, as one seeks in turn to expound them. It was Lincoln's charge that Douglas was reshaping the climate of opinion and reshaping, at the same time, the American soul. Jaffa sought to condense Lincoln's understanding here in this way: that "a free people cannot disagree on the relative merits of freedom and despotism without ceasing, to the extent of the difference, to be a free people."[30] In a related passage, Jaffa remarked, again construing Lincoln, that "if the majority favors despotism, it is no longer a free people, whether the form of the government has already changed or not."[31] Jaffa might have been sweeping with a literary flair, but what

---

[29] Debate at Charleston (September 18, 1858), in *ibid.*, p. 181.
[30] Jaffa, *supra*, n. 7, p. 336.   [31] *Ibid.*, p. 334.

was jarring for me recently was that I came to see that, on these points, he and Lincoln were being *quite literal*. And that is the thing that has to be explained.

The beginning of the explanation is to be found in that crisp summary Lincoln provided when he said that the "sacred right of self government" was so perverted in Douglas's construction that it would amount to just this: "That if any *one* man, choose to enslave *another*, no *third* man shall be allowed to object."[32] Lincoln spoke of men, not black men. For his point was that the argument in principle for slavery could not, would not, be confined to blacks. On this matter, there is no statement more penetrating and decisive than that fragment Lincoln had written for himself, when he imagined himself engaged in a conversation with the owner of black slaves. He had put the question of how that white owner could justify this enslavement of the black man. ("It is color, then: the lighter having the right to enslave the darker? Take care. By this rule, you are to be slave to the first man you meet, with a fairer skin than your own.")[33] In this fragment, Lincoln had also been reflecting the understanding of his political idol, Henry Clay. In one of the debates with Douglas, Lincoln recalled that someone had pressed on Clay the argument that blacks were an inferior race, drawn from an uncivilized land. And Clay responded, in a remarkable passage, that

> Whether this argument is founded in fact or not, I will not now stop to inquire, but merely say that if it proves anything at all, it proves too much. It proves that among the white races of the world any one might properly be enslaved by any other which had made greater advances in civilization. And, if this rule applies to nations there is no reason why it should not apply to individuals; and it might easily be proved that the wisest man in the world could rightly reduce all other men and women to bondage.[34]

With this ground, Jaffa was moved to suggest that the very willingness of certain Southerners to affirm the inferiority of black people,

[32] Lincoln, Speech on the House Divided, Springfield, Illinois, June 16, 1958, in *supra*, n. 24, v. II, p. 462.
[33] *Ibid.*, v. II, pp. 222–3.
[34] Clay, cited in Jaffa, *supra*, n. 7, p. 337.

as the condition that justifies their enslavement, was sufficient to prove that these Southerners were themselves unfit for self-government. Or, it might establish that they were no longer a democratic people, even when they were voting and mimicking the acts that describe citizens in a republic. For in their willingness to justify the enslavement of black people, they were affably putting in place the premises that justified their own enslavement.[35]

That may sound implausible and a bit farfetched, but that is the point that gets us closer to what I am more and more disposed to treat as the literal truth of the matter. I would make my approach to it in this way: People may go into voting booths and cast votes, and for all we can see, they are acting in the familiar modes of citizens in a republic, engaged in the act of voting, or manifesting a government by consent. But we know of course that we cannot always give a moral account, or even an accurate descriptive account, of what people are doing when we merely describe their outward behavior. Smith goes to the garage of his next door neighbor and takes the hose on the wall. But from that outward act alone we cannot say that he is engaging in a theft. He might have had permission to use the hose, or he might not have had permission, but there is a fire in his house and he is seeking to borrow the hose for a moment for a justified end. Before we can give an account of the act, or its moral significance, we need to know something about the purposes animating the actor, or his own understanding of the principles that inform his action.

Now, with that perspective in place, we might imagine that we are viewing an election, in Germany, in 1932. There are some good Germans concerned about the Versailles Treaty and drawn to Hitler and his program for dealing with the Depression. They know that he has a severe, illiberal program, shall we say, in dealing with the Jews. They know, too, that there is a risk that Hitler and his Nazi party may remove this government by consent and replace it with a dictatorship of some kind. This German voter may doubt that Hitler is fully serious in following through on his threats about the Jews, or that he would

---

[35] Hence, that stirring line, offered by Lincoln, which quickly spread through the ranks of men in the Union Army: "In *giving* freedom to the *slave*, we *assure* freedom to the *free* – honorable alike in what we give, and what we preserve." Message to Congress (December 1, 1862), in *The Collected Works of Abraham Lincoln, supra,* n. 24, v. V, p. 537.

really act upon his expressions of contempt for the Weimar republic. But in his willingness to vote for Hitler, he marks his willingness *to take a chance on these things.* In that respect, he would separate himself from the people who think that the avoidance of genocide, and the preservation of constitutional government, are things so important that they cannot be placed in the basket of things "we are willing to take a chance upon." On the other hand, this voter may indeed think that Hitler means it about the Jews, and the voter is quite willing, for his own part, to vote now to dispossess the Jews of their property and redistribute their businesses to deserving Aryans. The question then is: When this man casts a vote, is he affirming, with that vote, the principle of government by consent? Is he affirming, that is, the rightness in principle of a government that rules people only with their consent?

Apparently not, for he is not really concerned to preserve a regime of elections as an absolutely necessary condition of politics. Nor is he concerned to protect the right of his neighbors to enjoy an equal claim to that government by consent, a government that would protect their rights and their lives. The voter is acting to assert his interests, or his passions, quite apart from the form of the regime. If he is counting on a majority of Germans to vote with him in dispossessing the Jews, then he is merely affirming, through the ballot, the principle of the Rule of the Strong. If that is the case, the question then is: Does he have any ground of complaint when Hitler moves to suspend constitutional government after the Reichstag fire? For wouldn't Hitler merely be asserting now the same principle that the voter was acting upon in the voting booth? That voter would have no ground of complaint, for he was not in a position to offer a moral account, or a moral justification, for a "government by consent."[36] He had overthrown, or discarded that principle already, in his understanding, even as he was casting his vote. We might say, then, that he had gone through all of the outward acts, quite familiar to citizens voting in a democracy; but in point of fact, in literal truth, he had not been acting, in the voting booth, as a citizen in a democracy. And if a majority of the electorate had acted in the same way, with the same understanding, it could indeed be said that the outward forms of a republic had been present,

---

[36] For an interesting argument converging with this one, see Richard Neuhaus, "Can Atheists Be Good Citizens?," *First Things* (August/September 1991), pp. 17–21.

but that this group of voters had ceased being a democratic people. As Jaffa put it, "in choosing to enslave other men it is impossible not to concede the justice of one's own enslavement." Or again: the voters no longer composed "a free people, whether the form of the government has already changed or not."

I would bring the matter back then to our current situation, our present discontents. The doctrine of slavery, said Lincoln, meant that if one man sought to enslave another, a third man may not object. And my friend, Russell Hittinger, summed up our own situation in this way a few years ago: We have now created a private right to use lethal force, a private right to kill, for wholly private reasons.[37] One person may now claim to kill a second person, a second being, for reasons that may not rise above convenience, and under those conditions a third person may not object. That third person, or the rest of the community, may not object, because this is now, as we are told, a matter of "privacy." As Hittinger put it, imagine that a farmer in Vermont was told in the 1850s that if he objected to the prospects of slaves around him, he should not buy one. But he is also informed at the same time that he may not join with his fellow citizens in Vermont in deliberating about the question of whether the political community, in its laws, will recognize or honor this form of property. That is a matter of privacy, he is told, and it forms no part of the legitimate business of the polity. And now, in our own day, he is told that if he objects to abortion, he should not choose one for the women in his life. Yet, the *choice* of abortion, he is told gravely, remains a private matter, outside the laws. That is to say, whether the laws on homicide will be extended or contracted, to protect children in the womb or leave them unprotected, is no longer part of the legitimate business of the polity. And it is no longer part of *his* legitimate business, then, as a citizen or a member of the political community. But if the laws on homicide, or the protection of life, are not part of the purpose of a polity, or central to its legitimate business, what purposes on earth could be more apt or central?

We can readily anticipate the argument that would be offered in protest or resistance: Surely, it might be said, the claim for abortion

---

[37] See Russell Hittinger, "When the Court Should Not Be Obeyed," *First Things* (October 1993), pp. 12–18, especially p. 16.

is not as broad as Hittinger and I have stated it. Surely it would not be a claim that a person has a franchise, or right, of homicide in regard to *any* other person, and that the rest of us have been rendered powerless to object. Lincoln had sought to show that the argument for slavery, when cast in a principled form, could not be cabined, or confined to black people. But as the argument might continue, this claim over abortion is more readily and evidently cabined. And yet, is it? In the first place, we should take note of the obvious point that not everyone could be enslaved. One person could choose to enslave another, but only from that class of beings who were marked off as *available*; a class of beings who would not be protected from enslavement. In our own case we begin with a class of beings who are not protected from private killing or this private homicide. And yet if that claim to engage in private killing were so readily cabined to what would be it be cabined? Would it be: the right of a woman to end the life of the offspring contained in her own womb? But then we quickly learned, in the Baby Doe cases in the early 1980s, that the doctrine in *Roe v. Wade* would have to carry over to certain newborns.[38] The babies might come out with Down's syndrome or spina bifida, and we were told then, by jurists such as Thurgood Marshall, that the same rights of privacy contained in *Roe v. Wade* entailed now the exclusive, private right of the family to determine whether their newborn child had a life worth living, or a life worth preserving.[39] If the baby was slated for abortion, but in one of those rare cases, survived, then there were doctors and jurists ready to argue that the right to abortion entailed the right to an "effective abortion," or a dead child.[40] And very recently, of course, we have seen the case of the grisly partial birth abortion, with about 70 percent of the child outside the birth canal.

---

[38] See *Bowen v. American Hospital Association* 476 U.S. 610 (1986).

[39] See, for example, Marshall's comments during the oral argument in the Bowen case, U.S. Supreme Court, Oral Arguments, v. 8, Cases Nos. 84-1573-84-1560; October Term 1985, pp. 16, 23.

[40] Without pronouncing a judgment on the matter, the Supreme Court took note of these kinds of arguments in *Planned Parenthood v. Aschcroft* (1983). Justice Powell noted the testimony of a Dr. Robert Christ, that "the abortion patient has a right not only to be rid of the growth, called a fetus in her body, but also has a right to a dead fetus." Justice Powell pronounced this argument to be "remarkable in its candor." But as noted earlier, to describe the argument as "remarkable" is not exactly to pronounce it "wrong," and still less is it to supply the reasons that make it a wrongful

But once again we are told, quite explicitly, by the partisans of abortion that any yielding on this matter will *imperil the whole corpus of rights articulated in Roe v. Wade*. I do not then invent these connections in principle; the other side *insists* upon them. Ms. Kate Michelman insists, then, for the National Abortion and Reproductive Rights Action League, that the rights articulated in *Roe v. Wade* cannot be confined to the treatment of the child in the womb.[41]

But as I say, there had been no doubt, earlier, about a connection between *Roe v. Wade* and the right to dispose of infants born with serious handicaps or medical problems. There has been no attempt to conceal the reach of that doctrine in *Roe* by confining that doctrine to infants in the womb. We have been told, by many of the same people, arguing from the same book, that the right of privacy in *Roe* should entail the "right to die," or the right to assistance in dying for adults who lack the means, or the competence, to end their own lives.[42] Who were the candidates for this right? First, they were people in a supposedly terminal state, but who were not dying at a decorous enough speed.[43] Then there were comatose patients, who were not exactly terminal, but living in a state, we were told, that could hardly be called "living."[44] In a flight of metaphor, their condition was often described as "vegetative," as though a person, in a diminished state, had suffered a shift in kingdoms, from animals to plants. As the argument advanced another step, it was applied to people who were not

construction of the doctrines put forth by the Court. See 76 L Ed 2d 733, at 740, n. 7. We may remind ourselves that, without exactly saying so, Judge Haynsworth had been willing to install, in effect, the same understanding – of a right to an effective abortion – in his opinion in *Floyd v. Anders*, 440 F. Supp. 535 (1977).

[41] See her testimony in opposition to the bill on partial-birth abortions in "Partial-Birth Abortion: The Truth," Joint Hearing before the Senate Committee on the Judiciary and the Subcommittee on the Constitution of the House Committee on the Judiciary; 105th Cong., 1st sess., March 11, 1997, pp. 19–21. And see also the testimony from the representatives from other groups that have been engaged in the defense and promotion of abortion: the Planned Parenthood Federation and the National Abortion Federation, pp. 23–6, 31–5.

[42] See, as a notable case in point, the opinion by Judge Stephen Reinhardt, in *Compassion in Dying v. Washington* 49 F. 3d 790 (1996), the opinion that was overruled by the Supreme Court in *Washington v. Glucksberg*, 138 L Ed 2d 772 (1997).

[43] See *In re [Nancy] Jobes* 529 A. 2d 434 (1987).

[44] See, for example, *In re Guardianship of [Barbara] Grant*, 747 P. 2d 445, 452 (Wash. 1987) (en banc), modified, 757 P. 2d 534 (Wash. 1988), and *Bouvia v. Superior Court ex rel. Glenchur*, 225 Cal. Rptr. 297, 304 (Ct. App. 1986).

comatose, but conscious some of the time – and yet, not "what they used to be." They were people so impaired that their lives were wanting in fullness, or in the vigor that marked human flourishing.[45] In the case of Dr. Jack Kevorkian, the candidates may now include people who are simply depressed and have no wish to live. And indeed, as Michael Uhlmann has pointed out, the decision of the Ninth Circuit, in *Compassion in Dying v. Washington*, in 1996, would have established a right to die, or assisted suicide, that covered the patient so depressed, or so weary of life, that he simply wished to be quit of it.[46]

By the time we have moved along this route, the right to die entails the obligation of certain doctors to act as agents, or accomplices, in inflicting death. That is what a "right" to die means in its hard, operational side, or in its moral logic. If it is rightful for a patient to end his life, he should not be deprived of this good, or this "right," merely because he is incapable of effecting his own death. If he has a right, another person with the competence and means may have the obligation to minister to him, to act as his agent. The patient may also be too comatose to announce his own intentions or execute a formal will. And yet, why should patients in those conditions suffer *discrimination*? Why should they be deprived of a "good" made available to others? Once we establish the class of people who should not be deprived of this right; once we establish that doctors, or administrators, in a hospital, have the responsibility to administer this right; why should it not be available to orphans or to people without families? Why should it not be granted to them through the helpful intervention of strangers who happen to be doctors and administrators?

Again, I offer no fictions, or speculations. I merely note the train of cases *we have already seen*. These arguments have been brought forth already to show how the doctrine of privacy in *Roe v. Wade* should be extended, in mercy and liberality, to cover these cases. We move then, from children in the womb to newborns out of the womb; and from there we move to aged, or even middle aged, people, with

---

[45] See *In re Jobes, supra*, n. 43, and *Bouvia v. Superior Court ex rel. Glenchur*, n. 44.
[46] See, again, 49 F. 3d 790, and Michael Uhlmann, *Last Rights* (Eerdmans, 1998), pp. 1–44.

conditions terminal, but then not so terminal, unconscious but then partially conscious, or conscious but depressed. And then finally we arrive at a new "right" in the law for strangers to administer death to adults, well outside the womb, who have neither ordered nor consented to their deaths. When we view the sweep of this movement, we must put again the question, How would this claim to kill, for private reasons, be cabined any more readily than that principle of enslaving other men, whose reach and dynamic Lincoln saw with an unsettling accuracy? And Lincoln saw the direction of that tendency precisely because he saw the principle that lay at the heart of the thing.

I return then to that final, sobering connection: that a people who have made themselves suggestible to these things have ceased to be a democratic people. In regard to slavery, I think that argument, offered by Lincoln, can be understood as literally true. And if that argument at the core is the same thing, could the same charge be leveled today? Can we take it, not as a sweeping metaphor, but as a literal truth: that we are in danger of ceasing to be a democratic people, and that a regime, outwardly a republic in its forms, has been converted, in our lifetimes, into something radically different? As the measure of things, we would be obliged, earnestly, to consider, from what we have already seen and heard, whether the most educated people in this country have not in fact grasped hold of this right to abortion as though it were now the central right, the touchstone of our liberties, because it is the guarantor of sexual freedom. And sexual freedom seems to be taken now as the most fundamental freedom of all, perhaps because it is so evidently "personal." But in taking hold of abortion as a fundamental right, a right now bound up with the regime, people seem to have backed themselves into the position of affirming one or both of the following propositions:

(1) "I have a 'right,' anchored in the Constitution, to kill another human being, a child in the womb, if the advent of that being would adversely affect my interests, disrupt my plans, cause me embarrassment." That is, do we not find among some of our people an unashamed claim now of a right to kill for their own convenience? If so, that must be a novelty in our tradition, and could it be anything other than

sobering or terrifying? Still, there is enough of a lingering moral reflex in our people that most of them, I think, would recoil from that kind of a claim. To their credit, they seek to avoid that way of framing the principle. By in trying to avoid it, they find themselves backing into a second proposition, even more portentous yet – namely:

(2) "The being I would kill is *not* a human being, and it is not yet a real person. But any evidence from embryology or genetics would be quite beside the point, for the decisive question is whether *I myself* regard the being as human. Or to put it another way, my right here is the right to decide just who is a human being, on the strength of my own beliefs, and as it suits my own interests." That is, I may not have a right to kill any other human being as it suits my interests, but I have a right to decide just who is a human being when it comes to killing or disposing of that being, as *that* suits my interests. Either that claim reduces to the same thing, or it announces a principle, as I say, even more radical and unsettling yet.

I can report, from my own experience, that a surprising number of people, products of the best colleges and universities in the country, are indeed willing to affirm one or both of these propositions, as part of their defense of the right to abortion. And I would submit that a right to kill, cast in these terms, will not be cabined, any more than the claim to enslave could be cabined. But as we move through this series of discrete steps, absorbing the understandings that must come along with each step, there should no longer be anything unthinkable, or even startling, in that proposition I have put forth as the matter that had to be explained and justified: a people who have incorporated the understandings contained in these steps may no longer be a democratic people. To be sure, they are people quite used to the conventions of democracy. They are quite familiar with candidates, and they may even have a certain appetite for campaigns, with their color and drama and flavor. They may feel themselves enmeshed in the life of a democracy as they feel themselves enmeshed with the life of baseball when they are at ball games and following, intensely, their favorite team. But in all strictness they cannot count themselves as part of an association devoted to the end of securing the constitutional rights of other members of the community, for they cannot give an account any longer of why other human beings have a claim to be the bearers of "rights" in any strict sense. They cannot vindicate then their own rights, and for that reason, they are not in a position any longer to vindicate the rights of others.

For in the course of defending this new "right" to abortion, they have talked themselves out of the notion of "natural rights" held by Lincoln and the American Founders. But that understanding was absolutely necessary to the Constitution in the sense that, without it, one could not give a coherent account of the Constitution or the "rights" it was meant to secure. The partisans of abortion have meant to establish an expansive notion of rights; but the requirements of their own argument have compelled them to evacuate from the logic of "rights" its deepest meaning. In order to defend that right to abortion, they were compelled to reject the deep logic of "natural rights," for that logic would envelop even the child with rights as soon as the child begins to be. The partisans of abortion were driven then to put, in the place of natural rights, a rather diminished version of rights. But with that logic, or with that diminished notion of "rights," the partisans of the "right to abortion" cannot protect any longer my life, my freedoms, my rights, against the most arbitrary takings and restrictions. For the defenders of abortion have *removed the moral ground for the definition and defense of any of those rights.*

That may be a jarring point, but it may be brought home more gently and compellingly by piecing together the lessons that may be drawn through a series of vignettes.

I was in a conversation with a former student of mine, who had indeed been one of the most gifted students in a course on the Constitution. But then the conversation suddenly took a turn that surprised me. My student leaned in, with a sheepish smile, and "confessed" that he had never really heard the fuller argument for "natural rights," and he was inclined to be rather dubious about the notion. That did come as news to me, and I was curious: What were the grounds of his reservations, for how would he otherwise explain then the judgments he had reached and defended? If he had permitted himself no other grounds than legal "positivism" could supply – if he held that all moral judgments were reducible to the opinions that were dominant in any place – his judgments on the leading cases would become inexplicable. At this moment, my student drew on his considerable acuities, along with certain arts of presentation that he had acquired at Amherst. As the conversation unfolded, I raised the example of a homeless man in the gutter: He might be quite diminished in his sensibilities, and he may bear a responsibility for certain injuries done to himself. Nevertheless we seem to look upon him as one who merits not only our sympathy but a certain respect. Even in his diminished state, we regard him as a bearer of rights, and therefore we think we have some obligation to minister to him. And why was that? My student, drawing on his arts, then did what might be called a postmodernist riff: The established vocabulary came rolling out, in sentences, intervals, even cadences that seemed quite familiar. He now found himself trying to explain that notions of rights are "socially constituted" in different places, and we treat the derelict as a bearer of rights because of the way in which we, as a society, have come to view him. It had something to do with the lens of culture through which we had come to perceive and "construct" him. At that moment, I broke in and pointed out that he had just shifted, decisively, the terms of the conversation: He was talking about *his perceptions or ours*, about the lens *we* bring to the problem. But he had ceased talking about *him* – that man in the gutter. The question put out of the picture was whether *he* had anything about him that merited our respect or commanded our reverence for *his* life? Was there anything *intrinsic* to him that could be a source of rights, anything about him that commanded our respect?

I had returned, not long before, from my visit to the Holocaust Museum, and that experience I recounted at the beginning of this book: I had suddenly come up against the vat filled with shoes, and that encounter had brought back those unforgettable lines from Justice McLean's dissenting opinion in the Dred Scott case. Those lines, lingering with me, had led me to this question of how we had come to view that man in the gutter as a bearer of rights. McLean had said that the black man was a creature who bore "the impress of his Maker," that he was "amenable to the laws of God and man," and "destined to an endless existence."[47] He might be uneducated, diminished in his slavery, and yet McLean thought he was the bearer of a

---

[47] *Scott v. Sandford*, 60 U.S. 393, at 550 (1857). The fuller sweep of his remarks read in this way: "A slave is not a mere chattel. He bears the impress of his Maker, and is amenable to the laws of God and man; and he is destined to an endless existence."

certain dignity or sanctity because he was made in the image of some-thing higher. And to call back some earlier words, without that sense of human beings made in the image of something higher, it may indeed be harder to explain why that fellow in the gutter should claim anything called "dignity," or have even the slenderest claim to our respect.

As I had remarked previously, in this vein, we find ourselves in a curious situation in which so much of our language of politics and law is rooted in layers of moral understanding, and religious persuasion, which have fled from the recognitions of most of our people. Our words and terms often appear then as artifacts of a culture that has long departed. We casually speak of "rights," and without quite knowing why, we fold in the assumption that the persons before us have the standing of rights-bearing beings. Without knowing very much about particular persons, we nevertheless attribute to them, as human beings, a certain dignity, or a certain claim to our respect. Even if we inadvertently jar another person, we quickly beg his pardon – as though even the slightest injury still counted, still merited our apology.

We know that it is possible to speak of right and wrong without making appeals to faith or to God – for that is the very promise of "natural law reasoning." And yet, again, we may not realize just how much the notions of right and wrong are anchored in a sense of human beings as distinctly moral beings, with powers of reason that, in Aristotle's estimate, touched the divine. The most wondrous things about us may no longer be noticed, and from the other side, we may not be quick to see that, that when we scale down our sense of the "moral," or install a diminished sense of a "right," we may be diminish-ing also our sense of the persons who bear those diminished claims. So, at least, was the charge that Harry Jaffa came to level at a man he otherwise esteemed as a decent man and a political friend. Chief Justice William Rehnquist had defined himself, over the years, in scholarly commentaries, as a jurist who showed his conservatism by preserving a fidelity to the positive law. That was a thoroughly defensible posture, but it generated certain points of worry even for his friends when he ventured into a philosophic stream that delivered him to a scheme of positivism in moral and legal judgments. In a notable speech, in the 1970s, Rehnquist said that our moral views represent only our "value

judgments" until they are enacted into law. "It is the fact of their enact-
ment," he said, "that gives them whatever moral claim they have upon
us as a society." He went on to say that, if a society

> adopts a constitution and incorporates in that constitution safeguards for
> individual liberty, these safeguards do indeed take on a generalized moral
> rightness or goodness. They assume a general acceptance neither because
> of any *intrinsic worth* nor because of . . . someone's idea of natural justice
> but instead simply because they have been incorporated in a constitu-
> tion by a people.[48]

That passage has drawn a sharp critique from Harry Jaffa, who
unfolded its implications in this way:

> . . . To say that safeguards for individual liberty do not have any intrin-
> sic worth is to say that individual liberty does not have any intrinsic
> worth. To say that individual liberty does not have any intrinsic worth
> is to say that the individual human person does not have any intrinsic
> worth. This is to deny that we are endowed with rights by our Creator.
> To deny that is in effect to deny that there is a Creator. This is atheism
> and nihilism no less than moral relativism.[49]

But this is simply to say that conservatives, as well as liberals, can
fall into the premises of legal positivism, and even with the best of
intentions, they may not gauge the depth of the premises they are
accepting. What Jaffa finds, contained by implication in the writing of
conservative jurists, can be found routinely on the other side of the
political divide, with the premises of moral relativism made quite
explicit. An interesting example may be found, most recently, in
Professor Mark Tushnet's *Taking the Constitution Away from the
Courts.*[50] Tushnet evidently became seized with the conviction that the
Constitution must be taken from the courts when he sensed, on the
part of the Supreme Court, an alarming drift to the political right (a

---

[48] William H. Rehnquist, "The Notion of a Living Constitution," 54 *Texas Law Review*
693, at 705 (1976).
[49] These remarks, by Professor Jaffa, were contained in an address, "The False Prophets
of American Conservativism," delivered on Lincoln's birthday in February 1998.
The passage is contained on p. 12 of that typescript. Jaffa has elaborated on the
argument in print, though not exactly in the version found in the address of 1998.
See, for example, Jaffa, *A New Birth of Freedom: Abraham Lincoln and the Coming
of the Civil War* (Lanham: Rowman & Littlefield, 2000), pp. 87–8.
[50] Princeton: Princeton University Press, 1999.

drift discernible, it must be said, only to people of the most refined perceptions). And so, in a remarkable turnabout, Tushnet seeks to recover, for the Left in politics, Lincoln's argument on the limits to the reach of the courts. In the hands of Tushnet, that move has the purpose of permitting local governments and private corporations to persist with policies of racial preferences and affirmative action, even as the federal courts are more and more likely to regard those policies as unconstitutional. In a faint echo of Lincoln, Tushnet would deny the monopoly of the judges in interpreting the Constitution, and he would look beyond the Constitution for the standards of judgment used by politicians and ordinary citizens. He would appeal, as Lincoln appealed, to the Declaration of Independence, and to the "first principles" that marked the character of the American republic. Except for one notable thing: It is not the Declaration as Lincoln and the founders understood it. In Tushnet's rendering, the Declaration is purged of its moral substance. For one thing – and quite a notable thing – Tushnet's Declaration of Independence omits that tricky reference to the "Creator" who endowed us, in the first place, with unalienable rights. In a stroke, Tushnet removes what the founders understood as the source of those rights – and the Author of a Law outside ourselves, which even a majority is obliged to respect.

But that omission becomes the key to other omissions with an evident moral significance: In good postmodernist form Tushnet announces that "the Declaration's principles, the values that constitute the American people are always subject to change as the people change." But then how are they "principles"? They do not articulate truths, much less those truths, as Lincoln said, that were "applicable to all men and all times." If the principles of the Declaration are not really principles, based upon truths, then on what ground can we even claim their *goodness*? Why should we think that the political life based on those principles is better, or more just, than a politics based on premises wholly at odds with the principles of the Declaration? Tushnet, the offspring finally of postmodernism, delivers his valedictory:

> We are who we are because we are committed to the project of realizing the Declaration's principles. But we can start telling a different story

> about ourselves precisely because we constitute *ourselves*. [Italics in original.] We can, in short, change who we are . . .

> In taking that step . . . we would have to rethink how we understand the original Constitution, the post-Civil War amendments, and the New Deal and the Great Society programs. [But] the Declaration's principles provide a story line that is much closer at hand.[51]

A "story line"? In Tushnet's new method of constitutional interpretation, the text of the Constitution is displaced, first, in favor of the "principles" of the Declaration. Yet, those principles are detached from a Creator of nature and a moral law, so that they are not in fact, any longer, principles, but propositions of a contingent character, always subject to change. They "declare," then, in this version of the Declaration, no moral truths. They disclose no source of their rightness, and in the end we find that they provide only a "story line," a line we are free to change. What is left, after all of this, is not Lincoln or the founders, but Nietzsche. We are left simply as agents with a will, asserting our freedom to remake our own stories, or our own sense of the moral universe.[52]

Left or right, liberal or conservative, may come back then to the same ground. The conservatives may begin with a moral modesty, a reluctance to pronounce moral judgments, but that position turns, without much strain, into a posture of moral skepticism. The conservatives back then into a "soft relativism." But either way, the two sides may converge on the same point, and in either case, they end up undermining the moral logic that attaches to "rights." What Jaffa managed to capture here, or bring to a new level of awareness, was this implication: that the move to relativism finds both conservatives and liberals denying that any of us bears an intrinsic dignity, which can become the source in turn of rights with an intrinsic dignity. Yet, without that sense of things, we cannot give a coherent account of rights, and we have no "rights" in the strict sense: we have, that is, no claims of liberty or safety that others must be obliged to respect, even when those claims run counter to their own interests. For if we accord rights to people only because we think it would be useful to

---

[51] *Ibid.*, p. 191.

[52] See, in this vein, my own review of Tushnet, "Lincoln, Nietzsche, and the Constitution," *First Things* (April 2000), pp. 16–20.

us in the long run – that we would all benefit, by and large, by a regime of rights – why should we continue to respect those kinds of rights when they no longer seem useful to us?

That understanding may be conveyed finally, in the last vignette I would recall, and the last fragment I would put in place here. The scene is Brookline, Massachusetts, just a few years ago. It is just after the shooting that took place at an abortion clinic there, a shooting that took the lives of two women on the staff. The gunman, a young man crazed, eventually took his own life while in jail. A couple of nights after the shooting, there was a candlelight vigil. One young woman was there holding her daughter, born only about two weeks earlier. She explained to the interviewer that she was there for the sake of preserving, for her daughter, the same "reproductive rights" that she had enjoyed – meaning, of course, the right to have destroyed that child right up through the time of birth.

But if her daughter had possessed those reproductive rights as rights that were part of "women's rights," it becomes apt to ask: what was the source of those rights, and when did she acquire them? Were they a species of "natural rights"? If so, they flowed to her as a human being, or as a woman, and those rights would have come into existence as soon as she herself began to be, or began her existence as a female. But in that event, she would have been the bearer of those rights when she was in her mother's womb, and her mother could not have held a franchise then to sweep away all of her rights through the simple device of removing, in a stroke, the bearer of those rights. In short, if that child truly possessed "rights," her mother could not have possessed an unrestricted right to abortion.

But obviously, that could not have been the understanding of the mother, for her own "reproductive rights" evidently enjoyed a certain trumping power. They clearly overrode any rights possessed by the child. Plainly, the child had a claim to exist, as the bearer of rights, only when the mother decided to confer upon her the privilege of living. In other words, the child became a rights-bearing person only when the mother, in a grand Nietzschean gesture, said in effect, "I permit you to live. I confer upon you, now, dignity and standing." But if the child gains her rights in that way, *they could hardly be natural rights, and indeed they may hardly be rights at all.* For they do not begin – they cannot begin – with the sense that there is anything *intrinsic in the child* that we are obliged to respect, or any objective truths that we are obliged to respect as truths, *when they do not accord with our own interests.*

To the extent that we buy on to a "right to abortion," it must follow, inescapably, that we must buy on to this "story," or this construction of how we acquire our rights. No logic of natural rights can be squared with that right to abortion. But in that event, this most awkward tangle of construction produces that bizarre kind of "right" I mentioned earlier: a right that virtually extinguishes itself. Let us suppose then, for the sake of argument, what I would otherwise contest at every point: that there is such a thing as a "right to abortion." But the logic that must attend that right cannot draw on the logic of natural rights, or the sense that there is, in any of us, from the very beginning, an intrinsic dignity, the source in turn of rights with an intrinsic dignity. All rights then must be conferred by people in a position to confer them, and it must be clear that the only ground of their rightness lies in the act of their conferring. If those rights, or franchises, are conferred by the ruling majority in any place, it simply means, again, that those rights are thought to be consistent with the interests of the majority. When we come through this chain of steps, each clear in its import, what would that "right to abortion" now mean? It would be a right conferred only because it is thought to be consistent with the interests of those people who are affected most directly – or consistent with the interests of those who rule. The so-called right to abortion would be, then, a right that could readily be qualified, restricted, even canceled outright, if it were no longer thought to be consistent with the convenience or interests of others. Under those conditions, I would submit, we may still talk about a "right to abortion," but with no more significance than attaches to a "right to use the squash courts" at the club. It is a right that will always be contingent, always dependent on its acceptance by local opinion, always open to repeal at any point. It would bear no resemblance to what the partisans of abortion refer to these days as "abortion rights." For it would not in fact have the substance of a right in the deepest sense, the sense that attaches to natural rights.

If there is a dimension even further to this train of implications, it would begin with the recognition that the "story" that comes along with the right to abortion is a story that is not confined to abortion: it must determine, across the board, the entire spectrum of our claims to "rights." After all, the "story" that comes along with abortion is a story of how each one of us acquires our rights at our very beginnings as "rights-bearing beings." It is a story of the radical absence of rights, our nakedness of rights, until those rights are conferred by the powerful. It implies also the most emphatic judgment on the question of whether those rights have cognitive significance, objective standing as truths, or whether they depend at every moment on perception or the "social construction" of reality. And of course this account of rights implies something about us, in the same way, as the vessels of those rights. If there is no objective truth attaching to "nature," or human nature, if the very meaning of a human being is, as some radical feminists say, always contingent, always open to "contestation,"[53] then how could any of us be the bearers of *rights* that have objective standing? *Could our rights, after all, have an objective standing, while we ourselves do not?* The postmodernists, flexing their "literary theory," may be in a state of terminal cleverness, as they suggest the ingenious ways in which our natures may be reinvented, or reconceived, or effaced altogether. They say, with brashness, what they can hardly mean and they write with a serene want of awareness of the rights they are imperiling.

In short, the people who sign on to the "right to abortion" in the radical style of our current laws – a right to destroy a dependent human life at any time, for any reason – those people set in place the logic that deprives them of *all* of their rights. But not only "them": To the extent that this story line becomes necessary to the understanding of rights, it affects all of us with its radically diminished state. Hence, the conclusion that I set myself earlier the task of explaining: The people who talk themselves into this diminished logic of rights cannot vindicate that right to abortion, because they are not in a position to vindicate *any* set of rights, for themselves or others. They have made of themselves the most infirm allies, as fellow citizens, for they cannot be depended on any longer to come to our side in defending any of the rest of us, in the defense of our rights. For they can no longer offer a moral defense of those rights. And for the same reason, they cannot

---

[53] See Judith Butler, "Contingent Foundations: Feminism and the Question of Postmodernism," in Judith Butler and Joan W. Scott, eds., *Feminists Theorize the Political*, pp. 3–21.

offer any longer a coherent defense of the regime that began with the understanding of a Creator endowing us all, from our own beginning, with unalienable rights.

In one of his lasting phrases, George Orwell had taken note of a theory of intricate contrivance, and remarked that it had to be the work of intellectuals, for no ordinary man could have been that stupid. It may be breathtaking to contemplate the fuller implications that we have had to absorb in our law and our lives when we absorbed the novelty of a "constitutional right to abortion." But matters may be restored to the ground of sobriety when we recognize that the "right to abortion," and all of the theories of "autonomy" it has licensed, did not emanate from the conversation of ordinary citizens, or even from the arguments of politicians in the public arena. These doctrines have been promulgated by courts, and the supporting doctrines, growing more and more audacious, have been cultivated by the intellectuals resident in schools of law. When the matter of abortion is presented to the public, in surveys, ordinary people show that they have the wit to deliberate about the conditions under which abortions may be justified or unjustified. The conclusions produced by the public may not always display models of coherence, but they have been far more reasonable than the doctrines produced by the courts, as the judges have produced rationalizations ever more inventive in order to "explain" why even the most modest restrictions on abortion are not in the least tenable. The arguments that took place among ordinary citizens and their representatives were arguments anchored in a more natural language, not the jargon of the law schools, for they sprung from conversations, grounded in common sense, about the abortions that were justified or unjustified.

I would suggest then that the remedies can be found in measures that are quite modest, and grounded in arguments accessible to ordinary folk. The main remedy is to be found by ending the monopoly of the courts and judges, and returning the question of abortion to the arena of legislatures and the arguments of citizens in the natural discourse about "rights" and "wrongs." If legislatures are forbidden to legislate on the matter of abortion, then there will be no arguments in public. But if legislators are compelled to take positions again on this issue, then the conversation radiates outward: If something is at stake in the legislative arena, citizens will have some reason to be discussing the matter again in public meetings and private arguments. As Marx used to say, "the struggle of the orators on the platform evokes the struggle of the scribblers of the press; the debating club in Parliament is necessarily supplemented by debating clubs in the salons and pothouses. . . . When you play the fiddle at the top of the state, what else is to be expected that that those down below dance?"[54] In the politics of a republic, the conversations and the arguments at the center of power radiate outward. But there is no need for that conversation if legislatures have nothing to legislate, and they have nothing to legislate if the matter of abortion is removed from the political arena and reserved entirely to the governance of the judges.

It requires, however, no unsettling of the Constitution, no alteration in the American regime, in order to dislodge the courts from their monopoly of control on abortion and other matters. The remedy here lies in a simple restoration, and it needs no special contrivances, no new schemes of voting or constitutional amendments: It requires only recalling, for a new generation, Lincoln's understanding of the limits that must be part of the logic and character of the federal courts. That understanding reminds us, also, of the responsibility that must lie with the political officers of the government, as well as with the judges, to measure their practical judgments against the principles of the Constitution. Without wrenching the constitutional order, the issue of abortion, along with other matters of moral consequence, can be returned to the hands of executives, congressmen, and senators. It can be returned, that is, to the hands of officials who bear a more direct responsibility to the public, and who work under the discipline of giving an account of themselves to the voters who elected them. Yet, once that step is taken, and the issue of abortion is returned to the political arena, legislators as well as professors will be confronted with the next phase of the problem: What would be the constitutional ground on which the national government would legislate on a matter such as abortion? It is precisely because the matter had been confined almost exclusively to the jurisdiction of the States that it becomes

---

[54] Marx, "The Eighteenth Brumaire of Louis Napoleon" [1869], reprinted in Lewis S. Feuer, ed., *Karl Marx and Friedrich Engels, Basic Writings on Politics and Philosophy* (New York: Anchor Books, 1959), p. 333.

difficult to explain the ground of any federal jurisdiction over a matter seen as so vividly "personal." But here we may find ourselves dazzled to the point of distraction by the argument over constitutional formulas. Many things may fall into place when we ask the elementary question, What is the ground in the Constitution on which the Supreme Court had discovered, in 1973, a lurking right to abortion? If we can answer that elementary question, we have the main guidance we would need for a Congress interested in legislating on the same subject. At that point, we would find again that the solution would not lie in formulas overly intricate and contrived. The solution, or the remedy, would be rather modest, and it would find its ground in the axioms of the Constitution: not in theories, problematic and clever, but in the propositions that must ever be in place, because they are part of the very logic of the Constitution. And for that reason, as we used to say, they cannot be otherwise.

Seven

Finding Home Ground

The Axioms of the Constitution

I t was springtime in the Age of Clinton. The first spring, that is, in the first Congress, with a Democratic majority in both houses, and a Democratic president in the White House, the first alignment of this constellation since 1980. But that earlier Democratic president was Jimmy Carter, who professed to regard abortion as a regrettable thing, not to be promoted. He would do nothing as president to put the weight of the federal government in opposition to abortion, but neither would he do anything much to promote it. After the years of Reagan and Bush, the Democrats were once again in control of the Congress in 1993, but this time there was a president sprung from the generation of the baby boomers. He, too, professed in public to regard abortion as a regrettable thing – his hope, he said, was to make abortion "safe, legal – and rare." But the first two items revealed the most important part of his state of mind: that he regarded abortion as an eminently legitimate choice, and with those premises in place the last point in his trinity was quickly rendered a deception. For Bill Clinton would do nothing to make abortion "rare." In fact, quite the opposite: from the first moments of his presidency – in fact, even before he was sworn in as president – the documents were prepared for the first moves of his presidency, and in those moves he would rescind the executive orders of the Reagan and Bush presidencies that bore on abortion.[1] Gone, in a stroke of the executive pen, would be

[1] See *Public Papers of the Presidents of the United States: William J. Clinton*, 1993, two vols., bk. I (Washington: Government Printing Office, 1994), pp. 7–11.

the order that barred the performance of abortion in military facilities[2]; the directive that barred research in the transplantation of fetal tissue, in projects supported by federal funds, and the use of fetal tissue in experiments[3]; and finally, the "Mexico City policy" of President Reagan, which barred the use of monies from the American treasury to support programs abroad designed to promote abortion.[4]

Gone, too, would be the executive order of President Bush to deny federal funds to any program of "counseling" by private entities that promote abortion as a response to pregnancy.[5] Apart from that, the new Clinton Administration would seek to remove the restraints of the Hyde Amendment, in withholding the funds of taxpayers from the support of abortion. Abortion had been famously billed, after all, as a "private liberty" – a liberty so private that only a pregnant woman and her doctor had any legitimate standing in the decision. If that were indeed the case, it was hard to turn around and claim that this liberty had now a substantial "public" dimension: While the father of the child had no standing at all in the matter, the great public at large was somehow implicated in these private abortions, and the public as a whole deserved to be taxed then to support them. This was hardly the kind of matter that fitted the description of a "public good." As one notorious wag put it, "Unless [doctors or their patients] suffer from an overdose of literary symbolism or Russian novels, they know that the abortion they are experiencing is not being performed on the general public."[6] This sense of the matter formed the odd wall of limits that the public was willing to erect now: The public would be strangely acquiescent in accepting surgeries it regarded, in most instances, as wrong, but it would be unflaggingly resolute in its refusal to pay for them.

The Clinton Administration would set itself against this disposition, curiously settled in the public, and indeed the administration would

---

[2] *Ibid.*, at 11. The only qualification entered here was that the abortions would be paid for with private funds. The Hyde Amendment still barred the use of federal funds to pay for most abortions.

[3] *Ibid.*, at 9.

[4] *Ibid.*, at 10–11.

[5] *Ibid.*, at 10.

[6] See Arkes, "On the Public Funding of Abortions," in James Tunstead Burtchaell, ed., *Abortion Parley* (Kansas City and New York: Andrews and McMeel, Inc., 1980), pp. 237–64, at 243.

succeed in forcing a modification of this policy to cover abortion in the cases of rape and incest. The stance, however – the public posture – was far more significant than the funds it managed to snare: This was the first administration, since *Roe v. Wade* in 1973, to regard abortion as a "public good," as something to be promoted with funds drawn from the public. And as part of the same package, it was a "good" that justified the most strenuous efforts to remove any inhibitions on abortion that might still be lingering in the federal laws.

This was a rare moment, then, for the partisans of "abortion rights," and they sought to take advantage of it by bringing forth the Freedom of Choice Act. The object, put concisely, was to codify *Roe v. Wade*. The holding of any case could always be narrowed, over time, to the circumstances and the litigants in that case. But if the main provisions in *Roe v. Wade* could be enacted in a statute, the policy contained in *Roe* could be incorporated more explicitly in the laws of the land: They would be general in their application, not confined to the litigants in *Roe*, and they would be prospective – they would be valid and binding, presumptively, on all future cases.

The bill had been introduced in 1991, when the Democrats were in control of the Congress, but George Bush was still in the White House. Now, the alignments were different, and the prospects as good as they would ever be to pass a bill whose stated purpose was "To protect the reproductive rights of women by providing that a State may not restrict the right of a woman to choose to terminate a pregnancy." And yet, to the wonderment of all, it didn't happen. The partisans of abortion, expansive with their strength, with a Democratic Congress and an emphatically pro-abortion president, suddenly seemed to be jolted, as though they had found the end of their tether. Even in 1993, most of the public had never grasped that *Roe v. Wade*, and its companion case of *Doe v. Bolton*, had created a right to abortion for any reason at all, lasting through the entire length of the pregnancy. The public, and even most lawyers, managed to remain in a state of serene unawareness on that point. In the meantime, the judges preserved the cast of the laws created by the Supreme Court, and abortions could proceed apace, with no serious restraints remaining in the laws. But it was quite a different matter when that policy was to be made explicit and enacted in a statute. In the Judiciary Committee of the House, Congressmen Henry Hyde, Charles Canady, and others kept introducing amendments to bar abortions late in the pregnancy or to cast up other impediments. One by one those amendments were rejected by the majority. But one by one those amendments made explicit just what each member of the Congress was clearly voting for when he voted to imprint, in the laws, a policy of abortion on demand, with no restriction, no restraint, at any time in the pregnancy. Even for a party that was turning itself into the party of "abortion rights" this was, strangely enough, just too much. There was still a sufficient component of "pro-life" sentiment lingering in the Democratic party, especially in old Democratic enclaves in Missouri and Kentucky. And the result was that the movement to enact *Roe v. Wade* into a statute suddenly came upon its hard, sober limits. The votes were simply not there.

The Freedom of Choice Act had to be put to the side, and while it was, the Clinton Administration fell into some serious misadventures. The president's numbers in the polls took a dramatic plunge when the administration made one of its chief, early initiatives the campaign to break down the resistance to gays in the military. *Time* magazine, at this time, ran a cover with the headline, "The Incredible Shrinking Presidency." Mr. Clinton's problems were compounded as his wife undertook a mission to redesign the scheme of medical care and bring that complicated industry, with 14 percent of the gross national product, under the benign, deft management of the national government. The recoil from these measures finally produced an emphatic, and thoroughly unexpected recoil: The congressional elections of 1994 brought a gain for the Republicans of 52 seats in the House, and the first Republican Congress since Eisenhower's first landslide, in 1952.

The Republican party that took control of the Congress in 1994 was of course a party with a far different complexion from the party that took hold of Congress in Eisenhower's first term. It was a party strongly tilted now to the West and South. It was still the party of "producers" and businessmen in the sense of a party that was quite sensitive to the costs that were added to employment, in corporations and small businesses, as a result of expanding the taxes and regulations of the government. But since the days of Ronald Reagan, and the "culture wars" of the 1960s, the party had drawn to itself many of the so-called "cultural conservatives." The issue of abortion was nowhere on the screen in 1952; it was hardly imaginable as a national issue. But as the sentiment took hold in opposition to *Roe v. Wade*, and the

Democrats came to resist any restrictions on abortion, a new wave of Catholics and evangelical Christians was drawn into the Republican party. By some estimates, drawn from surveys, these new recruits among evangelicals made up about 40 percent of the voters in Republican primaries.

The party that took control of the Congress then in 1994 was a substantially pro-life party. In the first days of the Reagan Administration there had been an attempt to counter *Roe v. Wade* with ordinary legislation, a Human Life Bill. But that effort failed, and since that time the decisions of the courts seemed to entrench *Roe v. Wade* even further. Certainly, that was the overt message delivered by the Court – including three appointees of Presidents Reagan and Bush – in *Planned Parenthood v. Casey* in 1992.[7] The Congress would be compelled to work, at first, within the limits enforced rather severely by the courts, in alliance with Planned Parenthood and other groups defending the right to abortion. But it seemed to be understood that there were several places, touching the periphery of abortion, where the Congress could plant some new premises, and possibly have the effect of actually restricting a small number of abortions. That is where the bill on partial-birth abortion made its dramatic contribution. The sentiment in favor of that bill proved overwhelming, but with President Clinton in office, wielding the veto, the bill seemed to stand no chance of becoming part of the laws of the United States.[8]

Nevertheless, this issue offered an extraordinary vehicle for breaking out news that most of the public was bound to find disturbing – namely, that abortions could be performed for any reason right up to the time of birth. If even a Democratic Congress would not pass the

---

[7] 505 U.S. 833.
[8] The House passed the bill on November 1, 1995, by a vote of 288–139. The breakdown by party, however, was even more revealing. The Republicans voted for the bill by a vote of 215–15, while the Democrats voted mainly against the bill with a vote of 73–123. The bill passed the Senate on December 7, by a vote of 54–44. Forty-five Republicans were joined by nine Democrats in favor, 36 Democrats were joined by eight Republicans in opposition. After the two bills were reconciled, the slightly altered version passed the House on March 26, 1996, by a vote of 286–129. President Clinton vetoed the bill on April 10. The veto was overridden in the House by a vote of 285–137. But the vote fell short of the numbers necessary to override in the Senate, even though two Democrats (Nunn and Leahy) and one Republican (Spector) added their support to the motion to override. The final vote in the Senate was 57–41. See also Chapter 4, above, p. 105.

Freedom of Choice Act, a new, pro-life majority, was likely to have little trouble in summoning the votes to ban this grisly form of "abortion," performed on a child already in the process of "delivery." And yet, a serious question arose within the ranks of the Republican majority, and among conservative scholars, about the constitutional ground of that legislation. The first response seemed quite natural: What ground had the Democrats brought forth in 1993 when they had sought to enact the Freedom of Choice Act? What had they seen as the ground of an authority to enact a policy of legalized abortion and override all of the laws in the separate states casting up barriers to that policy? The expected, but utterly improbable answer was: the Commerce Clause. And so the drafters of the bill on partial-birth abortions came up with this language, reflecting a formula that would quickly be recognized: The bill would pick out, as the focus of its condemnation,

> Whoever, in or affecting interstate or foreign commerce, knowingly performs a partial-birth abortion and thereby kills a human fetus

But why, of all things, the Commerce Clause? Most notably, because the Commerce Clause had been associated with the expansion of the federal power, especially since the days of the New Deal. Whether it was used plausibly or implausibly – and in most instances, I think, quite implausibly – it seemed to be the most serviceable instrument for reaching *private* conduct. Of course, that clause had been conceived, from the beginning, as quite the contrary: It would be employed by the courts and Congress to deal with those impediments to commerce that were cast up by *the laws* of a state. The more characteristic, and dramatic, application would be found, say, in the classic case of *Gibbons v. Ogden* (1824): The Court, under Chief Justice Marshall, came down decisively against the State of New York when the state awarded monopolies to ships engaged in the coasting trade and barred ships licensed by Congress.[9] In other words, a state, acting through the law, barred people outside the state from engaging in commerce within its borders. All of that was quite different from the immanently implausible task of measuring the "effects" on interstate commerce if a business became vibrant, with sales diffused through the whole

---

[9] See, *Gibbons v. Ogden*, 22 U.S. (1 Wheaton) 1.

country, or if a strike threatened to close down a business trading widely across state lines. Justice James McReynolds once posed the telling question: Would the federal government actually have the power to order a *reduction* of wages on a ranch, or in a factory, if it were thought that an increase in wages would put the company out of business – and as a consequence, diminish the flow of goods in interstate commerce?[10]

It was arguable then that the Commerce Clause was used most properly when it dealt with obstructions to trade that were created, not by private parties, but by the laws of a state. But at the end of the nineteenth century and the beginning of the twentieth, the Commerce Clause was invoked more and more to extend the powers of Congress over private industry. There would be the moves to form an Interstate Commerce Commission, pass laws on antitrust, and use the leverage of the national government for the sake of promoting labor unions. These trends would deepen with depression and war, and they would finally cross a threshold of acceptance by the courts during the second term of Franklin Roosevelt. But as the Commerce Clause became used more widely as a device for reaching private conduct, it became serviceable at a sensitive time in the 1960s in the dispute over the Civil Rights Act of 1964. The Fourteenth Amendment offered ample means of addressing the discriminations enacted and enforced by the laws of a state. That was, after all, the very purpose of the Fourteenth Amendment. Still, that weighty instrument was almost entirely inapt when it came, say, to the policies of discrimination that were established as part of the conventions of private business and corporations, especially in the South.[11]

---

[10] McReynolds put it in this way:
> If a man raises cattle and regularly delivers them to a carrier for interstate shipment, may Congress prescribe the conditions under which he may employ or discharge helpers on the ranch? ... May a mill owner be prohibited from closing his factory or discontinuing his business because so to do would stop the flow of products to and from his plant in interstate commerce? May employees in a factory be restrained from quitting work in a body because this will close the factory and thereby stop the flow of commerce? May arson of a factory be made a Federal offense whenever this would interfere with such flow? If the business cannot continue with the existing wage scale, may Congress command a reduction? (*Labor Board v. Jones & Laughlin Steel Corporation* 301 U.S. 1 [1937], at 97–8).

[11] I say "almost entirely inapt": The one slender thread of possibility lies in the notion of certain customs, conventions, "uses," patterns of private practice that may virtually have the force of law. Or in any event, they reflect the climate of opinion that

When it came to the matter of abortion, however, and the people who were seeking to pass the Freedom of Choice Act, the main concern was to overcome those lingering parts of the laws in the separate states that might still offer a slight discouragement to abortion. These laws could no longer bar abortions, but they might mandate a waiting period of a day or two, or they might require the consent of parents for clients who were minors. If the concern now was to overcome those laws in the States, the Fourteenth Amendment should have been quite good enough. And yet, when Professor Laurence Tribe of the Law School at Harvard came to testify at the congressional hearings, he framed his own constitutional case for the bill by relying on the Commerce Clause. The arguments offered by Tribe tracked rather closely the arguments that had been made under the Commerce Clause in sustaining the Civil Rights Act of 1964. Veteran observers of the Supreme Court quickly recalled how problematic those arguments were. But it was apparently important for Tribe to draw on those arguments offered under the Civil Rights Act because he wished to present the "right to abortion" as part of the same movement: It was, in his estimate, cut from the same cloth, another fundamental "civil right." Indeed, as Tribe would have it, that right to abortion would be seen as one of the gravest rights that attached to citizenship, and on that ground it deserved now to be woven deeply into the laws.

When Tribe and his allies failed, when they gave way to another Congress and a different majority, turnabout was considered more than adequate fair play: If Tribe was willing to testify that the Commerce Clause supplied the constitutional authority for the Congress to legislate on the subject of abortion, then that was quite good enough for the supporters of the new bill on partial-birth abortions. Still, one scholar who supported this bill decorously declined to testify, rather than embrace the fiction contained here, that the power of the Congress to legislate on abortion was truly grounded in the Commerce Clause. Politically, the use of this formula was enough to answer any challenge raised by the other side, because the Commerce Clause had been offered, with a straight face, by Professor Tribe, and sup-

---

shapes the law or renders a law unenforceable. See, on this point, Arkes, *Beyond the Constitution* (Princeton: Princeton University Press, 1990), pp. 130–4.

ported, with faces equally void of puzzlement or embarrassment, by the congressmen willing to vote for the Freedom of Choice Act.

And yet, the question of what would get through the day, politically, was quite different from the question of whether the Commerce Clause really supplied the source of the federal authority to legislate on the matter of abortion. Those who were tutored in these matters were simply held back from lip-synching the kinds of constructions that were offered by Professor Tribe with his own, distinctive embellishments. But since Tribe's arguments were drawn from the arguments used earlier, in connection with the Civil Rights Act of 1964, it is worth recalling how those arguments ran. In his public testimony on the Freedom of Choice Act, Tribe had done a "riff," or an elaboration, of the brands of reasoning that had become familiar in the use of the Commerce Clause, in the cases that ran, say, from *Wickard v. Filburn* (1942) to *Katzenbach v. McClung* (1965). But in adding variations, he would find his inventiveness in stretching the scheme even further: Tribe was moved then to argue that, if states were free to impose restrictions on abortions, there would be more people driving on the highways, seeking out states with easier laws. He could write then, darkly, of "the human toll taken by this highway of anguish and frustration." It was a curious turnabout, to put it mildly. During the litigation over civil rights, the argument had been made that policies of discrimination, set in place in private inns and restaurants, would discourage black people from traveling between the states. And if black people did travel less, there would be fewer orders, along the way, for meat and drink and silverware. There was, mind you, no evidence presented that black people were indeed traveling less. Without proving or documenting a shortfall in traffic, that premise was simply *stipulated*. And from that assumption the conclusion was drawn that there would be a vast, depressing effect on interstate commerce. As the argument was fitted then to the Commerce Clause, the translation ran in this way: If there was discrimination against black people in interstate commerce, there would be a depressing effect on the interstate flow of meat and other services! (By that construction, as one friend put it, the problem would be dissolved simply by having the racists in the country eat more meat.)

But now that the lawyers and judges understood that they were trafficking in legal fictions, one improbable set of reasons seemed to license others. In one case, interstate commerce was injured because people were discouraged from traveling; but now the danger to commerce arose from the possibility that people might actually be *encouraged* to travel. By these kinds of reasonings, the federal government might claim the authority to close down strings of factory outlets in Maine because they caused large traffic jams in New England and the area north of Boston.

Professor Tribe was apparently quite willing to absorb the embarrassment, or wave it away, for he knew that this style of argument could not be dismissed out of hand without treating as ludicrous the arguments that were credited by the Court in upholding the Civil Rights Acts. Tribe also knew that nothing in this argument had to hinge on anything as elusive as empirical evidence. Indeed, he took care to point that out, for it was a feature of the argument that could be converted by him into an asset in the case of abortion: With the Civil Rights Acts, there had been no need to show even a reasonable estimate of the number of black people who were supposedly being discouraged from traveling between the States because they were inhibited by the prospect of racial discrimination. It was simply postulated that many black people *were* discouraged. In a similar way, Tribe claimed a comparable freedom now merely to assert that there would be a dramatic clogging of the roads, with a notably higher risk of accidents, if some states were actually permitted to impose restrictions on abortion.[12]

And yet, there is no need to engage in speculations about abortions, because we have some fairly precise figures on the volume of abortions performed every year. They were, for many years, at 1.5 million a year, and they seem to have tapered off recently to about 1.3 million. The irony here is that, if we alter the lens, and take a different view of the "victims" in these cases, the Commerce Clause would administer some striking surprises. For if the victims were not the women encouraged to travel, but the fetuses, or unborn children, getting poisoned or dismembered, the formulas of the Commerce Clause would work even more powerfully to uphold the power of the Congress to restrain abortions. For if it is legitimate to draw projections under the

---

[12] See Tribe's testimony on the Freedom of Choice Act of 1991, in *Hearings of the Committee on Labor and Human Resources*, 102nd Cong., 2d sess., May 13, 1992, pp. 31–6, at 32.

Commerce Clause, then it should be even more plausible to draw these inferences: The removal of 1.5 million new babies every year must surely have the most depressing effect on the market for baby food, diapers, bassinets, toys – to say nothing about the demand, in later years, for first cars and college educations.

In *Wickard v. Filburn*, in 1942, the Court showed how the Commerce Clause could help to reach even a private farmer, who was simply setting aside a certain portion of his wheat for the consumption of his own family.[13] The reasoning offered by Justice Jackson in that case was cited again by Justice Clark in *Katzenbach v. McClung*, in upholding the Civil Rights Act of 1964. In that passage, now nearly set to song, Jackson had written:

> That appellee's own contribution to the demand for wheat may be trivial by itself is not enough to remove him from the scope of federal regulation where, as here, his contribution, taken together with that of many others similarly situated, is far from trivial.[14]

If that reasoning is still plausible, then it is hard to see why the following argument should be anything less than clinching: That single abortion, performed on one woman, may seem to be a distinctly "private" act – as singular, and as private, as the decision of Roscoe Filburn to set aside a portion of wheat for his family. But when that private act of abortion is taken together with other, similar acts of abortion performed in this country, it contributes to a volume of abortions that add up, each year, to about 1.3 million abortions. And those abortions, in their bulk, produce the most emphatic, measurable effects on interstate commerce. They not only depress, massively, the market in the goods and services supplied to babies; but they also remove, from succeeding generations, a vast cohort of workers and taxpayers, who could supply revenue, reduce our deficits, and fund our system of pensions. If *Wickard v. Filburn* is still good law, then the reigning doctrines under the Commerce Clause would supply all of the authority the federal government would require to reach the subject of abortion and forbid even these "private" surgeries. If nothing else, it should be clear beyond caviling that an abortion

---

[13] See 317 U.S. 111, especially 122–4, 128.
[14] *Ibid.*, at 128.

interferes most emphatically with the freedom of a fetus to travel in interstate commerce.

The Freedom of Choice Act slipped mercifully into memory, without being enacted. But the same arguments under the Commerce Clause were hauled out again to support the bill to ensure Freedom of Access to Clinic Entrances, and that bill was passed, with votes from both political parties before the change in the political season and the advent of a Republican Congress. But then a minor jolt came in April 1995: The Supreme Court cast its first judgment in nearly 60 years in rejecting a federal law passed under the Commerce Clause. The law in question sought to ban the use of guns in the vicinity of schools. In striking down this law, in *U.S. v. Lopez*, the Court took the first step in rejecting the kinds of bizarre rationales that were treated seriously as arguments under the Commerce Clause. But until the case reached the Supreme Court, the lower courts had been upholding the Gun-Free School Zones Act, along with its rationale under the Commerce Clause. At the same time, the Freedom of Access act was being contested in the courts, and the judges upholding that act had been citing, as confirmation, the decisions in the lower courts in the Lopez case! Apparently, the recognition had not quite broken through yet: The decision of the Supreme Court in the Lopez case would now call into question the ground on which the lower courts have been upholding the Freedom of Access act. To the extent that the ban on "partial birth abortions" rests on the Commerce Clause, the Lopez case would imperil this new act as well.[15]

And with good riddance – not for the bill, but for the spurious reliance on the Commerce Clause. Scholars who might be labeled as "pro-life" would prefer to make an argument under the Fourteenth Amendment, but the Fourteenth Amendment deals with the action of states, operating through the laws ("No state shall make or enforce any law . . ."). It would require a rather more complicated argument to show how the Fourteenth Amendment would reach the decisions

---

[15] For a commentary on the paradoxes that attend the arguments over Lopez, see Arkes, "The Law and the Loss of Urbanity," in T. Willam Boxx and Gary M. Quinlivan, eds., *Toward the Renewal of Civilization: Political Order and Culture* (Grand Rapids, MI: Wm. B. Eerdmans, 1998), pp. 128–51.

taken by private persons to perform abortions. But there is an another argument to be made under the Fourteenth Amendment – and on that, more in a moment. In the meantime, it is worth at least some passing consideration of the devices that have been used far more typically when the political class has come to these intractable puzzles of the Constitution, and the politicians look for a way around the problem. The pro-lifers could get around the current problem in the style taken by liberal Democrats over the last 30 years, to legislate by indirection – to legislate, that is, without really legislating: The Congress could simply attach conditions for the enterprises that receive money from the federal government. In this manner, Congress does not presume to reach local schools or clinics counseling birth control, and it would strain its collective wit in trying to explain how the federal government could reach these activities that are local and private. Instead of facing that question, Congress merely offers grants and lays down conditions. If people do not find the rules congenial, they may merely forego the grant. In this gentle manner, the federal jurisdiction has been extended over the last 30 years without the need to show exactly how the Congress may legislate on any of these matters.[16]

But with the addition of the so-called Civil Rights Restoration Act of 1988, liberal Democrats have handed the pro-lifers an even more powerful tool, if they would care to make use of it: Even the most indirect aid may be taken as the definitive sign of "federal aid." And so, a student receives a loan from the federal government, and a private college becomes subject, in all of its phases, to the full panoply of federal regulations.[17] It would merely remain, for Henry Hyde and his colleagues, to use the same formulas that were engrafted on the law by their liberal counterparts. A private clinic or hospital may come under the federal regulations then if any patient receives medicare, but even less than that: if any patient receives a social security check, a student loan, food stamps, perhaps even a refund from the IRS. And through this device, again, it is conceivable that the federal government could effectively bar the awful procedure of partial-birth abor-

[16] For a review – and critique – of this matter of "legislating by indirection," see Arkes, *Beyond the Constitution, supra,* n. 11, ch. 9.

[17] The reach and logic of the Civil Rights Restoration Act – and its bearing on the problem of abortion – is something I treat more fully in *ibid.,* ch. 9.

tions without the need to explain how Congress can legislate on the matter.

But it seems not to have occurred to the Republicans in Congress that they can take this route; and for reasons of constitutional fastidiousness, they may be reluctant, quite rightly, to take it. If Congress legislates, it should legislate honestly, directly, and it should be able to explain the grounds of the federal authority. The actual ground of the law in this case is not so contrived or complicated, but the most direct explanation may also be the hardest for our lawyers to understand. It would begin with the fact that the problem of abortion, over the last 20 years, is a problem created distinctly by the federal courts. With *Roe v. Wade*, the Supreme Court indirectly nationalized abortion. In one stroke, the Court swept away almost all of the laws in the separate states that dealt with abortion. And for the past 29 years, local legislatures have been forced to shape their legislation in the mold permitted to them by the federal judges. A problem created in this way from the center of our political life may need a corrective coming at least initially from the center. It may require the Congress to provide the lead before legislatures at the local level will have a clearer sense of the way in which they too may begin legislating again.

But once we recognize the massive presence in this issue of the federal courts, we may suddenly notice the key to the jural problem that lawyers and politicians never quite seem to see, even while they strain over the puzzle. An adviser to the first President Bush asked me earnestly, years ago, "Can't we just agree to keep the federal government out of this issue?," and he was apparently taken aback when I respond, "Yes, if by that you mean the federal courts as well." We might be able to strike a deal, I said, if he and his friends were willing to support a use of the congressional power under Article III, Section 2, to alter the appellate jurisdiction of the federal courts. This power had been used famously in the past, in a liberal cause: to remove, from federal judges, the authority to issue injunctions in labor disputes and break the back of strikes.[18] In the current instance, that power could be used to take the federal courts out of the issue of abortion. The

---

[18] The reference, of course, is to the Norris-LaGuardia Act of 1932, 29 U.S.C. Sec. 113. See also *Lauf v. E.G. Shinner & Co.*, 303 U.S. 328 (1938).

matter could be left then mainly in the hands of the States and the local courts, with the possibility of an appeal, in the end, to the Supreme Court. But it was quite evident that this was not at all what the erstwhile adviser to the president had in mind when he suggested that the *federal government* recede from this issue of abortion.

And yet, why not?: Were the federal courts not part of the "federal" government? In a curious way, the federal courts seem to be placed outside the picture, as though they were acting merely as umpires, determining the powers that attach to the different branches of the government. But in a strange trick of the eye, the point seems to go unnoticed that the powers exercised by the courts are nothing less than the powers attached to a branch of the *federal* government. In the first piece I wrote on the subject of abortion, in 1972, I took note of Senator George McGovern, the Democratic candidate for president that year, and his curious attempt to finesse the matter of abortion. According to a report in the *Washington Post*, McGovern's settled thoughts on the matter now took this form: "[Abortion] is a deeply personal question with many people, a deeply religious and moral question. As a candidate for President, my position has been that the federal government should not intervene in any way on the question of abortion."[19] I raised then, in the winter of 1972, what turned out to be prescient question: Did McGovern's denial of jurisdiction to the federal government cover the federal courts as well? For as I noted, cases were already underway, appeals were being made to the federal courts, to overturn the laws on abortion in different states. If the federal courts sustained those challenges, they would in effect be "nationalizing" the issue of abortion. They would remove the matter of abortion from the domain of local law, and determine in effect that the Constitution was the source of an entirely different jurisprudence to govern and shape the laws on abortion. But that, of course, is precisely what happened. And as we might have expected, the announcement of *Roe v. Wade* elicited no protest from George

---

[19] *Washington Post*, August 10, 1972. McGovern continued: "From the beginning, this is one of those issues that has always been within the province of the states. The laws vary from state to state on this very difficult question. As far as I'm concerned . . . I intend no action in this field. I'm going to leave that where it is now." See also *The New York Times*, September 5, 1972, p. 1; September 25, 1972, p. 42; October 4, 1972, p. 32.

McGovern and the Democratic establishment. The opposition was not to the involvement of the federal government, but to laws that restrained abortion. If the federal government became the agency for sweeping away those laws, then there was, among the leading voices of liberalism, no aversion to the hand of the federal government controlling the laws.

Just a few months later, in January 1973, the Supreme Court announced the decision in *Roe v. Wade* and rather confirmed the state of affairs I had described. But even I had never anticipated the judgment that the Court would hand down that day, the first business day after the inauguration of Richard Nixon for his second term. In a single stroke, the Supreme Court canceled the laws on abortion in the separate states, or rendered them ineffective. The move was nothing less than a federal takeover, or a federal preemption, of the authority to legislate on abortion. The fact that it was accomplished by a court cannot disguise the fact that a power – and a distinctly legislative authority – was transferred from local governments to a branch of the federal government.

In the case of my interlocutor and friend, the adviser to the first George Bush, the interest in removing the subject from the federal government was quite sincere. Sincere, but entirely impracticable: Even if the federal government did not seek to legislate on the matter of abortion, there would be a persistent need to address the matter within the operations of the federal establishment. Would the National Institutes of Health (NIH) be permitted to experiment on embryos? Would it be allowed to carry out research with the tissues drawn from fetuses that were aborted in "elective" abortions? Would abortions be performed in the military and diplomatic outposts abroad? Would abortion be covered, and subsidized, in the extensive program of medical insurance for federal employees? And what restrictions would bear on the performance and funding of abortion in the District of Columbia, a jurisdiction directly under the authority of the federal government? These kinds of questions arose, as practical matters, only because of *Roe v. Wade*: They arose, and suddenly manifested themselves in all parts of the government, because the Supreme Court converted abortion into a procedure that was not only legal, but constitutionally protected. And for that reason, there is no way that an executive can address himself, practically, to any of these issues without putting himself into a line of inquiry that runs all the way back to *Roe v. Wade.*

By this point in the seasons of experience, we should be able to look past the cant and do a translation: When people urge, in a rhetorical flourish, to "get the federal government out of the matter of abortion," they do not mean to remove the federal courts. They mean to remove, rather, those parts of the federal government that show a more serious interest at times in restricting abortions. The courts would apparently remain, as before, unimpaired, unrestrained, in their authority to review the issue of abortion, in all of its dimensions, in statutes, ordinances, and executive orders at every level of government.

But it may be wise to draw on the wonderment of the young and ask simply, How can that be? We would seem to be at the threshold of a serious confusion in our very notion of the "federal government," and in the presence of that confusion, we may find our corrective in recurring, once again, to axioms or first principles. In *Cohens v. Virginia* (1821), Chief Justice Marshall observed that "the judicial power of every well constituted government must be co-extensive with the legislative, and must be capable of deciding every judicial question which grows out of the constitution and laws."[20] To put it another way, any issue that arose under the Constitution and laws of the United States had to come within the jurisdiction of the federal courts. And yet, even jurists are persistently taken by surprise by the corollary of that axiom: Any issue that comes within the competence of the judicial branch must come, presumptively at least, within the reach of the legislative and executive branches as well.[21] For how is it possible that the federal courts are competent to address abortion in all of its dimensions, while the doctors of the law ponder deeply over the question of whether Congress may legislate on the same subject?

What is engaged here is one of the deepest axioms of the Constitution, and yet it still seems to come as news to many lawyers. As it happened, no one explained the matter more compellingly than John Locke in his *Second Treatise*. Locke caught there the logic of the

---

[20] 6 Wheaton 264, at 384.

[21] The most pellucid account of this argument, or of the chain of propositions that make this understanding irresistible, can be found in James Wilson's magisterial opinion in *Chisholm v. Georgia*, 2 Dallas 419 (1793).

separation of powers by making the connection to the logic of morals itself, or what the philosophers call the "universalizibility" principle. Locke made the connection in this manner:

> And because it may be too great temptation to human frailty, apt to grasp at power, for the same persons who have the power of making laws, to have also in their hands the power to execute them. . . . [I]n well-ordered commonwealths, where the good of the whole is so considered as it ought, the legislative power is put into the hands of divers persons who, . . . have by themselves, or jointly with others, a power to make laws, which when they have done, being separated again, they are themselves subject to the law they have made; which is a new and near tie upon them to take care that they make them for the public good.[22]

To put it another way, the structure of the separation of powers works to impart this caution to those who legislate: You had better be careful in the laws you frame because you will not be given the right to direct prosecutions under those laws. Once you have passed any bill into a law, that law will be put in hands other than your own to administer – and those could be unfriendly hands, the hands of people who count themselves as your political enemies. Therefore, as a matter of high prudence, you should be careful not to legislate for others what you would not be willing to see applied, with its full force, against yourself.

By this reasoning, it is simply untenable under the Constitution that the Court can create new rights, and then assign to itself a monopoly of the legislative power in shaping those rights. The legislature understands that it will not have complete control over the administration of what it legislates, and the same wholesome discipline must extend to the judicial branch as well: The Court, too, should know that, if it does something inventive and original, it cannot keep a complete control over what it has wrought. That novelty must become the source of novel powers, then, for the Congress and the president as they, too, take their responsibility for the enforcement and interpretation of these new "rights."

Of course, there are complications here that cannot be papered over. There are powers of the executive, in directing the military, that should never come within the reach of judges. And if that is the case, I suppose it is arguable at least that there are certain matters within the

---

[22] Locke, *Second Treatise on Civil Government*, sec. 143.

reach of the courts that may not come properly within the reach of the Congress. Let us suppose, for example, that the Court came to the judgment that the First Amendment should be applied literally and categorically as it touches the press: that Congress literally may make no law abridging the freedom to publish. Let us imagine, further, that Congress and the president were fully persuaded by this argument, and found no ground for contesting this holding at the edges. Under those conditions, we might say that the Court pronounces on the freedom to publish, and as a consequence, the political branches find themselves receding from their claim to act upon the press through the instruments of the law.

But even to sketch in that scene begins to suggest why it may be deeply implausible. Most critically, it is simply not possible to mark off a whole class of activities (e.g., driving, painting, hitting balls) that may never have the consequence of inflicting harms. If driving can be directed, say, to an unlawful end, there is an apt ground for barring and punishing, under the law, certain kinds of driving (e.g., driving a getaway car, or driving in a lethal way). It seems to be well understood that contracts for murder are not legitimate contracts, and it should be quite as clear then that people should not be free to advertise, in the press, for people to enter into that contract. If Congress sought to bar, from the airwaves or the Internet, solicitations to murder, it is arguable that such solicitations form no part of the rightful freedom to publish. In that sense, we would find that even a sweeping rule will be far more porous than we might suppose. That is to say, it would be hard to form a categorical judgment that leaves any field entirely clear from the need for legislation. Congress simply could not be barred, categorically, from legislating on the press and publication, unless "publishing" had suddenly become an activity radically different from all others: an activity that could never be directed to a hurtful or wrongful end.[23] There can be, then, no class of activities,

---

[23] Alexander Hamilton anticipated this argument when he set down his own reservations about a bill of rights. Once again, the dubiety about a bill of rights did not spring from people who were hostile to rights, but from urbane men, with a more a refined jural sense, who grasped right away that the inventory of "rights" displayed a certain confusion between real principles and claims that were irreducibly "contingent." See Hamilton in the *Federalist* #84, *The Federalist Papers* (New York: Random House, n.d.) pp. 555–61.

no class of "rights," protected by the Constitution, that can somehow stand outside the legislative and executive power. To put it another way, there is no class of "rights" that the Supreme Court can discover, and which then lies outside the powers of Congress to address.

That problem deepens as the claim is made that the Supreme Court is articulating "rights" that should be protected against infringement by the States. If the Court articulates a right to an abortion, a right that arises distinctly from the federal Constitution, then the Congress would seem to have the presumptive authority to flesh out that right, to define it more fully, and protect it. The Congress has far more flexible instruments at hand than a court has in protecting that right against a state, mainly by providing the kinds of penalties that can overawe the officers of a state. But we may take matters to the root then in this way. The axioms of lawful government – the axioms that establish the separation of powers – would establish these inescapable points:

> If the national courts can reach judgments, in concrete cases, on any matter, then the national legislature must have the authority to flesh out the principles, on the same subject, with legislation that is impersonal, prospective, and not bound to the parties in litigation before the courts.

> If the federal courts can articulate new rights under the Constitution, the legislative branch must have the authority to fill out those same rights – to define them more crisply or sharply, and *in defining them, marking their boundaries.*

> If the courts can hand down judgments on abortion, then, on the same subject, cast in the same terms, the Congress must be free to legislate. Again, the one thing that should not be tenable, under the logic of the separation of powers, is this: that the Supreme Court may articulate new rights under the Constitution – and *then assign to itself a monopoly of the legislative power in defining and limiting those rights.*

The founders were quite alert to these kinds of points, about the axioms, or necessary truths, that anchored the Constitution. And so, for example, in the *Federalist* #80, Alexander Hamilton made what he thought was a self-evident point that "controversies between the nation and its members or citizens, can only be properly referred to the national tribunals. Any other plan," he said, "would be contrary to reason, to precedent, and to decorum." By "decorum" he meant, in the classic sense, the appropriate or reasonable scale of things. And that point, he said, would "rest on this plain proposition, that the peace of the WHOLE ought not to be left at the disposal of a PART."[24] The State of New York might have a reasonable policy in refusing to hand over, to a Bolshevik government in Moscow, the assets of Russian nationals held in banks in New York. But the diplomatic recognition of the Soviet Union hinged on that agreement to transfer assets to the new regime in Russia. Even if New York happened to be emphatically right in its judgment, the State of New York could not be given the leverage to undo a policy, arranged by the national leadership, to secure the peace and advance the interests of the nation in foreign policy. Justice George Sutherland was compelled then to explain, as the ground of the judgment, the axiom that could hardly be otherwise:

> [I]n respect of all international negotiations and compacts, and in respect of our foreign relations generally, state lines disappear. As to such purposes the State of New York does not exist.[25]

Many other examples may be cited,[26] but I recall only a few of them here for the sake of pointing out that the founders often wove these axioms, quite gracefully, in their own writings. And yet these arguments seem to have made only the least impression on "conservative jurisprudence" in our own time. On the matter of abortion, conservative jurisprudence has found a certain romance in the notion of federalism. The disposition among conservatives has been to address the problem of *Roe v. Wade* by overruling that decision and returning the matter of abortion to the states. That disposition has been encouraged by several understandings: There is the sense that states and local governments bear the main responsibility for the protection of life and the framing of laws on the family; that the federal government ought to be constrained, as a government of much more limited powers. But

---

[24] The *Federalist* #80, (New York: Modern Library, n.d.), pp. 516–17.
[25] See *U.S v. Belmont* (1937), 301 U.S. 324 at 331.
[26] The reader might consult my essay, "The Axioms of Public Policy," in David Forte, ed., *Natural Law and Contemporary Public Policy*, pp. 109–34, and *Beyond the Constitution, supra*, n. 11, especially chs. 1–4.

then there is a tacking on of a further assumption that may finally govern everything else: There is a lingering, unaccountable premise that "human life" and its beginning mark an inscrutable question to which reason offers no answers. It is not thought then to be a question to which the arts of judges can yield an answer. In that case, as the argument runs, it is a "political" decision; it must be made by consulting, of course, experts in medicine and embryology. But it must be made most decisively by consulting the "opinions" of the public on the points at which that vast, variegated public is finally willing to treat human life with reverence. And so, as Justice Scalia famously remarked in the Cruzan case in 1990, the point at which life becomes worthless or open to protection is not "set forth in the Constitution"; nor is it "known to the nine Justices of this Court any better than . . . [to] nine people picked at random from the Kansas City telephone directory."[27] The question of when human life begins is then, as he says, a "value judgment." Some societies, as he noted, cast that judgment in different ways, depending on what they "valued." As he remarked two years later in his dissent in *Casey*, "some societies have considered newborn children not yet human, or the incompetent elderly no longer so."[28] With this gesture, Scalia held out the possibility of a moral detachment he could not himself endorse. But with that construction, he implied that one judgment is no more plausible, or implausible, than another, which was apparently why the matter was to be treated as a "political" decision and thrown into the court of public opinion. And for that reason, he has held to the grooves of conservative jurisprudence in favoring a return of this matter to the states.

In taking that path, of course, he runs the risk of adopting, as the principle governing his judgment, an abstract principle of procedure, quite detached from the moral substance of the problem. To that mild complaint, Scalia would say, yes, that is exactly what I am doing, and it fits precisely the moral restraints bearing on a judge: By giving the matter back to the states and to people in the political arena, it would be precisely the purpose of the judge to avoid the moral substance of that issue. For the very point of the maneuver is to induce judges to hold back their hands – and to leave, in other hands, the authority to

---

[27] *Cruzan v. Director, Missouri Health Department*, 111 L Ed 2d 224 (1990), at 251.
[28] *Planned Parenthood v. Casey*, 505 U.S. 833, at 982.

reach judgments on matters of moral consequence. That is a plausible path of reaction, plausibly defended. But the statesman, including the statesman acting as judge, must be attentive to the way in which the circumstances of the case may disrupt his course of prudence and invert its ends. Nearly thirty years ago, in the immediate aftermath of *Roe v. Wade*, a decision to return the matter of abortion to the states would have been a decision to put the matter in the hands of a political class willing to resume the exercise of powers that had always been exercised, as long as legislatures had existed in America. As recently as 25 years ago, the political class in this country would have found it strange to assume that the issue of abortion was not part of the legitimate business of legislatures, that it should be regarded as a matter to be ruled exclusively by courts. But we have brought forth now a political class quite disposed to believe these things, and to be quit of issues, like abortion, which vex and divide their constituents.

And on the other side, we have brought forth a new generation of judges, fed on the notion that judges, in modern America, rule. The judge now finds his greatness, not in establishing himself as a model of judicious restraint, but as a figure wrapped in robes of majesty, rising above the gridlock of political men. He is majestically free then to impose the schemes of a more demanding justice that simply cannot spring from the genius and character of those forked creatures, of small ambition and even smaller imagination, who run for the legislature of a state. If the matter of abortion were returned to the states, it would not in fact be in the hands of political men and women, elected by the voters. The new breed of judges would readily find, in the constitutions of their states, a notion of "privacy" as discernible as any that can be found in the federal Constitution. There would be a comparable insistence on a limit to the reach of public law in affecting the most "private" of decisions – and the most private of all, of course, would be the decision to "terminate" a pregnancy. A jural posture of returning the issue of abortion to the states is, under the current circumstances, a largely empty gesture. I fear that it cannot serve the purpose that Justice Scalia has in mind, the purpose of returning the issue to the domain of public discourse, and to a judgment informed by the opinions at work in the public.

The strategy of returning matters to the states, under the banner of federalism, turns into the search for that "low door under the wall."

The old joke about pragmatism is that "it doesn't work," and neither does the low door under the law. It does not work, that is, as a finesse, or as a gesture of prudence, in avoiding moral judgments on the hardest questions. For it is ever the experience of politics that the moral judgments become inescapable, and the attempt to avoid them, with empty formulas, can produce only charades, and possibly make matters notably worse. Justice Scalia, with his own sense of modesty and restraint, would rather have the judges and the federal government avoid this troublesome matter of abortion, and yet we are destined to keep discovering that the substance simply cannot be evaded. If the matter is returned to legislatures in the states, the issue would lose its point unless the legislators understood that they were being asked to address the question of just who is protected by the laws on homicide, and who is left outside that protection. Surely, it must make a notable difference if legislators are tutored to regard that question in the first place, as Scalia regards it, as a "value judgment," to which there may be no right or wrong answers. For Scalia, the question is one that may lend itself to the taking of evidence, the pooling of opinions, and the settling of judgments. But in his understanding, the Constitution itself could not be the source of any principles of reasoning that could test the plausibility, or the arbitrariness, of these judgments. Scalia takes it for granted, then, that any state may plausibly enact the policy of *Roe v. Wade* and establish a policy of abortion on demand at any stage of pregnancy. That is to say, he assumes that the unborn child may be withdrawn entirely from a class of beings who are given some protection in the law. In that respect, the child may be treated as a being with even less of a claim to protection than the spotted owl and other privileged animals. If we are to take Scalia literally, all of this would be quite grievous; it would represent one of those risks of life in a democracy; but it would not encounter even the slightest barrier in the Constitution.

Yet, if I am correct here, even the efforts to skirt the question of abortion will find themselves running into the substantive questions at the heart of the matter. And if that becomes clear, it may suddenly become clear, too, that judges are not so constrained in their imaginations and their reach, even while they act with the discipline and restraint of judges. This matter may be brought home to us in a gentle way with a bit of a thought-experiment:

Through a series of constitutional amendments after the Civil War we forbade slavery or involuntary servitude, and sought to remove the lingering "badges and incidents" of slavery. The Thirteenth, Fourteenth, and Fifteenth amendments said nothing about blacks, but they provided that people should not be barred, on the basis of race, from the equal protection of the laws. Let us imagine for a moment that a state was allowing some black people to be kept in slavery, or that it was withdrawing the protections of the law, and allowing black people to be lynched. Imagine that a challenge is raised, but that the state insists that race has nothing to do with the matter: As a matter of common sense, the state says, the Civil War amendments were evidently meant to apply only to those blacks who were human. But not everything born of humans, it says, is human at all times or all stages. Certain people of a deep color, the state contends, are not clearly human, and so the normal protections of the law do not apply to them. In support of this position, the state produces an authoritative "color chart," to measure gradations in shading, and we are simply told, with the voice of authority, that these shadings mark degrees of "humanness."

Is it really conceivable that the commitments of the law could be subverted in this way? What is more likely to happen, of course, is that a suit would be brought on these terms: The authorities would be compelled to show that there was some ground of principle, or scientific evidence, to support the proposition they had simply stipulated in legislation. That is, they would be compelled now to show that the steps along the color chart truly marked off degrees of humanity, or discontinuities in nature, so that as soon as we exceeded, say, Shade 11, and moved to Shade 12, we were no longer dealing with a human being.

There is hardly a mystery, in our own day, as to how a court is likely to respond to an argument of that kind: The court is likely to say that the law was passed in a manner that was formally legal, but that it lacked the substance of justice. The law deprived people of their freedom, it withdrew the protection of their lives, on the strength of criteria that were finally *arbitrary*. For where was the evidence, after all, that a shift along the scale from a Shade 12 to a Shade 11, marked off any differences of moral significance; differences that would justify the enslavement of a whole class of human beings? In a

court addressing that question, Justice Scalia would probably offer the
most telling explanations, as he calls again on his arts as a teacher.
What he seems to be passing by so far is the recognition that the
problem of abortion would present him with a problem substantially
the same, in its main, defining features. That problem would require
of the judges no arts more arcane or inscrutable than the arts they
would readily engage in dismantling a policy of marking degrees of
"humanness" along the gradations of a color wheel. After all, if a legislature allowed abortions up to the third trimester, or if it permitted
abortions in the case of children who were likely to be infirm or
retarded, why would not the same style of reasoning come into play?
Why would it not be quite as plausible for a judge to ask, What sep-
arates the child in the womb at six months from the child at six months
and a day? How could that child have crossed a barrier between the
nonhuman and the human? What attributes, necessary to her standing as a human being, did she not have the day before, when she was
24 weeks old?

The conclusion of the judges should be the same: In all of these
instances, the law is based on distinctions, or classifications, that are
finally arbitrary, in the sense that none of them can supply the ground
of a moral justification in taking a life, or removing certain people from
the protections of the law. Whether a human being can speak yet,
whether he is affected with Down's syndrome, whether he is healthy
or infirm, heavier or lighter, wanted or unwanted – none of these
things can have a bearing on the question of whether anyone deserves
to live or die.[29] In that sense, they provide distinctly "arbitrary"
grounds on which to cast a class of persons outside the protections of
the law. They would be quite as arbitrary as the difference between a
Shade 11 and Shade 12 on a color wheel.

If I am right, there is no inscrutable, or even unusual, question presented to the courts by this problem of abortion or the need to settle
on an understanding about the beginning of human life. The question requires no canons of reasoning different from the principles that
the judges are well practiced in applying to the run of cases that come
before them. In that event, the judges have, well within their means,

---

[29] On this critical matter of attributes that are "lacking in moral significance," see
Arkes, *First Things* (Princeton: Princeton University Press, 1986), pp. 168–9.

the principles of reasoning that would allow them to judge any policy that would withdraw the protections of the law, for the most arbitrary reasons, from a whole class of human beings. One might as tenably say then that the Court already has, within its competence, all of the institutional wit it would need in order to articulate a "right," on the part of people, not to suffer that withdrawal of the protections of the law. If the Court can articulate such a right, it should be able to explain then, without much further strain, just which part of the Constitution may supply the ground of that right. And in turn, any right that the Court can articulate in this way, with a grounding in the Constitution, the legislature should be able to vindicate. The legislature should be able to act, that is, for the same ends, with measures no less precise or authoritative than anything a court could produce.

An exercise no more extravagant than the one I have described here would be quite sufficient then to provide, for the unborn child, a "right" to receive the protections of lawfulness – or, to put it another way, a right not to have the protections of law removed for arbitrary reasons. And I emphasize that nothing in this argument depends yet on the clause of the Constitution that is finally invoked as the ground of that constitutional right. As we approach that question, the clearest case would arise if governments at the state and local level withdraw the protections of the law, for arbitrary reasons, from this whole class of the population. There is a broad warrant for the federal government, under the Fourteenth Amendment, to counter any actions of a state that imperils the "life, liberty or property" of "any person." A state could endanger those rights through its own operations, or it could do it quite as clearly by granting permissions to engage in private killings. And no, there would be no getting around this clause through the device of claiming that the unborn child is not a "person." As we have seen, the Civil War amendments could not be circumvented by claiming that they covered, say, only blacks who were persons or humans. As Justice Story often reminded us, what may not be done directly may not be done indirectly. The Fourteenth Amendment seeks to protect whole classes of people from having the protections of law withdrawn on the basis of attributes, such as race or color, that cannot supply a moral justification for taking, or endangering, the lives of human beings. The Equal Protection Clause offers the means, and the logic, of extending that same principle to any other group imperiled in the same way (e.g., on the basis of hair color). That offspring of homo sapiens, resident for a moment in his mother's womb, cannot be placed outside the protections of the law through the sleight of hand of changing the label – by calling him a "snark" or a "fetus" instead of a small human being.

Faced with laws of that kind *in the States*, a federal court could aptly hold them invalid. The judges would not need to pronounce a final, authoritative rendering on the beginning of human life. It would make a point quite sufficient, and telling, if a court simply held that human beings could not be converted into nonhumans, in this arbitrary way, through the vulgar shifting of labels. Rising to the same recognition, and acting on the same constitutional ground, the Congress would be free then to legislate to bar legislation of that kind, and punish its enforcement.

But of course this was not the kind of problem that brought the matter of abortion into the federal courts. In most states, the public held steady in support of the settled laws that forbade or restricted abortions. In a few states, however, such as New York, California, and Hawaii, there were notable moves to "liberalize" abortion – or, to put it in that other way, withdraw the protections of law from those vulnerable beings in wombs. In those states, the federal courts could indeed have become more active in challenging those policies, and the judges should not have been cowed by any concern for being labeled "judicial activists." For the decision they reached would still be bounded, and contained, by the principles that work to confine the decisions of the courts, and open them to the checking of the political branches. That understanding, too, seems to have fled from memory, and it would be worth calling it back, in a moment, to recall the most powerful fences that constrain judicial activism. Those fences allowed judges to act properly, and fully, as judges, without the vice of taking over the whole government. If the judges had taken a more advanced position, in fending off these moves to lessen the inhibitions on killing, the decisions would have articulated concerns and principles, and summoned the country. But just how much resonance they produced would have depended, critically, on the response they elicited from legislatures and executives, at the federal level, as well as in the states. And if those moves by the judges had elicited no confirming response, the energy or "activism" of the judges would have been decorously contained.

But let us take things from another angle: Let us return for a moment to the time before these changes were afoot in the states to "liberalize" the laws on abortion in the late 1960s. Evidently, the laws were porous enough to admit abortions. Some were performed legally, under a permission to carry out abortions when they were necessary to the life or health of the mother. With an elastic definition of health, not exactly approved in the laws, abortions were apparently taking place in a kind of nether world – in respectable hospitals, but in the shadow of the law. Still, with all of the compromises, the main cast of the law was settled in the commitment to protect nascent life, or that life in the womb, from its first moments. To change the laws required an immense burden of effort, in overturning understandings long settled in the law, to say nothing of the modern evidence of embryology and the resistance of the medical profession. Far more promising was the prospect of persuading a handful of judges, especially federal judges, who were more insulated from politics with permanent tenure. To ask a federal court to overturn these laws in the states was to argue, in effect, for a new constitutional right, a federal right, anchored in the Constitution. Let us assume that the courts responded, as they would indeed respond later, in the decisions that led to *Roe v. Wade*. But let us assume that the political class continued to operate on the traditional understanding of the separation of powers: the courts could articulate rights, but they could not themselves have a monopoly of control, especially legislative control, of the rights they were discovering. As the courts declared new rights to abortion, the Congress would regard itself as fully authorized to legislate about those rights. On what ground, though, would the Congress have legislated?

The Court itself would have supplied a plausible ground for the legislation when it supplied the ground for this new right. If the Court had found that right in a "liberty interest" under the Fourteenth Amendment, or a right of privacy contained in the Ninth Amendment, the Congress could have gone on to define that right more precisely. But in doing that, it could have entered into a conversation about the things that a right to abortion might not encompass: Congress could have asserted, for example, quite tenably, that a "right to abortion" could not include the right to kill a child at the point of birth when it was not necessary to end a "pregnancy." That "right" might not entail a right to destroy a child in the womb because its advent was inconvenient, or because it interfered with the plans of the parents. In all of these ways, the Congress would have the means of putting the question back to the Court of what, more precisely, could have been comprehended in a "right to abortion." It is entirely conceivable, in fact, that once the conversation between the branches unfolded in this way, Congress might have led the courts, step by step, to confine any right to abortion to instances in which the life of the mother was endangered. That is to say, once Congress was engaged, once the monopoly of the courts was broken, the judges could have been led, as they have been led in the past, to modify or alter their decisions. And in this case, they could have produced a law on abortion that mirrored more fully the range of opinions in the country. They were the opinions, of course, that were woven into compromises in different parts of the country as claims of rights were qualified, distinguished, contained, as legislators sought to deal, politically, with a vexing question that divided the community.

But we may come to see yet other alternatives if we pull back the curtain and simply notice that rather obvious point that has been so curiously obscured to us – namely, that the intervention of the federal courts is indeed the intervention of the federal government. One thing we might notice then, in looking back on the 1960s and 1970s, is that the threat to the lives of unborn children did not come principally from the laws in the states. It would become clear that the threat did not emanate from the states, but from the federal government: It emanated from that branch of the federal government whose decisions went unnoticed as interventions of the federal government and the flexing of the federal power. Once the matter is seen in that way, it becomes arguable that the Fifth Amendment may now become engaged. Before the Fourteenth Amendment nationalized the Due Process clause, the Fifth Amendment sought to protect persons against the deprivation of "life, liberty, or property, without due process of law." That amendment was understood as a restraint precisely, and solely, on the federal government. In the case of abortion, Congress could be said to confront a situation in which the protections of the law were not being removed by the agencies of a state, but by officers of the federal government gone astray in the use of federal powers: Most notably, they were judges who now took it, as their mission, to remove the laws in the states that restrained the killing of unborn children. Under those conditions, Congress could have flexed its powers to protect life against a federal judiciary that was sweeping away any restraints of "due process" in the states and offering, in effect, an unmodulated license to kill. For in effect, the Supreme Court was issuing new licenses to engage in private killings, for wholly private reasons. Congress might have acted by statute to bar the judges from interfering in that way with the protections erected in the laws of the states. Or the Congress might have acted with its powers under Article III, Section 2, to alter the jurisdiction of the federal courts. But there should be no constitutional puzzlement about the authority of the Congress to legislate when the attack on lawfulness, or the protections of law, emanate from branches of the federal government itself.

That proposal might be received with some wariness, because it is unfamiliar, and yet even more unfamiliar it seems – and more radical in its appearance – is the understanding held by Lincoln, Jackson, and Jefferson on the limits on the judicial branch. Robert Bork, in his recent book, *Slouching Toward Gomorrah*, had been moved to make a truly radical proposal: that decisions of the Supreme Court might be overturned by votes in both houses of Congress. He soon backed away from that proposal, which he had been mulling over in print. For that kind of scheme did indeed promise an alteration in the structure of the separation of powers. What seems to be missed in all of these discussions is the recollection that Lincoln had set forth the most precise understanding on limiting the reach of the federal judges, but without the need for any alteration in the principles of the Constitution. In Lincoln's understanding, there would be no need for judges to stop acting in the style of judges. They would still be free to expound the law, by its spirit as well as its letter. They could be free to appeal to the natural law, or even to engage in arts of imagination that strained credulity. Still, with all of that, there were certain conditions that confined the judgments of the courts, and limited any damage they might produce. At the same time, those limits to the courts were reinforced by the presence of the political branches, with officers who bore interests of their own. And those restraints worked with even more effect when those political officers in the government grasped the responsibility that necessarily flowed to them, in their positions, to weigh the bearing of the Constitution on the measures that came under their hands.

Lincoln's argument had its ground in Chief Justice Marshall's legendary opinion in *Marbury v. Madison* in 1803. Indeed the opinion is so legendary that people cite the legend with a certain conviction even though they no longer remember very precisely the ingredients in Marshall's argument. It might be said, in fact, that *Marbury v. Madison* is a case far more often cited than read. For people have the impression that Marshall articulated in that case a claim for the Supreme Court to stand as the sole, authoritative interpreter of the Constitution within the American government. Several writers over the years have sought to deliver the reading public from this misunderstanding, and perhaps even get the word to one or two lawyers. To that venture in the public interest, I have joined my own slender contribution to those of others.[30] I would not press upon the reader now the fuller briefs offered on that subject; I would draw here some of the most important points, and invite readers to consult the fuller arguments at their own leisure.

In *Marbury v. Madison*, Chief Justice Marshall argued that the Constitution had to be regarded as "fundamental law," for if that were not the case, the Constitution would lose its function, and meaning, as a control on the legislative power. Marshall pointed us to the elementary recognition that there were two kinds of laws: To make a "law" of the United States required a vote in two houses of Congress, plus a concurrence by the executive. But how did we know that this was the rightful way of making laws? No procedure of that kind had been set down in nature. This was the necessary form for making "laws" of the federal government only because it was prescribed by the Constitution. It was the Constitution, after all, that provided a legislature of two chambers, and required the concurrence of the executive before any bill, passed by the Congress, became a "law." That a "law" was made in this way was a matter determined, then, by the "fundamental law" of the

---

[30] See my book, *First Things*, *ibid.*, pp. 416–22, and the citations contained there, and also, notably, Robert Clinton, *Marbury v. Madison and Judicial Review* (Lawrence, KS: University Press of Kansas, 1989).

Constitution. That is, there was the *ordinary law*, composed mainly of statutes, and the "basic law" (what the Germans called the *Grundgesetz*), *the law that tells us just how we get laws*. Marshall's opinion was rooted in the assumption that this sovereign distinction was part of the axioms of the law. The "fundamental law" claimed a certain logical precedence over an ordinary statute. In a conflict between a statute and the Constitution, precedence had to be given then to the Constitution. Again, that precedence had to be implicit in the understanding of the Constitution as a restraint on the legislative power.[31] With that premise settled, Marshall could make the observation, now seeming rather obvious, that "those who apply the rule to particular cases, must of necessity expound and interpret that rule. If two laws conflict with each other, the courts must decide on the operation of each."[32]

As Marshall described it, then, the judicial duty was modestly drawn. Marshall simply recognized that the judges had an obligation to be governed by the Constitution as they sought to settle the particular case that was submitted for their judgment. As Professor Herbert Wechsler would later observe, "Federal courts, including the Supreme Court, do not pass on constitutional questions because there is a special function vested in them to enforce the Constitution. . . . They

---

[31] See 5 U.S. (1 Cranch) 137, at 176–7. Chief Justice Marshall set forth the explanation in this way, in returning to the root:

> That the people have an original right to establish, for their future government, such principles as, in their opinion, shall most conduce to their own happiness, is the basis, on which the whole American fabric has been erected. The exercise of this original right is a very great exertion; nor can it, nor ought it to be frequently repeated. The principles, therefore, so established, are deemed fundamental. And as the authority, from which they proceed, is supreme, and can seldom act, they are designed to be permanent. This original and supreme will organizes the government, and assigns, to different departments, their respective powers. It may either stop here; or establish certain limits not to be transcended by those departments.
>
> The government of the United States is of the latter description. The powers of the legislature are defined, and limited; and that those limits may not be mistaken, or forgotten, the constitution is written. To what purpose are powers limited, and to what purpose is that limitation committed to writing, if these limits may, at any time, be passed by those intended to be restrained? The distinction, between a government with limited and unlimited powers, is abolished, if those limits do not confine the persons on whom they are imposed, and if acts prohibited and acts allowed, are of equal obligation. It is a proposition too plain to be contested, that the constitution controls any legislative act repugnant to it; or, that the legislature may alter the constitution by an ordinary act.

[32] *Ibid.*, at 177, 178.

do so rather for the reason that they must decide a litigated issue that is otherwise within their jurisdiction and in doing so must give effect to the supreme law of the land."[33] But in that sense, *nothing was claimed for the judges that could not have been claimed for other officers of the government.* If, for example, the president were faced with an act of Congress that drafted into the military service only members of a minority race, would he be obliged to judge the measure only on the grounds of utility? Would he be constrained to ask only, Will it work? Or would he be warranted in considering whether the measure was compatible with the principles of the Constitution? If he came to the judgment that the measure was at odds with the Constitution, would he not be obliged, quite as much as any judge, to give primacy to that question of principle in the cases that came before him?

This was the understanding held by Thomas Jefferson and Andrew Jackson, as well as by Lincoln, and without that understanding, Lincoln's resistance to the Dred Scott case would not have been intelligible. In that notable case, the Court held that blacks could not have the standing of citizens to sue in the courts, and that no man could be deprived of his property in slaves, even if he brought that property into territories in which slavery had been forbidden by Congress. As Russell Hittinger has pointed out, Lincoln could not have taken his oath of office in 1861 if swearing to uphold the Constitution meant swearing allegiance to the Constitution as it was interpreted by the Supreme Court. If the Dred Scott decision had been considered part of the "law of the land" as though it were woven into the text of the Constitution, Lincoln could not have taken the oath, for he had led a national movement to resist and overturn that decision. But at the same time, Lincoln's position, in relation to that case, incorporated a respect for law and for the judgments of the courts. As Lincoln put it, "We do not propose that when Dred Scott has been decided to be a slave by the court, we, as a mob, will decide him to be free." But he and his party would "oppose that decision as a political rule which shall be binding on the . . . members of Congress or the President to

---

[33] Herbert Wechsler, "The Courts and the Constitution," 65 *Columbia University Law Review*, 1001, at 1006 (1965). The same point was made by Justice Sutherland in *Adkins v. Children's Hospital*, 261 U.S. 525, at 544 (1923).

favor no measure that does not actually concur with the principles of that decision."[34]

During his first Inaugural Address, Lincoln returned to the matter, so evidently critical in our law and politics at this moment of crisis, and he restated the understanding in this way: He was willing to accept the judgment of the Supreme Court as "binding in any case, upon the parties to a suit, as to the object of that suit, . . . [and] limited to that particular case."[35] What he was not obliged to accept was the *principle* or the broader rule of law that the Court was trying to create in the case. As Alexander Hamilton had remarked in the *Federalist* #78, the Court had no control of the sword or of the purse – it had "neither force nor will, but merely judgment; and must ultimately depend upon the aid of the executive arm even for the efficacy of its judgments."[36] The power of the Court would ultimately depend, then, on the force of its reasoned argument. With that sense of the matter, Lincoln insisted that other officers of the government could not be obliged to accept any new "law" created by the Court unless they, too, were persuaded of its rightness. To construe things in any other way threatened nothing less than the overturning, or conversion, of a republican government: For it would mean that "the policy of the government, upon vital questions, affecting the whole people, [could] be irrevocably fixed by decisions of the Supreme Court, the instant they are made, in ordinary litigation between parties, in personal actions." And in that event, said Lincoln, "the people will have ceased, to be their own rulers, having, to that extent, practically resigned their government, into the hands of that eminent tribunal."[37]

Lincoln had led a political movement, summoning support throughout the country, in opposition to the holding in the Dred Scott case, and by the second year of the administration the political branches would indeed act directly to register their refusal to be bound by the principle in that case. In June 1862, Congress abolished slavery in all of the existing territories of the United States, and in any that

---

[34] *The Collected Works of Abraham Lincoln*, Roy P. Basler, ed. (New Brunswick, NJ: Rutgers University Press, 1953), v. III, p. 255 (debate with Douglas at Quincy, October 13, 1858).

[35] *Ibid.*, v. IV, p. 268 (First Inaugural Address, March 4, 1861).

[36] *The Federalist* #78 (New York: Modern Library, n.d.), p. 504.

[37] Lincoln, *supra*, n. 34, v. IV, p. 268; emphasis added.

might be formed or added in the future. The historian J. G. Randall would write of this legislation that "Congress passed and Lincoln signed a bill which, by ruling law according to Supreme Court interpretation was unconstitutional."[38] The president and Congress had acted in the most explicit and direct way to counter the decision of the Court in the Dred Scott case. They did not pass a constitutional amendment; they countered the Court through an act of *ordinary legislation.* In the conventions of our own day, lawyers are inclined instantly to say that this kind of act must be unconstitutional on its face. But that reaction already absorbs, as a premise, the assumption of judicial supremacy that Lincoln – as well as Marshall and Jefferson – had rejected. The moves of Lincoln and the Republican Congress made eminent sense, though, if one understood that the political officers of the government must have the responsibility to consider the bearing of the Constitution on the measures that come under their hands. The political officers must have then, perforce, a responsibility to interpret the Constitution – and therefore they must have an ample warrant for refusing to follow principles, or broader rules of law, that they regard as indefensible.

But even before Lincoln and the Congress confronted the decision in the Dred Scott case directly in legislation, there was a dramatic test of Lincoln's argument in the very first days of the administration. A young black man in Boston had sought a passport to study in France, but he had been denied the passport on the strength of the Dred Scott decision: As the rationale ran, black people could not be citizens, and therefore it was reasoned now that they could not carry American passports. For the same reason, a black inventor in Boston was denied a patent under the laws of the United States. Both cases were brought to the administration by Senator Charles Sumner of Massachusetts. Neither case involved a slave litigating over his freedom. In both cases, agencies of the federal government had applied the *principle* of the Dred Scott case to circumstances quite remote from that case. The Lincoln Administration quashed both decisions. It issued the passport and the patent, and it came forth with an opinion of the Attorney General, Edward Bates, declaring that, in the understanding of the

---

[38] James G. Randall, *The Civil War and Reconstruction* (Boston; D.C. Heath & Company, 1937), p. 136.

Lincoln Administration, free blacks born in the United States were in fact citizens of the United States. In all decisions coming under its hand, the executive would act on that premise – even though it ran counter to the principle proclaimed by the Court in the Dred Scott case.[39]

These moves were comprehensible – and defensible – only with the understanding held by Lincoln, and one might indeed ask, How could they have been anything other than defensible and compelling? But now, as they say, we "fast-forward": It is the late 1980s, and a committee is constituted to advise the National Institutes of Health on the matter of experiments with fetal tissues. Even some of the conservative members of the committee are under the impression that the NIH must be governed by *Roe v. Wade*, that it must regard elective abortions as legitimate. In that event, the tissue drawn from fetuses in these "legitimate" surgeries must be tissue legitimately drawn. But if we take Lincoln's understanding seriously, it must have been possible for the Reagan Administration to say, in the style of the Lincoln Administration, that "This Administration will respect *Roe v. Wade* as it bears on the litigants in that case. But it will not accept the principle proclaimed in that case, and apply that principle to any measure that comes under our hand. This Administration cannot accept then a right to destroy an unborn child either early or late in pregnancy, a right that can be exercised without qualification, on the strength of any reason whatever." This kind of an argument, put forth by the Reagan Administration, could have been wrong only if Lincoln had been wrong in the understanding that governed the cases of the two black men in Boston. But I would suggest that there is no way, under the Constitution, that Lincoln could have been wrong.

And yet, this understanding, with a long tradition in the United States, seems to evoke, even among judges, a sense of wonder and surprise, as though they were hearing it for the first time. But even without the awareness of the doctrine, this understanding has persisted in our political practice. In the early 1980s the Supreme Court struck down the "legislative veto," the arrangement that allowed the admin-

---

[39] These cases are recalled in my book, *First Things, supra*, n. 29, p. 421. The opinion rendered by Attorney General Bates can be found under the heading of "Citizenship" (November 29, 1862), in *Opinions of the Attorneys General*, v. X, pp. 382–413.

istration to put certain policies into effect, until they were vetoed by
one or both houses of Congress. The occasion for the decision was
United States v. Chadha,[40] a case dealing with immigration. At that
time, the legislative veto had been incorporated, in one form or
another, in nearly 200 statutes. But instead of receding from the
arrangement, Congress continued to find utility in the legislative veto,
and kept reenacting it in different forms. In other words, with a sense
of things reflecting Lincoln's, the Congress and the president
respected the judgment of the Chadha case *as it bore on the litigants
in that case.* But the Congress insisted on narrowing the understanding of the case to a decision dealing with immigration. At the same
time, it was not willing to accept the broader principle, or rule of law,
that the Court had articulated in that case. The political branches
would still regard themselves as free to adopt the legislative veto, until
they became persuaded in the fullness of time that the arrangement
was truly wrong, truly incompatible with the Constitution.

One of those who apparently shared this view, or this refusal to
abandon the legislative veto, was Senator Gary Hart of Colorado. That
fact became prominently known because Senator Hart chose to stage
a public act of deploring when President Reagan, in the mid-1980s,
declined to modify his judgment that the War Powers Act of 1973 was
unconstitutional. That act had sprung from the reaction to the war in
Vietnam, and it appeared to have, for Hart, a meaning bordering on
religious significance. Hart railed at the president for daring to suggest
that, as president, he could indulge his own convictions about the constitutionality of any measure. Hart insisted then that

> the President . . . is bound by the laws of the United States, whether or
> not that President likes them, and whether or not that President even
> believes them to be constitutional. The president must obey the laws of
> the country. The President is free at any time to submit changes to the
> law.
>
> But if President Reagan does not believe the War Powers Act is con-
> stitutional, I suppose there are ways in which that can be tested in the
> Supreme Court.[41]

---

[40] 77 L Ed 2d 317 (1983).
[41] *Congressional Record* (October 28, 1983), S14869.

With a surprising blitheness – or perhaps because he simply had not noticed – Senator Hart passed by the rather unsettling fact that the Court, several months earlier, had struck down the legislative veto in the Chadha case. But that veto was at the heart of the War Powers Act. The very point of the act was distrust of the president, and so the act allowed the president to commit troops only for a period of about 90 days without a sustaining approval by the Congress. Which is to say, it was the worst of legislative vetoes, for Congress could in effect veto the deployment of troops, and undermine a military project, without the need to offer reasons and reach an explicit decision. Mere silence, mere inactivity, would count as a veto.

If Hart had been serious in his claim, that decisions on constitutionality depended entirely on the Supreme Court – that political officers, such as presidents and senators, were simply obliged to obey the rulings set down by the Court until the Court changed them – then his complaint against President Reagan should have dissolved instantly. For once the Supreme Court had struck down the legislative veto in the Chadha case, that decision should have been enough to strike down the War Powers Act as well. And yet, that was not, evidently, the understanding held by Hart. Hart continued to act, and speak, as though the War Powers Act was constitutional, that it retained its standing in the laws. In that event, his position could be explained only in this way: He would apparently respect the decision of the Court as it bore on the case of Chadha and the other litigants. But he would not accept the broader principle articulated in that case, the principle that pronounced the wrongness of the legislative veto. As a political officer of high standing and constitutional responsibility, Hart would reserve his freedom to reach his own judgment on the constitutionality of the War Powers Act, quite apart from anything the Supreme Court had to say on the subject.

That is to say, Hart had struck a posture of high outrage because President Reagan had dared to claim for himself precisely the same freedom and authority that Senator Hart claimed, without being much aware that he was claiming it. I take the incident to make this point, which may now transcend the differences of the parties: The fact that Lincoln's understanding can be found woven into the practice of liberals as well as conservatives may be but another sign that the logic of that position is simply inherent in the logic of the Constitution itself.

People find their way back to Lincoln's understanding in the way that Hart did, without being the least aware of Lincoln's teaching, or the reasoning that informs this way of acting. There would appear to be something in the structure of the separation of powers that permits Congress to get around the Chadha case as it does. But if we then summoned our powers of reflection to explain what that "something" is, or the rationale that informs it, the persistent surprise is to find that we had discovered yet again Lincoln's argument.

As these recognitions settle in, there may be a recognition, also, of that other truth so much belied in the cliches that prevail in the public discourse over law: namely, that the Supreme Court does not really have any distinct power, named in the Constitution, to render the *final* judgment on any issue of contention in our constitutional law. The deeper truth here, apparently harder to accept, is that none of these institutions bears that kind of authority to settle the law *finally*. That is the case, in part, because the questions are, as we used to say, "open textured." There are always dimensions open, or to switch the figure, strands still dangling. It would appear that the Supreme Court established a right to abortion as clearly as any right can be promulgated by the Court. But not long after *Roe v. Wade*, the Court decided that the right to an abortion did not entail the right to an abortion paid for by taxpayers. Nor did it involve a right to have the abortion performed by an unlicensed practitioner, in some establishment other than a hospital or medical clinic. Did it involve the right of a minor to order an abortion without even informing her parents? Or getting the consent of her parents as would be necessary in any other surgery involving a child "under age"? Would the right be incompatible with requirements of "informed consent," in which the woman electing an abortion was provided with detailed information about the development, and condition, of the child she is carrying?[42] And finally, as

---

[42] It was not until *Planned Parenthood v. Casey* in 1992 that the Court finally came down decisively on the side of sustaining measures of that kind as quite compatible with the freedom to choose abortion. Aristotle once observed that an action taken in ignorance was not a voluntary action. And it could hardly impair any notion of a "freedom to choose" to establish that the woman doing the choosing also understood precisely what was being done in the surgery – and the condition of that child to whom it was being done. For the passages dealing with this topic, see 505 U.S. 833, at 881–6.

Justice White suggested, might that right to abortion mean, not the right to order an abortion for convenience, but mainly when the life of the pregnant woman was endangered by the pregnancy?[43] The questions never stop coming, because the moral texture of the problem cannot be removed. There are always other angles, raising questions about the restrictions that may be justified or unjustified. And as long as the questions arise, the larger issue may always be reopened. Persistently, grounds could be found for the Congress and the president to put the matter back to the Court, and suggest a different way of conceiving the rights articulated in *Roe v. Wade* or other cases.

It makes far more sense to see the experience of our government as an ongoing conversation among the branches, a conversation that can never quite be closed. When Lincoln and his Congress confronted the Court over the Dred Scott case, they invited the Court to take a sober second look at what it had done. And at times, the Court has done just that. Indeed, the argument had been made quite forcibly on the other side in the 1960s that it was *the Congress* that was necessary to settle the law finally in a way that the Supreme Court could not. That argument was sounded importantly during the argument over the Civil Rights Act of 1964. In a string of cases, the Court had reversed convictions for civil rights demonstrators sitting in at segregated lunch counters and department stores in the South. It was arguable that the federal courts would find the means of knocking down virtually all of the prosecutions directed at these demonstrators for "trespass." But each case would have to be litigated separately, with the expenses of litigation borne by the defendants. And it was not always to be assumed that the rule of law announced in relation to a soda fountain in a drug store would apply to a large department store, or to a restaurant with a more selective clientele. The decisions of the courts, pasted together case by case, could not claim to settle the law in the same manner as a statute passed by Congress – a statute that would apply at once, prospectively, to all similar cases, in all parts of the country.

It speaks no treason then to remind ourselves that the Supreme Court cannot be the supreme legislative chamber, or the institution that rations to the Congress its permissions to legislate. Nor can it be

---

[43] See Justice White's concurring opinion in *Harris v. McRae*, 448 U.S. 297, at 327–9 (1980).

the institution that, *by itself,* settles the law on any question. To set these things in place is not to set the stage for a counterrevolution carried out against the Court and its works. It is to set the ground for a renewed conversation, which begins with the recognition that the shape of our constitutional law is indeed established, properly, in a conversation among the branches. That conversation may draw on the interests and sentiments at work in the country, leavened by an awareness of those principles that must constrain or discipline our judgments. Judges have been given the leisure to cultivate a more professional sense of those principles: The arrangement of permanent tenure rather implies that judges will act in a style quite different from that of other politicians, in taking as their vocation the expounding of those principles. Still, judges are not the only ones who are guided by a sense of equity, consistency, and even by a certain awareness of principles of right and wrong; principles that will not always vary with measures of degree and circumstance.

That sense of the problem may be even more fitting to us now, when the country is reputed to be highly divided over the issue of abortion, and when there seems to be a growing unwillingness on the part of people to talk about this matter in public. But that loss of practice has not been a matter of inadvertence. It has been the precise, predicted result of a state of affairs in which judges inserted themselves into the most contentious "political" issues of the day. After the courts set upon a course of desegregating the public schools, the judges were being lured, more and more, to take on other contentious questions that produced gridlock in the political process. In Felix Frankfurter's time, they were being invited to break through the shell of local structures of power and order the reapportionment of state legislatures.[44] And once the judges crossed this barrier, once the inconceivable became routine, it was no longer so unthinkable that judges might take on, for themselves, the task of ordering changes in taxes or the placement of public housing. If one pieced together the warnings that threaded through Frankfurter's opinions, his argument might have been

---

[44] See Frankfurter's dissent in *Baker v. Carr,* 369 U.S. 186 (1962), pp. 266–330, and his opinions in Civil Rights cases such as *Screws v. United States* [in dissent], 325 U.S. 91 (1945), *United States v. Williams,* 341 U.S. 70 (1951), and *Monroe v. Pape,* 365 U.S. 167 (1960).

restated in this way: If the judges began to take on the hard, political questions, the danger was that ordinary politicians would all too quickly cultivate the willingness to acquiesce. For if judges were willing to "take the heat" on questions like the raising of taxes or ending segregation, then why not leave those decisions to the political men and women best able to take that heat, because they were insulated from the need to run for reelection? When the Supreme Court, in 1989, looked as though it were taking the first steps to return to the matter of abortion to the political arena,[45] one television station interviewed state legislators in Oklahoma, and found them altogether quite averse to taking on this subject. After all, it was a subject that vexed their constituents. The courts had taken this issue out of the political realm, and the politicians were more than willing now to have it removed entirely from their hands – and their responsibility.

Indeed, the life of a politician could be rendered all the more tranquil and secure if other issues generating controversy – issues such as taxes – could be removed in the same way from "politics" and managed by the judges. But then how would politicians fill their days? Answer: by running errands for constituents, and delivering services in an apolitical way, a way that elicits gratitude and insures a continuance in office. In this manner, the intervention of the judges not only works to expand the powers of the courts, but to transform the character of politicians. Under the regime of judicial leadership, we cultivate politicians who have the reflexes of civil servants: They do not see their function as that of crystallizing issues, sharpening questions of principle, or drawing the lines of division. They find their interest rather in rendering "services" in an apolitical way. They could serve then, in effect, under conditions of permanent tenure, in the style of bureaucrats. And that style of things would be secured, along with their positions, if politics could be rendered less turbulent and contentious.

The conflict, in a republic, radiates outward until it affects ordinary citizens, drawn into those arguments. Or they are drawn in if something of consequence is at stake, and political men find an interest in agitating the public in the hope of discovering support. But the chains of causation may run the other way: The political class may find its

---

[45] See *Webster v. Reproductive Health Services*, 492 U.S. 490 (1989).

interest in tranquilizing politics, and removing, from the political arena, the issues of moral consequence. That trend works to alter the character of citizens as well as politicians, for it is the muteness then that radiates outward. Politicians stopped speaking about abortion because it was a matter that riled people in their districts and imparted a rancorous tone to things. It became easier to deflect the matter by saying that it was an issue for the courts, that it didn't belong in the grubby world of politics. Surely, decisively, the point was conveyed that this was something that respectable people do not talk about in public, any more than they go about at parties looking for ways of starting brawls. In time, then, even ordinary people have come to see abortion as a matter so inscrutable, or so productive of incivility and discord, that only lawyers and judges can deal with its layers of complication. It is not, then, the kind of issue that ought to agitate us in our political life – apparently, we are to be agitated, most properly, mainly by the issues of taxes and regulation. It would appear that the protection of life, once thought the first concern of the polity, had ceased to be a central part of the business of the political community. The principal task of politics would become instead the "management of the economy," a task that the founders did not regard as part of the competence or the purposes of the government.

Everything would seem to converge then on producing a politics of muteness. Issues of moral consequence, precisely because they are issue of moral import, are thought unsuited to our political life and the judgment of politicians. Hence, my friend, the seasoned lawyer in Washington, turning on me and asking whether I really wanted "politicians" making decisions on the question of whether the laws would recognize homosexuality as a new, legitimate style of sexuality. But in that case, who were the experts so constituted now to render those judgments of moral substance on the meaning and purpose of sexuality? Would the decision really be left to each one of us to decide the issue for himself? To the members of the North American Man-Boy Love Association? Or to the partisans of polygamy and incest? Hardly. Even the proponents of gay rights do not profess to go that far. And indeed, the move for sexual liberation does not brook any such willingness to respect the judgments that people preserve for themselves and their own families. The landlord who is reluctant to rent space in his house to a gay couple could not apparently invoke the benefits of tolerance and "choice." He is more likely to suffer the penalties of the law, to be punished for his retrograde view of morality.[46] The forces that seek our respect for all species of "sexual orientation" have shown their intent, in fact, to legislate, to have their own ethic of sexual freedom recognized as the one, rightful ethic, the ethic that deserves to be favored and enforced with the law.

In other words, a politics of muteness is not a politics that recedes from judgment and from the uses of the law in teaching moral lessons. It simply produces a victory for one moral teaching, while it seeks to quash into silence the people who would express a rather different moral understanding on the matter of sexuality and abortion. But if this sense of things is accurate, the problem points to a remedy quite simple and modest: It is a matter of restoring speech to the mute. That means: resuming a conversation among the branches of the government, restoring a certain confidence among political men and women that they are not less able than other people to conduct a serious conversation about matters of moral consequence. That conviction, planted again, would soon stir the same kind of conviction among ordinary citizens. Those convictions could be restored with remarkable ease if politicians simply show again, with their own example, that there is nothing illegitimate in this kind of conversation, that it is fitting and necessary for grown-ups.

If the task is to restore speech to the mute, my own suggestion has been to engage the question at the simplest point, with the most modest measure of all. That proposal has been simply to preserve the life of the child who *survives* the abortion. The mere statement of an end, or an objective, does not supply the reasons, and the main point behind this simplest of proposals is to start launching the conversation and bringing forth those reasons. Once launched, that conversation would no doubt sweep well past this most modest of proposals, because even people who count themselves as "pro-choice" express a willingness to accept restrictions on abortion at different stages, for different reasons.

This opening gambit, or modest proposal, managed to attract considerable support among pro-life organizations, and yet it encountered

[46] See my piece in the Symposium in *First Things*, "A Culture Corrupted," *First Things* (November 1996), pp. 30–3, at 31.

the most serious resistance among the groups with the most active operations of lobbying in Washington. As I noted previously, the leadership at the National Right to Life Committee thought the measure just too modest – and largely unnecessary. When an abortion ends with the surprise of a baby born alive, several lawyers pointed out that the dominant inclination was to save the child. They could not see then what practical difference a bill would make. But what they really could not see, or what they apparently discounted, is that the reasons may matter. The philosopher would recognize the point more quickly: Two owners of restaurants in Amherst behave in the same way; they both decide not to discriminate against their customers on the basis of race. They behave in the same way, and yet their behavior may spring from maxims, or premises, that are strikingly different. One owner operates on the axiom that it would be wrong to draw adverse inferences about people on the basis of race, an attribute that cannot control or "determine" moral conduct. The other owner operates on this maxim: "Always accord the rules of the establishment with the mores that are dominant in any place." Amherst is a liberal town, and so it would be bad for business if one acquired a reputation for discriminating on the basis of race. The two owners seem to be acting in the same way, but the behavior is animated by reasons dramatically different, and those reasons in turn mark off notable differences in character.

In the same way, it does not so much matter that there is an inclination, prevalent in most places, to preserve the life of a child who survives the abortion. The trick is to explain the grounds on which that child, marked for disposal, now generates an obligation to respect and preserve its life. For any explanation of that kind could not be easily squared with laws that are compelled to look upon the child in the womb as something less than a human being – or as a being, in fact, with no moral significance, with not the slightest moral claim upon us. I have suggested attaching to any bill on this kind an assertion: that the claim of the child to the protection of the law cannot pivot on the question of whether anyone happens to want her. Now, if that assertion is not true, or if it were contested, then we would put the burden on those who contest it to tell us wherein it is wrong. If that proposition does not hold, we may earnestly ask, What *is* the ground on which we establish the claim of the child to the protection of the law? If that reason does not explain it, let the judges or the opposition supply the reason that does. Or on the other hand, if they would resist this move to preserve the life of the child, they would acknowledge that the argument for abortion must in fact spill over into an acceptance of infanticide. And if their principles really bar them now from rejecting infanticide, then they should be free to claim their proper name.

But from that elementary point, a certain unraveling may take place. If we established the premise that a certain dignity attaches to that child – even the child marked for abortion – that premise would have to start altering the way we can view the unborn child, even earlier in the pregnancy. If his life had a claim to our respect, quite apart from whether anyone "wanted" him, the question naturally arises as to when he acquired that sanctity – or when he was ever without it. It is, as I have said many times over, a modest proposal, but once the premises are planted, those premises could begin dismantling the whole argument in favor of "choice" or abortion. And that is why I suspect that the partisans of abortion rights would seek to resist that move at the very threshold, even when it seems to put them squarely, explicitly, in defense of infanticide. But this matter was not long for speculation. In the summer of 2000, the bill was actually introduced, and as we anticipated, the National Abortion Rights Action League came out in opposition. We would soon learn the answer to these questions, and learn more than we ever wished to know.

Up until recently, my own reckoning had been that the partisans of "abortion rights" would never be willing to resist to the point of defending infanticide, that even Bill Clinton would not have refused to sign a bill to protect the child who survived the abortion. And on the Republican side, I never thought that the Christine Todd Whitmans would threaten to walk out of the Republican Convention if the party simply committed itself to the rejection of infanticide. But I can no longer profess to the same confidence or surety. Just over the past few years there has been a drift in liberal opinion to take a more benign, or less rejecting, view of infanticide. The appointment at Princeton University of a notable defender of infanticide has been taken, in this respect, as a telling sign. I was surprised myself to find at least one U.S. senator who had noticed this appointment, and who was quite concerned about the import of that move. But whether things have in fact drifted in that direction or not, the drift can be arrested only by an attempt to raise the issue sharply and force the country to face it more directly. My own surmise has been, of course, that once the conversation is opened, it will set off its own dynamic, and that dynamic will work in the direction of expanding the protections for unborn children.

That momentum would not be diminished in its import because it happens to take place one small step at a time. Some people simply recoil from the notion of abortions late in pregnancy, when the fetus resembles something they see more clearly as a child. Some are affected when they hear that heartbeats can be heard at 18 to 20 weeks with a simple stethoscope; that fingerprints are discernible and unique by about 12 weeks; or that the child in the womb may be swallowing and moving its tongue at the ninth or tenth week.[47] Some people are opposed to taking the life of a small human being for the sake of avoiding embarrassment. Some are opposed to taking the life of a child, at any age, when the abortion is animated by the concern that child is likely to be deaf or afflicted with Down's syndrome. The process may move in this way, case by case, but it has, with each move, a distinctly moral significance, for at each turn people are earnestly pondering the question of whether any defect in the child, any disability or attribute, would be a justified ground for taking a human life. As people start assembling the reasons, in a chain of decisions, they may begin to point to principles even more sweeping, and lead on to a conclusion even more astounding.

But that is all a speculation. For all we know, people may draw few inferences. The reasons they settle upon in one case, they may not see at work in another. They may see, for example, that racial discrimination is wrong in swimming pools, but they may not see just yet that the same principle may cover tennis courts or the rental of cars. In the same way, they may be slow to see the fuller reach of the principles they are affirming when they move across the cases on abortion. Yet, all of that is part of the risks of political life. Some people have a keener sense of principles and reason; others happen to be more plodding, and have trouble in connecting their actions with their reasons. But even if this process works to save only a handful of lives, there is the

---

[47] For a review of these stages, see Arkes, *First Things, supra*, n. 29, pp. 363–6.

whole world contained in those lives. They are lives, nevertheless, and they are not to be belittled. If the conversation runs into a wall very early, if we do not manage to persuade one another to advance the protections of life, then at least we will have gone as far as an exchange of reasons can carry us.

It is not, after all, as though we purposed to settle this whole matter in a game of pool or squash or a boxing match. It matters profoundly that the process we have been pursuing is not a game, but an argument in the most serious sense – the exchange and weighing of reasons over matters of right and wrong. It is an enterprise fit for grown-ups and for people who count themselves as citizens fit for a republic. Those kinds of citizens should be able to give a moral account and a moral defense of that regime, the regime that lives off and through the rendering of reasons in public. The citizens, so engaged, may not have the wit or the philosophic reach of that first generation, of men such as James Wilson or Alexander Hamilton. But to the extent that they involve themselves in that same enterprise of giving reasons, and making their most compelling arguments, they are living the lives that the founders meant our people to live. They may live, also, with a proper deference to the courts, and a reverence for what the presence of courts marks in a regime of law. But with Lincoln, they would understand that they cannot permit the policies of this continental republic to be fixed by a majority in a court of nine persons, based on cases arising "in ordinary litigation between parties, in personal actions." For in that case, as Lincoln said, the people truly "will have ceased to be their own rulers" and "practically resigned their government, into the hands of that eminent tribunal."

But the last word may belong here, as elsewhere, to Chesterton, so distant from us, but so persistently and uncannily close to us. Governing oneself, he said, is rather like writing a love letter or blowing one's nose: It is something that a man ought to do for himself even if he does it badly.

Eight

Spring Becomes Fall Becomes Spring

A Memoir

I sought to offer, in these pages, a reflection on currents long at work in our law; currents that have produced, over the last 20 years, moral transformations that run deep. So deep, I have argued, that a large portion of our political class have now absorbed premises that detach them from the premises of the American Founders, and the Constitution they brought forth. Regrettably, those currents will not soon be altered by anything shifting in our political seasons. But this book has also been, in part, a chronicle of events unfolding even now in our politics, and of plans that have, as their end, a remaking of the laws. In that part, the book has been a memoir, set down by one who has been a participant at the periphery of our politics. As I have argued here, that "right to abortion," so seductive to many people of standing in our politics, has been the vehicle by which many of these people, highly schooled, highly placed, have talked themselves out of the logic of natural rights. That problem was posed in the sharpest way in the litigation over the bills on partial-birth abortion, as the political class had to put the question of whether that right to abortion would find a limit anywhere. If there was no barrier in infanticide – in the destruction of children at the point of birth – there might be no barrier anywhere in that vast field encompassing "homicide" in all its varieties.

And indeed, as I have noted, the spillover has already taken place. From the child in the womb, the license to end life has been extended to newborns afflicted with disabilities – and then to people at the other end of the spectrum of age. One after another, rationales have been brought forth in the name of "privacy" to end the lives of people who may be disabled or depressed, and the moral logic in the argument soon refuses to withhold this "good" from patients who had not had the foresight to will it for themselves. This sense of things was sharpened, as I say, as federal courts found one reason or another to begin striking down the laws on partial-birth abortion passed in 31 states. The judges, as a distinct segment of the political class, were making it clear that they would have none of this. They would brook not the slightest restriction on the right to order an abortion for any reason, at virtually any time, even when a child emerged in birth.

For the sake of testing – and challenging – that ethic, now congealing more firmly into place, I had brought forth, in my own writing, the proposal for that "most modest first step" of all, the proposal simply to preserve the life of the child who had survived an abortion. As the federal courts began to strike down the bills on partial-birth abortion, those decisions began to form a design that was unmistakable. Those decisions forced an appeal to the Supreme Court of the United States, but as those decisions accumulated, with only a rare dissenting judgment, the odds were mounting that the highest Court would finally accept the reasoning and the judgments that were finding a consensus among their colleagues in the courts below. To recap, I had sounded the alarm on this trend of events in the spring of 1998. With the help of friends in the academy, in the press, and on Capitol Hill, I sought to force a confrontation of the issue in principle by bringing the issue, even more plainly, to the question of a child born alive, quite separate now from the woman who had borne the child. No danger would conceivably arise to the health or the interests of that woman as the law sought to protect the child.

As it happened, my earlier chapters here offered a rather precise anticipation of what was to come. The jolting, and galvanizing, event came in June 2000. The Supreme Court, in a narrow vote of 5–4, struck down the law on partial-birth abortion in Nebraska, and by inference, in the 30 other states that had passed a law of this kind. The decision was *Stenberg v. Carhart*, and from that moment, in the summer of 2000, a new chain of events was set in motion.

In that chain of events, I became, inescapably, a central participant, as I made the case in public for the bill to protect children born alive. I would testify before the Committee on the Judiciary in the House, and I would become even more active, in trying to connect people on

Capitol Hill, in garnering support. It may be slightly awkward to offer an academic account of a political happening in which I would figure. But since I was the principal mover of the legislation, it would be a strange account of events that discreetly brushed me out of the picture. I will try to offer an account suitably detached, and yet it may also enhance the narrative that it offers an account, so to speak, from "within": that it conveys an understanding, not by interpreting the action from without, but by reporting how the action was understood by the principals.

I would offer then a kind of afterword or epilogue, on the events that began moving in train, with remarkable, vast promise, even in a season of melancholy for the pro-life movement. From the spring of 2000 to the fall of 2001, I would set down an account of how the arguments in the book made their way in the Congress, and from there into the swirl of our politics. From *Stenberg v. Carhart* through *Bush v. Gore*, the action in the Congress, and the events of September 11, 2001, that day of infamy, it was a year of dramatic, surprising turns. As the bill to protect children born alive made its way to passage, the trauma of September 11, the attack on the World Trade Center and the Pentagon, produced an upheaval in the country. The words were on everyone's lips, that nothing, thereafter, in American life, would ever be the same. And yet, the events had disclosed nothing new in human nature or in the possibilities for evil. From that perspective nothing had changed. But for the moment, old antagonisms were muted or put in abeyance, and while nothing promised to change in the lines that divided politics in America, it was evidently a time when the American people, in an altered state, were looking at many things anew.

From the spring of 2000, to the summer and fall, the story moved quickly, in discrete, dramatic steps, amplified by the phases of our political season and the stages of the presidential election. The tale to be told here is at once striking and intricate, but the telling would get lost in the parts without a quick overview of the sweep of events. Compressed as a prelude, it would run in this way:

Everything began in June, when the Supreme Court finally heard an appeal from the decisions in the various states on partial-birth abortion. In a closely divided Court, matters seemed to hinge on one vote, that of Justice Sandra Day O'Connor. In the end, she tipped the balance to the side of the liberal coalition, striking down virtually all of the laws on partial-birth abortion in 31 states. With the decision in *Stenberg v. Carhart* there was no longer any practical alternative for the pro-life groups but to fall back on that proposal I had been making for a long while, and which I set forth in this book. The National Right to Life Committee, which had held back with dubiety and reservation, now threw its weight behind the bill. With some deft drafting, that measure was introduced in the House by Representative Charles Canady of Florida, the chairman of the Subcommittee on the Constitution of the House Committee on the Judiciary. The bill was styled the "Born-Alive Infants Protection Act." I was given the privilege of leading the testimony on the bill in July 2000, in the hearings in the House. To the astonishment of the people at the National Right to Life Committee – but consistent with the predictions made by others of us – the National Abortion Rights Action League (NARAL) actually came out in opposition to this bill, to protect children born alive.

But NARAL was cautioned by its friends in the House not to be drawn into opposition on this bill. And so, against all of the passions and reflexes of the partisans of abortion, the opposition was deliberately muted. The bill then sailed through "mark up" in the Committee on the Judiciary. That willingness to recede, to let the bill pass without an argument, induced the managers to accede to my own proposal that the bill be attended by a "preamble" or a list of "findings," which could make more explicit the premises that the bill sought to plant in the law. That simple act would raise the level of tension, and make it harder to avoid the argument. That it did, but surprisingly it raised the tension among the Republicans before it inflamed the Democrats. The result was that the findings were deleted, out of delicacy toward the pro-choice Republicans, and the bill then passed quite as readily in the full House. But by this time, the political conventions were held, the presidential election was underway, and the question was whether George W. Bush would take advantage of these events. Might he recast the argument over abortion now – and disarm his opponents – by offering to begin with "the most modest first step of all," in saving the life of the child who survived the abortion? And yet, from Mr. Bush, and his camp there came nothing. Without that signal of support or interest on the part of the Bush campaign, the Born-Alive Infants Protection Act was never introduced into the Senate. In the aftermath of the election, it became clear that there was no point in reviving the bill on partial-birth abortion, for it had little prospect of entering into force until there had been a change in the Supreme Court. And so, as summer gave way to fall and winter, and the turn of the year finally brought a new administration, the Born-Alive Act was now being treated in Congress as the lead move. It was in fact *the only move* that could set in place the ground for any serious legislation, establishing limits to abortion and possibly offering protections for the unborn child. But then suddenly the bill was caught in all of the reverberations and aftershocks of "Bush versus Gore."

When the dust had cleared, a Republican Administration would be installed with its party in control of both houses of Congress for the first time since Eisenhower's first landslide, in 1952. But the result was produced with one of the closest elections, and for the first time since 1888, the victor in the electoral college did not have an edge in the popular vote. With Republican losses in the Senate, that body was divided 50–50. The Republicans would be able to take control only with the election of Bush and the advent of a Republican Vice President, in Dick Cheney, who could then tilt the control of the Senate. But the close division simply amplified the disputes that lingered from the close election and from those differences marked on the map between the "red and blue" counties. They were the differences that marked the "culture wars" in the division between Bush and Gore. That division would be reflected in the tensions that finally tipped Senator Jim Jeffords across the line to the Democrats.

With the switch of Jeffords, the Republicans lost control over the scheduling of business in the Senate. And so, even if the Born-Alive Infants Protection Act could gain overwhelming support in the House, it might not even be scheduled for a vote in the Senate. Unless, of course, the Republicans were fueled with conviction to put that bill into play – or unless President Bush would finally discover his voice. In his reflexes he was deeply sympathetic to the pro-life side, and he had, on his staff, accomplished writers who could write, in support, with real effect. And so it was in the end a political question, Could the President finally be induced to speak?

The Supreme Court, June 2000. The augurs had not been favorable. On a rainy day at the end of April, I made my way to the Supreme Court to hear the oral argument in *Stenberg v. Carhart*, the case that challenged the bill on partial-birth abortion in Nebraska. The remarkable points in the opinion by Judge Kopf have already been discussed previously, and the question was whether this opinion would survive a review in the Supreme Court. It was evident even to the dimmest observer that Justice Sandra Day O'Connor would be the swing vote. The question was whether O'Connor would be willing simply to sustain the conservative party on this issue through the simple – and conservative – expedient of having the Court hold back its hand. The properly conservative and judicial response would have been: Let us wait and see if there is such a case. There was, after all, a rationale for courts working under the discipline of waiting for real cases in controversy. Let us see whether the Attorney General of Nebraska, armed with this new statute, uses it to launch prosecutions against doctors performing abortions that were never proscribed in this legislation.

When the oral argument was held, then, on *Stenberg v. Carhart*, the attentive listener was waiting to hear any questions from Justice O'Connor that could register that conservative stance or those points of caution. But the silence was telling. From Justice O'Connor there was not the slightest intimation that those concerns were anywhere in her thoughts. The inference seemed inescapable: O'Connor would be folded in with the liberal bloc, to strike down the law in Nebraska. Two months later, at the end of June, in a chamber crowded with lawyers and the press, that inference was confirmed. And Justice O'Connor was indeed confirmed as the swing vote. In this case, that meant swinging away entirely from the Reagan–Bush appointees, including Justice Kennedy, who had been her partner in defection, along with Justice Souter, in the plurality opinion in *Planned Parenthood v. Casey*, eight years earlier. As Kennedy made plain now, in tones of injury and disbelief, O'Connor had staged a defection from a defection: In order to align herself with the liberal bloc in this case, she had to repudiate that carefully crafted middle course that Kennedy thought he had signed onto in *Casey*.

In his astonishment, mixed with anger, Kennedy was willing to do his version of Claude Rains in *Casablanca*: he was "shocked–shocked" that O'Connor would be willing to walk away from her own holdings in *Casey* and other cases. The Court in *Casey* had built on the Webster case in 1989 in insisting that the state had to be conceded an ample measure of authority to act on behalf of the unborn child, as life worthy of respect. In Kennedy's reading of *Casey*, a woman might be conceded a critical autonomy in making decisions on abortion, and yet "the State's constitutional position in the realm of promoting respect for life is more than marginal."[1] In this case Nebraska "deprived no woman of a safe abortion and therefore did not impose a substantial obstacle on the rights of any woman."[2]

Weighed in the balance in these cases was mainly the claim, made by the doctors who performed these abortions, that this kind of procedure *might* be better for his client. But as Justice Kennedy pointed out, Dr. Carhart used the D & X procedure "for every patient in every procedure, regardless of indications, after 15 weeks' gestation."[3] This was not a doctor who was apparently refining his procedures in accord with a refined measure of the condition of his patients. And yet, O'Connor was now intimating that Nebraska might salvage its law if it merely permitted the D & X to be performed when "the procedure, in appropriate medical judgment, is necessary to preserve the health of the mother." The judgment, that is, of Dr. Carhart. But as Kennedy remarked, it should have been as plain then to Justice O'Connor, as to anyone else, that "the assurance is meaningless. . . . A ban which depends on the 'appropriate medical judgment' of Dr. Carhart is no ban at all."[4]

That critical point, directed against the central pretense in the case, was echoed also by Justice Thomas, in the main dissenting opinion, the opinion read from the bench: "Justice O'Connor's assurance that the constitutional failings of Nebraska's statute can be easily fixed . . . is illusory. The majority's insistence on a health exception is a fig leaf barely covering its hostility to any abortion regulation by the States – a hostility that Casey purported to reject."[5]

It was O'Connor's thin strand of justification, in her concurring opinion, that the law in Nebraska might have been sustained if the

---

[1] *Stenberg v. Carhart*, 530 U.S. 914, at 964. "Casey made it quite evident . . . that the State has substantial concerns for childbirth and the life of the unborn and may enact laws 'which in no real sense deprive women of the ultimate decision.' 505 U.S. at 875 (joint opinion of O'CONNOR, KENNEDY, and SOUTER, JJ.). Laws having the 'purpose or effect of placing a substantial obstacle in the path of a woman seeking an abortion of a nonviable fetus' are prohibited. 505 U.S. at 877. Nebraska's law does not have this purpose or effect." *Ibid.*, at 965.
[2] *Ibid.*   [3] *Ibid.*, at 972.   [4] *Ibid.*   [5] *Ibid.*, at 1013.

legislators had only been far more fastidious in marking off the lines of their definitions, so that the ban on abortion would not spill over to affect the D & E procedures.[6] But as Thomas and Kennedy argued, there was virtually no chance that any functional person could have mistaken the D & E for the procedure of killing a child at the point of delivery. With the D & E, as Dr. Carhart had testified, the surgeon used the traction created by the opening between the uterus and the vagina to tear the parts of the child from the rest of the body. And so, what the abortionist was left with at the end, he said, in a memorable phrase, was "a tray full of pieces."[7] "No one," then, said Thomas, "including the majority, understands the act of pulling off a part of a fetus to be a 'delivery.'"[8] Therefore, no ordinary citizen – let alone doctors or lawyers – would have suffered any confusion as to what exactly the law had meant to forbid.

For Justice Scalia, holding back in wry detachment, it seemed curious that so much outrage should be vented, so much forensic effort should be expended, in mapping Justice O'Connor's betrayal of the settlement in the Casey case. To Scalia, it was merely the shedding of self-delusion. Scalia evidently thought it a venture in self-hypnosis to suppose that there had been any such settlement in *Casey*. The outcome in the Stenberg case was not, as Kennedy claimed, "a regrettable misapplication of *Casey*." But rather, as Scalia argued, it was "*Casey's* logical and entirely predictable consequence." Kennedy had apparently found, in that decision, an intricate weave, designed by the most refined jural minds. Scalia looked past the contrived phrasing, with its airs of subtlety finely worked, and he saw, beyond the artifice, a principle of action far more elementary: namely, "the Court's inclination to bend the rules when any effort to limit abortion, or even to speak in opposition to abortion, is at issue."[9]

When the case was viewed with the eyes of the common man, one could see, as Scalia said, a "method of killing a human child . . . so horrible that even the most clinical description of it evokes a shudder

---

[6] *Ibid.*, at 947–51.
[7] Quoted by Kennedy in *ibid.*, at 959.
[8] *Ibid.*, at 991.
[9] Scalia, dissenting opinion in *Stenberg v. Carhart, supra*, n. 1, 953–6, at 954.

of revulsion."[10] But for Justice Breyer and the majority, it was not apparently possible to restrict even this egregious form of abortion without imperiling the whole corpus of "abortion rights." That was plainly the meaning of the concern, expressed by Breyer and O'Connor, that the law could spill over and affect even D & E abortions, the most common form of abortions performed in the second trimester and beyond.

As Breyer conceded, there were "no reliable data on the number of D & X abortions performed annually," and therefore there were no reliable studies to confirm that this procedure was safer for most patients, or for any particular patient. Breyer found himself fashioning then a judgment of this kind: If the attending doctor thinks that the surgery might be safer for his patient, then the withholding of the procedure for that patient could indeed be a threat to her life or health. He could also lean on Dr. Carhart in extracting some possibilities that could conceivably arise in principle. And so, with this reasoning, the alternative procedure of D & E carried grave risks, which could be avoided by the D & X:

> The use of instruments within the uterus creates a danger of accidental perforation and damage to neighboring organs. Sharp fetal bone fragments create similar dangers. And fetal tissue accidentally left behind can cause infection and various other complications.[11]

But with that style of argument, Breyer was taking a radical step, nowhere acknowledged in his argument. The method used quite typically in performing late abortions was now seen as far more hazardous in principle than this novel form of abortion, as gruesome as it was. For the sake of gaining that speculative advantage for the pregnant woman, it was now thought legitimate to kill a child with about 70 percent of its body dangling from the birth canal. Would the implication not be obvious? On the same premises, would it not be even safer to deliver the child whole and simply let it die? For the doctor could then wholly avoid the insertion of instruments into the uterus. Or he could avoid the dismembering that would allow fetal parts to be left behind, where they could be the cause of infection. With these steps, the Court had backed into the acceptance of the method known as "live birth

---

[10] Ibid., at 953.   [11] *Ibid.*, at 926.

abortion," the form of abortion that had been brought to light recently at Christ Hospital in Oak Lawn, Illinois: A baby is delivered live from the mother and simply put aside, unclad, and left to die. With the opinion in *Stenberg*, Breyer and his colleagues brought themselves to the threshold of accepting infanticide outright, and it takes but the shortest step to cross that threshold. Whether it was the design of the judges or not, the decision in *Stenberg* did indeed form a design, and the effect of that design was to prepare the public mind for an acceptance of infanticide, unfolding in the gentlest way, step by step.

Leaving the Court that day was hardly a buoying experience. Nor was it exactly a ground of elation that the Court had confirmed the line of argument I had been offering since the spring of 1998, when I had sounded the warning, in the *Weekly Standard*, on the trend of decisions in the lower federal courts. I had argued that the most tenable course was to go back to that most modest measure of all, to preserve the life of the child who survived an abortion. That would not only be a position certain to prevail; it would also put in place the premise that the laws on partial-birth abortion had never quite filled in: It would establish the cardinal point that the child was in fact an entity, whose injuries somehow counted; a being who came within the protection of the law. Those arguments, set forth years earlier, now seemed to have met the moment. For when the jolt came in the Stenberg case, the pro-life professionals seemed to have a sense, at once, of the next move. Or they were at least willing to look now, with eyes unclouded, at arguments they had been too quick in the past to dismiss as far too modest.

The critical move, opening everything else, came from Douglas Johnson at the National Right to Life Committee. He had been an old friend in the movement, and in friendship he had never concealed from me the reservations he had borne over the years toward this "most modest first step" of all. But now, the strategy of partial-birth abortion had been blocked. It would take at least another appointment to the Court, and the election of a candidate who would make the right appointment, before the path for that bill could be opened again. Until then, another attempt to pass the bill on partial-birth abortion in Congress could help stir sentiments anew, but it would be a gesture without consequence. Under these circumstances, Johnson saw that the move to protect the child who survived the abortion could be the only plausible card to be played. With his willingness to play it, he opened all the doors. For as Charles Canady remarked, in one meeting on Capitol Hill, National Right to Life was simply the most important player on the pro-life side. The group had the lobbyists, did the work, turned out the witnesses and the studies. From the standpoint of sheer person-power, it was futile to do anything without the support of National Right to Life. Nor would any pro-life politician waste much time on a proposal that found the pro-life groups divided, with National Right to Life in opposition.

Canady, the Congressman from Florida, was the chairman of the Subcommittee on the Constitution. He was also quick and resourceful, and not disposed to waste a moment, for he had put himself under term limits, and he would be leaving the Congress at the end of the term. He was 46, a graduate of Haverford and the law school at Harvard. But he was also a new father, and ready to give up the grinding schedule of Congress for another life on the bench or in politics back in Florida. He was determined, however, to get something done before his time ran out in the chairmanship, and he quickly saw that the bill to preserve the child born alive offered the best practicable measure at this moment. As modest as this bill was, Congress would actually be legislating to forbid a killing, and to establish at least a limit to that sweeping "right" to abortion. Of course, that end could have been accomplished by the bill on partial-birth abortion, but that bill had been blocked by President Clinton's veto. Clinton was still in office, but this bill to preserve the child born alive was a bill that even Clinton would find it hard to veto. And this bill surely would pass.

Canady went to work then with his staff right away, drawing what he could from my notes and my previous drafts. In recounting that effort, it is hard to understate the contributions of Bradley Clanton, who had become the main counsel to Canady in the drafting of this bill. Brad Clanton was only around 31 at the time, and he proved, through the turns of the legislation, a model of clearheadedness. He was amply tutored in the law, but to that training he brought a quick wit. He could see around corners, he was alert to every shade of meaning in the bill, and nothing got past him. When the staff dealt with the sections defining, precisely, the conditions of a live birth,

Clanton was able to draw from the draft produced several years earlier by Clark Forsythe, who had been the chief lawyer at Americans United for Life.[12]

But then Charles Canady added a deft touch of draftsmanship by drawing again on the genius that went into play, four years earlier, with the Defense of Marriage Act. The question had naturally arisen then about the grounds on which Congress could legislate on the matter of marriage. To that question, there was a substantial answer, and yet the drafters had found a delicate way of approaching the problem: Congress was the author of the federal code, and Congress clearly had the preeminent authority to pronounce on the very meaning of the terms contained in its own legislation. As it turned out, there were several hundred references to marriage or to spouses in the federal code. It fell then to Congress to stipulate that all references to marriage would mean only references to a legal marriage, constituted by a man and a woman, as husband and wife.

Canady would now draw on the same playbook. Once again, Congress would pronounce on the meaning of terms in the federal code. In this case the Congress would stipulate that all references to "persons" in the federal code would now encompass a child who was born alive following an abortion. To pronounce in that way on the meaning of terms in federal law was not to enlarge the federal jurisdiction. The law would simply take that jurisdiction as it stood, and it would make the simple point that children who survive abortions were indeed persons who came within the protection of the law. In that respect, the child who had survived an abortion would be *placed on the same plane as other newborns protected by federal law.* That law, as it stood, did not mandate heroic surgery. Its concern, rather, had been with the withdrawal of medical care from children who were afflicted with spina bifida or Down's syndrome. If lifesaving care was typically ordered up for other newborns, it could not be withdrawn for babies

---

[12] He had now become its president. In Forsythe's draft, now taken up by the committee, a child "born alive" was taken to mean "the complete expulsion or extraction from its mother of that member, at any stage of development, who after such expulsion or extraction breathes or has a beating heart, pulsation of the umbilical cord, or definite movement of voluntary muscles, regardless of whether the umbilical cord has been cut, and regardless of whether the expulsion or extraction occurs as a result of natural or induced labor, caesarean section, or induced abortion."

suffering these disabilities without constituting the most palpable discrimination based on the disabilities of these children. In the same way, this new measure, to protect the child born alive in the aftermath of an abortion, would not have mandated heroic surgery that was likely to be futile. It would simply establish that the condition of being marked for an abortion did not remove the child from the class of rights-bearing persons. That the child might emerge injured or poisoned or afflicted with deficits – or that the child was conspicuously "unwanted" – did not mean that his life could be disregarded now, as though he counted for nothing, with a life not worth living, and without the slenderest claim even to exist.

But of course, in the style typical of legislative bodies, this modest bill, elegantly crafted by Canady and the staff, was encumbered with a clumsy title, with the usual run of "nouns as adjectives." And so, the bill would be called "The Born-Alive Infants Protection Act of 2000" [H.R. 4292]. Its operative parts were contained mainly in these two sections, with the word "abortion" not coming in until the very end, to endow the rest of the language with its fuller significance:

SEC. 2. DEFINITION OF BORN-ALIVE INFANT.
    (a) . . . – Chapter 1 of title 1, United States Code, is amended by adding at the end the following: "§8. 'Person', 'human being', 'child', and 'individual' as including born-alive infant
    "(a) In determining the meaning of any Act of Congress, or of any ruling, regulation, or interpretation of the various administrative bureaus and agencies of the United States, the words 'person', 'human being', 'child', and 'individual', shall include every infant member of the species homo sapiens who is born alive at any stage of development.
    "(b) As used in this section, the term 'born alive', with respect to a member of the species homo sapiens, means the complete expulsion or extraction from its mother of that member, at any stage of develop-ment, who after such expulsion or extraction breathes or has a beating heart, pulsation of the umbilical cord, or definite movement of voluntary muscles, regardless of whether the umbilical cord has been cut, and regardless of whether the expulsion or extraction occurs as a result of natural or induced labor, cesarean section, *or induced abortion.*"[13]

---

[13] For the text, see *Born-Alive Infants Protection Act of 2000*, Hearing before the Subcommittee on the Constitution, Committee on the Judiciary, House of Representatives, 106th Cong., 2d sess., July 20, 2000, p. 10; italics added.

But as we met in Charles Canady's office, contemplating the text of the bill, I invoked the late Felix Frankfurter, in the appeal he once made to restore "preambles" to legislation. That venerable style had the advantage of making clear the premises or the purposes that were acknowledged by the legislators who had framed and enacted the law. In this case, the bill was, as we had often said, the "most modest first step" that was conceivable on abortion. The significance of this measure would be found in the premises it planted in the law, and in the lessons that the bill would teach. In that respect there was a change from the original draft, of several years earlier, that bore noticing. In a section prepared by Clark Forsythe, the original draft had stipulated civil penalties for doctors and medical facilities.[14] The dropping of those penalties might have been a mistake, for the law then would command the protection of children without offering the prospect of a serious penalty to doctors who ignored the law. But the purpose of this law was to plant premises and teach, and Charles Canady had thought that this character of the law would become even clearer if it avoided any threat of prosecutions.

Still, if the object was to teach, then there was a case for making the underlying principles of the bill more explicit, by setting them forth in a preamble to the legislation. Charles Canady appreciated the case, but his political sense cautioned him to hold back: This measure, he was convinced, would pass, and lay the groundwork for others. But he feared that if its premises were set forth so boldly, that could furnish quite enough cover for Bill Clinton in staging a veto. A few months later, Canady would find reason to change his mind. In that shift would hang an interesting political tale, which revealed, in a flash, the desperation of the Democrats and the dimness of the Republicans.

In the meantime, though, the text was settled, and Charles Canady introduced the bill. When the bill was assigned a number – when it became H.R. 4292 – it was set down for hearings at the end of July. In a gesture of courtesy, the staff invited me to lead the testimony, because I had been arguing in print for this approach for a dozen years.

---

[14] In the draft prepared several years earlier by Clark Forsythe, the bill provided that any physician violating the act "shall be subject to a civil penalty of not less than $10,000 and not more than $50,000, in addition to any other remedy or penalty that may be available under federal or state law." And in a parallel section it was provided that any "medical facility" violating this law would be subject to a "civil penalty of not less than $20,000 and not more than $100,000."

But I would be joined, in making the legal and moral arguments, by two friends: Robert George, now the McCormick Professor of Jurisprudence at Princeton, and Gerard Bradley, Professor of Law at Notre Dame. We would be joined also by three women who had a direct experience with babies born alive, surviving abortions. Jill Stanek and Allison Baker had served as nurses at Christ Hospital in Oak Lawn, Illinois, and there they had suddenly come upon the experience of "live birth abortions." These were cases of babies "induced," in the course of an abortion, with the object of delivering them intact, and then permitting them to die, with no attendance or care apart, perhaps, from what was called "comfort care."[15] For Stanek and Baker, the scenes jarred with their natural sense of nursing and the care of babies. Their reactions would eventually get them into trouble with their superiors. Baker had moved, in the meantime, to Charlottesville, Virginia, but Stanek had remained at Christ Hospital, dangling in a kind of probation because she had drawn such an unwelcome attention to the way in which Christ Hospital practiced its vocation. Still, with her position hanging in this way by a thread, Jill Stanek had chosen to appear and testify.

The third woman, with "practical experience," and a story to tell, was 23-year-old Gianna Jessen. She bore the name of her adoptive parents, for her own mother had cut her ties when she had marked her daughter for an abortion late in term, at around seven and a half months. The method of choice was the saline abortion. But the child had survived the poisoning, and her presence, with a beating heart, seemed to cast up a reproach to other people in the ward disposing of other babies in her condition. For some reason, as yet untold, the care was not withdrawn in her case. She had ingested enough saline to cause many deficits, and afflict her with cerebral palsy. And yet, through therapy, and the steady support of her adopted parents, the disabilities over time seem to be shed in layers. I had seen her, several years earlier, at a pro-life dinner in New York, simply come onto a stage, singing "Amazing Grace," and the audience, slowing catching on to her story, was moved to quiet tears. In her appearance now, before the committee, she apologized for a head cold that affected her voice, but as she recalled the gradual easing of her afflictions, she

[15] *Supra*, n. 13, p. 38.

remarked that "I am so thankful for my cerebral palsy. It allows me really to depend on Christ for everything."[16]

On a stage at the Waldorf Astoria, this young woman, with a song sprung from her soul, was measured precisely to the occasion. But in the Rayburn Building, in the structure of a legislative hearing, her piety mixed with her story seemed a bit out of scale, and some of my colleagues confessed later that they were a little taken aback by it. They were afraid, that is, that the flexing of this Christian piety was not measured, in the same way, to the sobriety of the arguments that formed the currency of the committee. Their concern was that she would appear, to the committee, just too earnest, too evangelical. I record that sense of the moment right now, because in looking back at the transcript of the hearing, the tones become modulated, and the transcript of her words, read for themselves, I find irresistibly moving. Stripped of the emotive tones that were part of her speech, the words themselves, and the story they convey, have a power that runs beyond the tone that the rest of us could pick up that day.

But it fell to me to lead the testimony, in setting out the argument and the explanation. The case I made to the committee encompassed the argument that I have already set forth, in its fullness, in these pages.[17] But I would recall here the points I sought to accent for the committee when we were compelled, in the hearing, to compress our presentations to around five minutes. I began by suggesting that the bill introduced by Congressman Canady "offers the gentlest and the most modest first step of all in engaging the question of abortion." But that measure, I said, "runs to the root, and it offers the best chance of drawing all sides into a conversation and achieving the kind of settlement that I think can be achieved only by the political branches of this country." That conversation could draw in many people who were "pro-choice," and it would begin at "the earliest point at which the interests of the mother and the child can be detached. Nothing in the move to protect the child impairs any right to abortion or any right to end a pregnancy, because the abortion and the pregnancy have ended."

---

[16] *Ibid.*, p. 55.

[17] That testimony can be found in *Born-Alive Infants Protection Act of 2000*, Hearing before the Subcommittee on the Constitution, Committee on the Judiciary, House of Representatives, 106th Cong., 2d sess., July 20, 2000, pp. 17–34.

I reminded the committee of the cases that made this problem so plausible right now: There was *Floyd v. Anders* and Judge Haynsworth's intimation that the right to abortion meant the right to an effective abortion or a dead child. There was the trend of cases on partial-birth abortion, culminating in the decision, just three weeks earlier, in *Stenberg v. Carhart*. I pointed out that Justice Breyer's opinion for the majority was "at one with the argument that would justify delivering the baby whole and letting it die if that procedure would be arguably safer for the mother." Breyer had set the ground, in other words, to defend precisely the kinds of abortions that were taking place now at the Christ Hospital in the suburbs of Chicago; the abortions that would be described shortly by Jill Stanek and Allison Baker. There was nothing, then, in the least speculative about this problem. It could not be regarded any longer as "far-fetched or inconceivable" that the right to an abortion meant the right to a dead child. And so the burden of argument now had to shift: "The burden, I am afraid, truly lies with our friends on the other side to make it clear that the right to an abortion does not entail for them the right to infanticide."

I anticipated the argument we were likely to hear – that, "yes, we would like to protect the child, but we don't want to take the first steps in getting the federal government involved in abortion." And we were likely to hear this argument even from people who had been supporting the Freedom of Choice Act years earlier. When it came to enacting *Roe v. Wade* into the statutes of the United States, these people had not seen any barriers to the authority of Congress to legislate on abortion. But I reminded the committee, also, that the *federal courts* had been addressing abortion for more than 30 years. Were the federal courts somehow not part of the federal government? That question was meant to draw the committee back to Chief Justice Marshall in *Cohens v. Virginia*, and to the deeper axioms of the separation of powers. I condensed the argument in this way:

> [I]f the Court can articulate new rights under the 14th amendment, civil rights or a right to abortion, the legislative branch must be empowered also to vindicate those same rights and, in filling them out, marking their limits. The one thing that should not be tenable under this Constitution is that the Court can articulate new rights and then assign to itself a monopoly of the legislative power in shaping those rights.

I concluded then by returning to the root point:

> The ground on which we take this simplest of all measures will clarify
> our understanding of the human person as a bearer of rights. To rework
> a line of Lincoln's, we might say that in securing this simplest of all
> rights, we secure the rights of us all, born and unborn. And to take one
> other line of Lincoln from another occasion, . . . this is the simplest of
> steps, and as Lincoln once said, [may] the vast future not lament our
> having failed to take it now.[18]

I was followed by Jill Stanek and Allison Baker, who reported that
in the Christ Hospital in Oak Lawn, Illinois, abortions were performed
on women in the second or even third trimesters of a pregnancy. The
method of choice was the so-called "induced labor abortion," which
was also being called now "live birth abortion." As Stanek explained,
the procedure worked in this way:

> [T]he physician insert[s] a medication called Cytotec into the birth canal
> close to the cervix. Cytotec irritates the cervix and stimulates it to open.
> When this occurs, the small, preterm baby drops out of the uterus, often-
> times alive. It is not uncommon for one of these live aborted babies to
> linger for an hour or two or even longer. One of them once lived for
> almost eight hours.[19]

The experience that apparently proved revelatory for Stanek came
when another nurse was on her way to the Soiled Utility Room with
an aborted child, with Down's syndrome, who had survived the abortion. She was on her way, with the child, to that room with discarded
towels and other debris "because his parents did not want to hold him,
and she did not have time to hold him."[20] In another case, a live
aborted baby was simply left in the Soiled Utility Room, wrapped in
a disposable towel. But Stanek's reflections were sharpened by the
account of still another case, with a woman more than 23 weeks pregnant. As Stanek consulted the tables, the child at that point might have
been part of a group with a 30 percent survival rate. As it happened,

---

[18] *Ibid.*, p. 20. I make a slight correction here to offset the stenographer, who would
set down what she had taken in by ear even when it made little connection with
the text. In this way, the transcript converted "may" into "made" and "likely" into
"lucky" – as in "we are lucky to hear this even from people who were supporting
FOCA years ago. . . ."

[19] *Ibid.*, p. 37.   [20] *Ibid.*, p. 38.

the child survived the abortion. Stanek was moved then to consider that "if the mother had wanted everything done for her baby, there would have been a neonatologist, pediatric resident, neonatal nurse, and respiratory therapist present for the delivery, and the baby would have been taken to our Neonatal Intensive Care Unit for specialized care.[21] Stanek ended with a heartfelt plea to provide, for the unborn, the same care given to "big people." Abortion, she felt more and more, was "killing America. . . . killing our consciences" – sentiments that put her, of course, quite at odds with the policies of the hospital in which she was employed.

In the arguments over abortions at the point of birth, I had taken the line that the importance of the question was quite separate from the number of cases. But Stanek and Baker, in their testimony, had brought news. This happening, of a baby surviving an abortion, was not all that rare or uncommon after all. Here was a cluster of cases found in just one suburban hospital. And if Justice Breyer's opinion in the Stenberg case were widely diffused in the land, other hospitals might soon discover the advantages to the pregnant woman in doing abortions in the style of Christ Hospital in Illinois.

In balancing the advocates, the committee arranged to have Stanek and Baker followed by a spokesman on the other side. Matthew Hile was a clinical psychologist and a Research Associate Professor at the University of Missouri–Columbia Medical School. Hile told the story of his own infant daughter, born 14 years earlier, with deficits not exactly named in his account, but apparently affecting the central nervous system and the right side of the brain. He drew on his journal in offering a report of the strain of the family and the child, as the child was sustained with a feeding tube and other devices. At the same time, much agonizing went on among the doctors as to what it was practicable to do for her. The father, regarding himself as tutored in the law, was evidently given to worry about the interventions of the Reagan Administration. But his journal reflected no sign that he and his wife and the hospital were ever in danger of any reproaches offered by the federal government, or any prospect of the law intervening. The prospect had to arise of putting the child on a ventilator, but the parents did not choose to do that. The child died in her mother's arms,

[21] *Ibid.*, p. 39.

having lived for 31 days. From these sad days, lived again through his notes, the father drew this lesson for the committee: "I urge you to leave these agonizing decisions to those most involved, the physicians and families who care deeply about their children."[22]

But the "lesson" did not seem to make contact with the question before the committee in any of its dimensions. Apparently Mr. Hile had not been threatened by the Reagan Administration, or by any prospect of prosecution, state or federal. The decision to withhold a ventilator from the child had not been questioned or reviewed. The baby had received a combination of care, medical and maternal, and she died in her mother's arms. Why would the Born-Alive Act have mandated any more heroic care than the law would have mandated for the Hiles? There was no danger arising for the Hiles that had not already arisen from the earlier federal statutes, which had been concerned with the withdrawal of medical care from newborns afflicted with disabilities. The objection of the Hiles would seem then to have run more aptly to that earlier statute than to the bill to protect the children who survived abortions. But putting that aside, Mr. Hile sat on the Medical Ethics Committee at the St. Louis Children's Hospital, and so it became apt to focus the moral question: How would the "lesson" he offered have any bearing on the cases described by Stanek and Baker? Clearly, there was no disposition on the part of the parents, in these cases, to do what was even remotely practicable in caring for their children. The question was whether those children did not have, nevertheless, a certain right to receive the care offered to other newborns; the kind of care that had now come within the protections of the law. Did anything in Hile's experience "establish" or prove that these children were less deserving of the care tendered other children? Did anything in his journal show that these children were less than human beings – or could anything in the journal have "proven" that these children genuinely counted for nothing unless they were "wanted" by their parents?

As the hearing went on then, with some kindling of disagreement, the main legal and moral questions remained. In a second panel, Gerard Bradley, from the law school at Notre Dame, recognized that the bill did not track the distinctions between the "viable" and

---

[22] *Ibid.*, p. 53.

"previable," cast up in the jurisprudence of abortion. But those distinctions had to do with pregnancy, and this bill, he reminded the committee, dealt with born persons. The pregnancy was over. As Bradley put it, abortion "refers to terminating a pregnancy and has really nothing to do with terminating children." In the jurisprudence of abortion, the courts often talked around a difficult issue by using that strange expression "potential" life. Of course, if there was already a pregnancy, marked by a pregnancy test, that test gauged nothing other than the presence of life, not merely potential life. As Bradley observed, "The *Roe* Court often referred to 'potential life,' and used that term interchangeably with the 'fetus,' or the child *in utero*. All these terms were contrasted to the child born alive." To cast a protection over the child born alive is to do nothing that touches a pregnancy, and it cast up no restriction on abortion. The rights proclaimed in *Roe v. Wade* would remain unimpaired.[23]

Or that would be the case – unless the right to abortion must indeed spill over to give parents a bit of choice about the child born alive. Justice Breyer's opinion in *Stenberg* was already pointing in that direction. Robert George's testimony offered a complement then to Bradley's by dealing with that other end of the problem. George concentrated his testimony on the drift within the American academy to the acceptance of infanticide. Exhibit #1 was the appointment to Princeton of Professor Peter Singer, a man who had cut his distinctive figure in the academy by offering an explicit defense of infanticide. Singer had once done a piece with the title, "Killing Babies Is Not Always Wrong." He had since backed away from some of the flourishes in that piece, but on the main thesis he had not altered. As George summarized the matter, Singer had not receded from his denial that "it is always wrong intentionally to kill innocent human

---

[23] As Bradley put it, in summing up:

> Another way to terminate a "pregnancy" [apart from abortion], it is equally clear, is to give "birth." Having given "birth" by completely expelling the child from the womb, the Act assures equal protection of the law to the person just born. The woman is not then prohibited, by this or any other act, from securing or completing an "abortion." From the moment of birth on, "abortion" is, according to standard medical usage, impossible. No "pregnancy" remains to be terminated (*Ibid.*, p. 132).

beings, nor has he abandoned his claim that newborn human beings are not 'persons' with a right to life that must be respected and protected by law. He continues to insist that human beings only become 'persons,' and acquire a right to life, sometime well after birth."[24] The people who had arranged the appointment of Professor Singer were well aware of his views; indeed those views had formed the main part of his attraction. His elevation was, for them, a means of making a dramatic point in public: namely, that we should recede from any opposition to infanticide that was overly emphatic. Viewed with a new lens, that traditional aversion to the killing of children would not be treated as a commitment anchored in principle, but as a social prejudice. And as with all prejudices, it should be subject to erosion with the advent of new and better reasons.

As George crystallized the matter, "The legitimization of infanticide constitutes a grave threat to the principle of human equality at the heart of American civil rights ideals. If weak and vulnerable members of the human family . . . can be defined out of the community of, 'person,' whose fundamental rights must be respected and protected by law, the constitutional principle of equal protection becomes a sham." As George understood, the argument over abortion was part of the more complicated argument over natural rights. For that reason the appeal, with this act, to make a decisive judgment on infanticide was part of a move to summon people, again, to the ground of their own, natural rights.

But then there was Mel Watt. The congressman from North Carolina. No encounter in the subcommittee for me would have been complete without the presence of Congressman Watt. And for Watt, it was plain, my presence was a persisting source of puzzlement and irritation. A year earlier, I had testified before the committee on Lindsey Graham's bill on the Unborn Victims of Violence. During the questions, Congressman Watt remarked that he and some of his colleagues had trouble in referring to an unborn child. He wondered whether it would make any difference to refer simply to a "fetus." What difference it made was brought out in the exchange; and the congressman did not find

[24] See George in *ibid.*, p. 143.

that exchange congenial, to put it mildly.[25] He did not find the current bill any more to his liking, but he had worked out his angle of approach: Instead of confronting directly the moral premises contained in the bill, he would raise a problem of prudence in draftsmanship. He had been advised by staff that there were "some 15,000 sections of the U.S. Code and over 57,000 sections of the Code of Federal Regulations in which the terms 'person,' 'human being,' 'child,' or 'individual' are used." The bill, he said, sought "this one singular purpose," and he suggested that there might be something out of scale in a bill that would seek a purpose while threatening to affect other parts of the federal code. Of course, all bills have a focus or purpose. And because they impose restrictions, or allocate benefits, they can hardly avoid identifying the "persons" who are the objects of the restraints or the benefits. In any event, Watt professed now that it would be necessary to read the 15,000 references to "person" in the federal code before the conscientious legislator could cast a vote for the bill.

He would return to that issue later in his questions to me and ask whether I had managed to canvas, even in part, those 15,000 sections of the federal code that mentioned "persons" or human beings. I

---

[25] That exchange may be found in *The Unborn Victims of Violence Act 1999*; Hearings on H.R. 2436, before the Subcommittee on the Constitution, Committee on the Judiciary, U.S. House of Representatives, 106th Cong., 1st sess., July 21, 1999, pp. 126–8. The encounter contained this exchange:

Mr. WATT. . . . Is there something in this bill, is there something critical to this bill that the word "child," as opposed to "fetus" is important?

Mr. ARKES. It may not make much of a difference, Congressman, unless there is –

Mr. WATT. Well, it makes a lot of difference to me.

Mr. ARKES. Well, if I can finish the sentence.

Mr. WATT. All right.

Mr. ARKES. Unless it strains the coherence of what you are doing, which is why you protect –

Mr. WATT. Unless it is what?

Mr. ARKES. It strains the coherence of what you are doing. Are you assuming that it is an animal protected by the Endangered Species Act, or are you protecting it precisely because you are aware that it is a human being? If it is a human being, it may not really matter whether you call a human fetus or a child. That rather begs the question. So I think it is perhaps important for you to understand why are you protecting it.

Mr. WATT. Well, Mr. Arkes, if you are not going to be serious with me, I am not talking about animals.

Mr. ARKES. I am quite serious.

reported that I had looked into several of them, but that this kind of inquiry really had not been necessary. I offered, as an analogy, the example of Edward Bates, Lincoln's first Attorney General, resisting the decision in the Dred Scott case. Bates came forth with an Opinion of the Attorney General, dealing with the matter of "citizenship," and he announced that, in the understanding of the Lincoln Administration, all free blacks in the United States would indeed be considered "citizens" of the United States. With that move he seemed also to incorporate Lincoln's understanding that the reference to "persons" in the Privileges and Immunities Clause covered, in its terms, all people, black as well as white.[26] But then I put the question: What if someone had responded at the time, in the style of Congressman Watt, and said, "there are 15,000 references to 'person' in the federal code" – and were we really to reach such an emphatic judgment before we looked into each one of these references and gauged the sweep of what we were doing?

I had not known Mel Watt well enough to anticipate his reactions, but those who did know him found his response at this moment quite characteristic. The transcript records the action:

> **Mr. WATT.** Mr. Arkes, I have – and maybe this is just a personal thing to me. But I get real offended when people try to put everything that I ask into some racial context. I asked you a simple question. If you haven't analyzed the impact on other things, that is fine. That is why I started out by trying to reassure you that this was not a trick question. But what we are talking about today has little, in my opinion, to do with Dred Scott, and so, I mean, just – . . . Because I happen to be black, you don't have to give me a black response today. A simple yes or no answer –. . . .

---

[26] Lincoln had made this argument at other times, and in his First Inaugural Address, he shaped it in this way:

> [I]n any law upon this subject, ought not all the safeguards of liberty known in civilized and human jurisprudence to be introduced, so that a free man be not, in any case, surrendered as a slave? And might it not be well, at the same time, to provide by law for the enforcement of that clause in the Constitution which guaranties that "The citizens of each States shall be entitled to all privileges and immunities of citizens in the several States"?

The Collected Works of Abraham Lincoln, Roy P. Basler, ed. (New Brunswick, NJ: Rutgers University Press, 1953), v. IV, p. 264. It was a refined, yet still audacious move, to presume that free black people had the standing of "citizens." But it was an assumption in which Lincoln could follow Jefferson.

Mr. ARKES. May I say that I am offended by this attempting to keep blocking off an – I am trying to give you a proper answer to the question, because –

Mr. WATT. The question is: Have you done any analysis –

Mr. ARKES. Yes, Mr. Watt, I have.[27]

When I had begun drawing on the example of Edward Bates, Watt had interrupted, trying initially to block that path of response, and faced with that move, I remarked, a bit vexed, that "I guess I get in trouble in this committee offering that rare thing called an analogy."[28] But now that Mr. Watt was evidently determined not to acknowledge the principle in the example, I tried to make it a bit clearer. Still, it was not exactly an optimal moment for laying out an explanation – while fending off attempts to derail the speaker:

Mr. ARKES. . . . if you don't like the analogy of race, I could simply take the ball rolling down the inclined plane. If somebody says –

Mr. WATT. Well, keep going, then.

Mr. ARKES [continuing]. We have the principle by which that ball [rolls down the inclined plane, and people then say] have you tried this with the yellow balls, the blue ones – if you are clear on the principle, then you are clear that that principle will not be affected even by the numerous instances that arise under the law.[29]

If the conditions of the "discussion" in the committee truly had allowed the courtesy of completing two or three sentences in sequence without an interruption, the problem could have been restated in this way: Once we are clear on the principle by which the ball rolls down the inclined plane, as the angle of inclination is altered, then we no longer have to ask whether it was a blue plane or a yellow one, a metal ball or a wooden one. For the point is that the *principle* is virtually indifferent then to the multitude of *instances* in which that principle can be manifested. Regrettably, this is a confusion that has often afflicted the minds of judges, even on our highest courts. And so, for example, if we understand that it is wrong to draw adverse inferences about people on the basis of race, we would no longer have to ask whether racial discrimination would be quite as wrong in regulating

---

[27] See *supra*, n. 13 (Hearing on the *Born-Alive Infants Protection Act of 2000*), pp. 62–3.
[28] *Ibid.*, p. 61. [29] *Ibid.*, p. 64.

access to tennis courts or swimming pools, as to schools. As the argument came to bear on the bill at hand, our contention was that there was no defensible ground in principle to remove a newborn from the protections of the law because she happened to survive an abortion. For there was no conceivable set of circumstances in which the innocence of the child would be impaired. And in that case, there could be no conceivable set of circumstances that could justify removing that child from the same protections of the law that were available to other newborns.

Nine years earlier, when I had been seeking support for this "modest first step" on abortion, Douglas Johnson, the chief lobbyist for the National Right to Life Committee, had feared that the measure was just too modest. He thought that even the most unyielding partisans of "abortion rights," would be able to vote for this measure. But now, as I was waiting to testify on the bill, he handed me a paper with late news: The National Abortion Rights Action League had actually come out, that day, with a forceful statement in opposition to the bill. NARAL, sensing exactly what was taking place, denounced the bill in a press release proclaiming, "Roe v. Wade Faces Renewed Assault in House":

> The basic tenets of *Roe v. Wade* were the subject of yet another anti-choice assault today, as the House Judiciary Subcommittee on the Constitution held a hearing on H.R. 4292, the so-called "Born-Alive Infants Protection Act." The Act would effectively grant legal personhood to a pre-viable fetus – in direct conflict with *Roe* – and would inappropriately inject prosecutors and lawmakers into the medical decision-making process. . . . In proposing this bill, anti-choice lawmakers are seeking to ascribe rights to fetuses "at any stage of development," therefore directly contradicting one of *Roe's* basic tenets.
>
> The bill also attempts to inject Congress into what should be personal and private decisions about medical treatment in difficult and painful situations where a fetus has no chance of survival.[30]

The fact that the child had emerged from the womb apparently made no difference for its standing: It was still a fetus. And it would be a fetus, presumably, as long as it was marked for abortion. It would never attain the name of "child" or person. All of that quite fit the

---

[30] National Abortion Rights Action League, press release, July 20, 2000.

premises and the lens with which NARAL looked out on the world. And yet the reaction was in a way a credit to NARAL. Many congressmen were still baffled by the modest reach of the bill, but NARAL was supremely attuned to every shading of principle. Some pro-lifers still did not exactly "get it," but the leadership in NARAL understood that this simple bill actually ran to the root of things.

One who saw the same thing was Congressman Jerrold Nadler, Democrat, from New York City, and a member of the subcommittee. He recognized at once the import of the bill, but he sensed that NARAL was creating a peril for itself in overreacting. What Nadler saw was a "trap," as he would later call it. He did not see an effort to plant premises and lay the groundwork for steps in the future; he saw mainly an attempt to embarrass the defenders of abortion by luring them in to vote in favor of infanticide. Sensing what he saw as a trap, Nadler was evidently grasping for a way to accommodate this political move without exposing his allies to a deep embarrassment.

> **Mr. NADLER.** Mr. Chairman, I confess that I am very confused on this bill. I have read all the material on it. As far as I can tell, it changes the law in no way at all, . . . I know that the pro-choice forces are very fearful of this bill. I am not sure that they are not mistaken.
>
> . . . My understanding today is that any baby that is born, whether it is born after 9 months of pregnancy or it is premature or whatever, if it is in good health, it lives, fine; if it is in desperate shape, it is up to the parents and the doctors to decide whether to take heroic actions, ...
>
> I will ask Mr. Arkes, how would this bill change that in any way, if at all?[31]

I responded that Nadler was indeed "partially right," that the current bill was simply building upon the law already in place. But what Nadler had not recalled was the legislation, from the mid-1980s, dealing with the Baby Doe cases, the problem of withholding medical care from newborns afflicted with Down's syndrome or spina bifida. With that move, the decisions taken by parents and doctors and hospitals could conceivably come under a review from the legal authorities. In comparison, this new bill, to protect children who survived abortions, would not add even a further degree of complication.

[31] *Supra*, n. 13, pp. 68–9.

As far as one could tell, the presumption was rather universally established that local law, in the States, would cast its protections over children born alive. What Nadler had not recognized, however, was that this presumption, so firmly settled, had already been unsettled by the advent of that new right to abortion. After all, what accounted for Judge Clement Haynsworth's novel claim, in 1977, that the protections of the law, normally cast over any newborn, would not apply to that child marked for abortion?

By his own admission, Congressman Nadler had come late to this body of law. But his political instincts were still sound. Whatever the shape of the law, he knew that it would not be good for NARAL to come out so dramatically in opposition to a move to bar outright infanticide. When the hearings broke, Nadler suddenly had around him a cluster of women, observers from various groups intensely interested in preserving abortion rights. In the presence of their anxiety, he was evidently seeking to offer counsel. And what he seemed to be counseling now was prudence. From the atmospherics, and from the clues of his own commentary, I drew my own impression of the advice he was tendering, and in a later conversation he essentially confirmed the inferences I had drawn.[32] He urged his listeners to consider that the legislation was really quite modest, that it made a change in the law that was barely perceptible. The bill would indeed plant premises, but it could do little harm if those premises went largely unnoticed. And the way to leave them unnoticed was to avoid drawing any conspicuous attention to them. That, however, the opponents would surely do if they allowed themselves to be drawn into a public argument, which would only draw more attention to the bill and insure that the deeper premises of the bill were absorbed by a wider public. His counsel then seemed to be: play rope-a-dope; go with the punch – mute the opposition – and avoid the kind of argument that would give to the bill the significance that its framers had sought.

That advice apparently took hold, for when the time came for the mark up of the bill in the full Committee on the Judiciary, the bill

---

[32] It was a friendly conversation in passing, in the Members Dining Room of the House, June 29, 2001, when I was having lunch with a former student, Thomas Davis, a congressman from Virginia.

sailed through with a vote of 22-1. Only Mel Watt lingered in opposition. The vote was telling, and it yielded information at several levels, some confirming and some alarming. It confirmed that the bill would be virtually impossible to oppose, that we could expect it to move through the Congress at a level that could easily command veto-proof majorities. Yet, on the other hand it was sailing through all too readily, and that indicated that Jerrold Nadler's counsel had taken hold. The opponents would put up at best token resistance. Their strategy would be to deprive us precisely of the debate we were inviting, the kind of debate that would lay bare the radical premises that now governed the laws on abortion. The question now, in turn, was whether the managers of the bill could read these signs and respond with their own countermove.

The natural response, in coping, was to raise the price, to make the opposition a bit more costly. Charles Canady had backed away from the move to add a "preamble" to the bill, out of fear that it would draw a veto. But now it was clear that the opposition was afraid to vote against the bill – and it was quite as clear that, if the defenders of abortion ever had their opponents caught in a comparable situation, they would not have hesitated for a moment in squeezing them just a bit harder. The task then was to raise the level of tension for them. There were evidently more than enough votes to spare, and indeed the managers could have taken the risk even of bringing the vote down to levels that might not have survived the veto. For as important as it was to enact this measure, it was quite as important that the issue be joined, and the public drawn into the debate. The obvious step then was to bring back the preamble, or make quite explicit now the premises that this bill would plant in the law. The moment had been lost for presenting those premises as a preamble. But there were precedents for coming in later with a set of "findings" to attach, as a predicate for the bill.

At the direction of Chairman Canady, Bradley Clanton set to work to prepare the findings. Robert George and I submitted our drafts, and as Clanton brought the items together in a new composition, he brought forth a compelling statement, unfolding an argument. The findings began with the things nearest at hand: the recent judgment of the Supreme Court in *Stenberg v. Carhart.* Judge Haynsworth had once intimated, and now the Supreme Court had affirmed, that by the logic of abortion rights the law might not be able to protect even the child born alive. That logic, it was noted, was now being played out in the examples of "live birth abortion," a practice made known to the committee through the testimony of Jill Stanek and Allison Baker. The findings then drew to a set of assertions or conclusions:

PURPOSE – It is the purpose of this title –

(1) to repudiate the flawed notion that a child's entitlement to the protections of the law is dependent upon whether that child's mother or others want him or her;

(2) to repudiate the flawed notion that the right to an abortion means the right to a dead baby, regardless of where the killing takes place;

But those propositions in turn had to imply that the child had an intrinsic dignity that commanded the concern and protection of the law. The findings expressed the matter by continuing in this way:

(3) [the bill would] affirm that every child who is born alive – whether as a result of induced abortion, natural labor, or cesarean section – bears an intrinsic dignity as a human being which is not dependent upon the desires, interests, or convenience of any other person, and is entitled to receive the full protections of the law.

That findings of this kind should be incorporated in the bill by the chairman was a consummation that ran beyond anything that the drafters of the bill had come to expect. And there the matter stood, then, at the end of August, as the Democrats, following the Republicans, held their national convention. Al Gore bounced back in the polls, wiping out the lead that George W. Bush had gained in the "bounce" of his own convention. By Labor Day the presidential campaign would open with its full force, and Congress would return. That the Born-Alive Act would be brought to the floor of the House was virtually certain, for this was Charles Canady's last term, and he was determined to see this measure passed. With the committee and the leadership resolved to move ahead with the bill, it was set down for a debate and vote on the floor for September 26. But then the surprise hit. Or perhaps it was a series of surprises. Or perhaps they were no surprises at all, but a confirmation of everything we had argued. We had contended that the presence of the findings would raise the level of tension, for they would make even clearer the moral understandings contained in this modest bill. What we had not anticipated – what came truly as a surprise – was that the explosion would erupt, not among the Democrats, but within the ranks of the Republicans. The story played out, from that point forward, might constitute a minor Book of Revelations. The bill would move toward passage with jolts, and sudden, winding detours, but the tumults of that day astonished Charles Canady, along with the rest of us. They surprised, that is, even the people who made their vocation in politics. And they delivered a rather sobering reflection of that part of the political class in which we found our own political friends. The part that proved even more sobering was that, over the course of the next year, the unfolding of events would merely confirm the state of things revealed to us that day in September.

That resistance would flare up, in response to the Born-Alive Act, hardly came as news. In fact, it had been our policy precisely to encourage that resistance and force the debate. Nor did it come as a surprise that the proposal would stir uneasiness in the ranks of the Republicans who were pro-choice, or even more emphatically pro-abortion. But that section of the party in Congress had been dealt with, cabined, comforted in the past. They would eventually acquiesce in measures brought forth by a party that was, after all, dominantly pro-life, and they would acquiesce all the more readily when the measures brought forth touched only the periphery of the issue. It was hard to imagine then that any serious opposition would flare within the party over this, "the most modest step" of all, for this measure did nothing to restrict the freedom of women to have abortions. But as modest as this measure was, it did run to the root in principle, and the opposition turned out to be acutely sensitive to that point. Years earlier, I had pronounced it inconceivable that Christine Todd Whitman, the pro-choice governor of New Jersey, would stage a walkout from the Republican convention if the party proposed merely to protect a child born alive. And yet, that is very nearly what took place now, in the Republican delegation in the House.

On the morning of the 26th a group of so-called "moderate" Republicans demanded a meeting with the Republican leadership of the House over the matter of the Born-Alive bill. Only within the jargon of the American media would people be labeled as "moderates" when they refused to contemplate the restriction of even a single abortion out of an annual volume of 1.3 million. What these so-called moderates threatened now, to their leadership, was the prospect of joining with the Democrats in adjourning the House if the managers really went to the floor with those "inflammatory" findings. This was in the fall, just as the presidential campaign was heating up. And this threat came from the same Republicans who had bent themselves out of shape, virtually giving in to Bill Clinton on every spending bill, lest they give Clinton a pretext for closing down the government yet again, and yet again saddling them with the blame. No question of policy seemed to justify a willingness to go to the edge with Bill Clinton and face him down, with so much at stake. But the prospect of passing a bill on abortion to save a child born alive – *that* was apparently the kind of measure that would move these "moderate" Republicans to risk all.

Charles Canady, called into the meeting, could hardly believe the conversation. As he recalled later, he found himself wondering whether his colleagues really thought that there was, in their districts, a powerful constituency that would be moved to a spasm of retaliation if it looked as though their Congressman were too ardently opposed to infanticide. As one veteran remarked later, any politician worth his campaign chest could always declaim, "I am pro-choice – but *this* goes too far. We have to draw the line at infanticide." As Canady listened to the members venting their concerns, he assumed that the leaders would do what it was the function of leaders to do in this kind of setting. The complainants had not offered any reasons to show the wrongness of the bill, or the inaptness of the findings. Canady anticipated that the leadership would show a certain sympathy, and then try to find a formula to soften the bill – put in a qualifier here or there, drop or add a clause. They might also try to show people how to play the issue, and assure them that they could hardly damage themselves in their districts by voting for a bill that simply protected a born child.

Canady was not prepared, though, for what happened next: Henry Hyde, of all people, leaned in, acting as the statesman, and pulled the rug out from under him. Hyde was the chairman of the full Judiciary Committee, and a man much respected and beloved among the pro-lifers in the country. He had also gained a wide public visibility as chairman during the impeachment of Bill Clinton. Hyde enjoyed a wide affection in the Congress, and within the ranks of his own party that affection was undergirded by the fact that, apart from being a committed pro-lifer, Hyde was also a reliable "team player." In the spirit once explained by Tocqueville, Hyde had become practiced in the art of merging his own interests with the interests of all the rest, and subordinating his own concerns to a sense of common ends. As Hyde explained to me later, when I caught up with him by phone, he saw the face of real anxiety on several colleagues gathered round him. The practical concern was that these were people "hanging by a thread" in their congressional districts. They were congressmen such as Steven Kuykendall, in San Diego, elected with a razor thin margin the last time out. The serious pro-lifer, experienced in politics, understood that the pro-life cause could be advanced only within the ensemble of one of the main national parties. The pro-lifers required allies, including people who were pro-choice. Joined within the party, they were willing to reciprocate for the support given them in turn on other matters of concern (say, on taxes and regulation). It was indeed part of the alchemy of political parties that they could induce people in this way to reconcile interests that were often at odds. And in the way that alchemy worked now, Henry Hyde understood this irony: he could preserve a House under the direction of pro-lifers – with pro-lifers in charge of the Judiciary Committee – only if the party could hold a Republican House. Holding Republican control in a House closely divided meant going to the aid of Republicans who were pro-choice or even adamantly pro-abortion.

Still, it was a matter of practical judgment: Was it really necessary to gut the section that accomplished the purpose of the bill – the section that would dramatize to the public the premises that shaped the current laws on abortion, the premises that were being challenged now in the bill? But what seemed to set in, with Hyde and others, was part of the code of the House: and that was a willingness to regard the member himself as the sovereign expert on the things that would make life, in his district, untenable for him. With that sense of things, Hyde made what seemed a magnanimous gesture: The committee would go to the floor without the findings. And it would go with a rule limiting the debate to 45 minutes.

A day or two later, after the vote had taken place, I managed to reach Charles Canady at home, and he was still in a mild state of disbelief. Hyde's gesture might have been magnanimous, but it seemed to purchase no gratitude, no goodwill, no tempering of passions. The most committed defenders of abortion still registered their outrage that such a bill should be brought to the floor, with or without the findings. Douglas Johnson of the National Right to Life Committee had remarked, years earlier, that even Nancy Johnson (R–CT) would vote for this bill. But he was mildly astonished to find now that he could not have been more wrong. Encountering Charles Canady on the floor, Nancy Johnson turned her back and would not even look at him. At times, in fact, she appeared so consumed with anger that she could hardly speak.

On the floor, Charles Canady opened for the committee. He recalled the cases that made this legislation necessary, and he drew on the testimony offered by Jill Stanek and Allison Baker, on the experience of "live birth" abortions. Mel Watt acknowledged that he was the one vote in committee against the bill. "My name is one, I guess." Rather than confront the argument in the bill, he would glide round it by repeating the concern he had voiced in the committee: Congress should be more cautious before enacting a bill that touched so many parts of the federal code. And to make matters worse, Congress would be adding to a "litany of terms" in the code that Watt found barren of meaning – "that litany," he said, "being person, human being, child, individual, and another term which a has no definition either, that term being born alive."[33] But as Gerard Bradley had noted in the hearings, Congress typically acted by legislating benefits or penalties that were assigned to different classes of persons. When Congress referred to taxpayers or citizens or residents or spouses, it presumably meant to distinguish any of those persons, say, from household pets. If Congressman Watt was to be believed, he spent his life legislating on the rights and wrongs done to persons or individuals, while finding utterly inscrutable the categories of beings who were the objects of his protection. And because he found "born alive" a term without

[33] *Congressional Record* (September 26, 2000), p. H8158.

significance, he would vote benefits and penalties for persons, apparently, even without any firm ground of knowing that any of these persons actually existed at the time they were receiving their benefits or penalties.

Jerrold Nadler picked up on the theme he had sounded in the hearings, but the skirmish over the findings moved him to a new level of vituperation. He assured his liberal colleagues that the bill would not change the law, or change it much. Why then did he urge his colleagues to vote for this bill? "Because of its dishonest sponsorship," he said, "because of the dishonest purpose behind it":

> The purpose of this bill is only to get the pro-choice members to vote against it so that they can then slander us and say that we are in favor of infanticide. If I had any doubts about that, the manager's amendment and the Dear Colleague letter with it – [a reference to the amendment containing the findings, though here Nadler was interrupted. He resumed.]
>
> . . . Mr. Speaker, I believe the only real purpose of this bill is to trap the pro-choice members into voting against it so that they can slander us. . . . [T]hat is why I voted in the committee in favor of the bill. . . . so that we do not step into this trap.[34]

In a striking way, then, the reactions of both parties confirmed the understanding that lay behind the move to add the "findings" and make the premises of the bill explicit. The explosion set off among the Republicans revealed, quite undeniably, that congressmen understood at once the meaning of those findings, and why their presence made such a profound difference. Nadler revealed the same understanding in his reactions, but the outrage covered the decision he was spared now from making or revealing: If the findings had been added to the bill, would Nadler then have urged his colleagues to vote against an attempt to bar infanticide? Thanks to the deleting of the findings, that was a path that Nadler and his friends would not have to take, and a choice they would never have to face.

With the bill stripped of its provocative parts, and with the begrudging acquiescence of the Democrats, the bill sailed through, with votes from both parties. The final vote was 380–15. Of the 15, two were

---

[34] *Ibid.*, p. 8157.

Republicans, Nancy Johnson of Connecticut and Ben Gilman of New York. Other pro-choice Republicans chose, tellingly, to sit out the vote – for example, John Porter of Illinois and Connie Morella of Maryland. Thirty-five congressmen decorously held back from showing up for the voting, including young Rick Lazio, running against Hillary Clinton for the Senate in New York. Absent also was Jim Rogan, one of the managers for the impeachment, who was running in a tight contest for reelection, in a district reputed to be fiercely pro-abortion.

The day had its bitter tastes, but at the end of that day, some perspective was in order. A proposal I had been arguing for, as the Bible said, coming in and going out, in the morning and the evening, had finally taken hold. Congressmen and staffers, and many others in the country, had been persuaded, with the result that the bill was in fact introduced, and the rationale had been understood. Well, there it was, with a vote of 380–15, a resounding win by any measure.

But more than that, there the issue was now in the center of things, during the height of the presidential campaign. Presumably, the bill would go to the floor of the Senate, and as it approached passage, Mr. Bush would be asked his opinion. Without doubt, he would endorse the bill – or at least, so it seemed – but the question was whether he would take advantage of the occasion that this bill represented. He could offer now the "most modest first step" of all on abortion, a proposal that was bound to be received as disarming. Only about 22 percent of the public was willing to support abortion "on demand" – abortion performed at any time, for any reason at all. No one but the most hard core defenders of abortion would find the Born-Alive Infants Protection Act, joined by Bush, as anything other than reasonable. If Republicans in the northeast were forming into a cast of opposition, here was a chance to melt them. With Republicans in the northeast delivered from their intransigence on this issue, the politics of the northeast could have been made far more fluid. At the same time, Bush could have made himself a far stronger candidate among Catholics in Pennsylvania and Michigan. A moderate but firm pro-life position would have marked Bush in the role of FDR as an "enemy of his class" – and made him even more interesting to the Catholics who had become Reagan Democrats.

That, at any rate, was how the situation looked at the end of September, with the presidential campaign moving into high gear. And after the vote in the House, I must confess to a certain buoyant confidence. In retrospect it is hard to see what justified that confidence, for in all these respects my expectations were disappointed. My main consolation is that just about everyone else was wrong as well. The most accomplished political observers were routinely guessing wrong in this season. It might be said that all calculations had swerved from the knotty truth of things, a truth that was never quite revealed in the polls surrounding the election. For it is arguable that the polls did not pick up the deep division in the country marked by the "culture wars." The election, it turned out, was really about those so-called cultural or moral issues after all, and yet one side had been notably reluctant to wage that campaign. To our puzzlement, at first, and then to our deep astonishment, the Born-Alive Infants Protection Act never made it to the floor of the Senate in the course of the campaign. The word went around Capitol Hill that the bill never made it to the floor because Trent Lott, the leader of the Republican majority, had no particular interest in bringing it to a vote. But the fact that nothing, persistently, happened could not be entirely attributed to inadvertence. The further word circulating in Washington was that, of course, Lott would have brought the bill to the floor if he had received any directing word from the Bush campaign that it suited the interests of the campaign to draw attention to that issue and bring it to the point of judgment.

That the Republican majority did not bring the bill to a vote, and that Mr. Bush would preserve a silence on the matter, were two non-happenings that seemed more and more connected. And so, as the campaign wore on, it became less and less surprising that Mr. Bush, on these matters, would say absolutely nothing. Not that he failed to speak on abortion, for he was willing to join an emphatic opposition to partial-birth abortion. His party and the Congress had staked out heavy majorities in favor of that measure, and he could safely align himself with his party, even when it meant expressing a willingness to condemn and restrict a certain kind of abortion. But if Bush had been willing to condemn the killing of a child mostly extruded from the birth canal, would it not have been even easier – and less freighted with political peril – to condemn the killing of children who had emerged in a live birth in the course of an abortion?

That paradox seemed to point to only one plausible answer: That Bush should endorse a policy adopted by his party, and by most of the Congress, would have appeared inescapable and altogether excusable. But that he should now talk about yet another kind of abortion, on a matter that would come as news to the public, would seem to betray an unseemly willingness to *talk* about this issue. And in some circles of the Republican party, the willingness to talk about this issue, when it was not strictly necessary, was taken as the sign of an immoderate soul, edging perhaps on the fanatic.

As the season wore on, Bush rose and fell in the polls, he needed a surge of support from Catholics, especially in Pennsylvania and Michigan . . . and yet Bush never found a reason to speak about the Born-Alive Infants Protection Act. He would not express an endorsement, even in a press release, and so things remained all the way through to the fateful election day of November 7. After that date, it was hoped, a George W. Bush made reticent by caution, would be freer to speak. Nor did there seem much doubt that the Born-Alive Infants Act would take its place within an ensemble of measures shaped by an administration that would define itself, in its main cast, as conservative and pro-life. All of that would become clearer with the configuration of support and division that emerged on election day.

The lines of the culture wars would be written plainly on the map that emerged even during that bizarre election night in November 2000. Of course, the arguments over the election have continued to this day, and they have produced a bitterness that will probably endure well past the next presidential election. But the political warfare in Florida was a reflection of the remarkable constellation revealed by the morning after the election. The election could not have turned so decisively on the outcome in Florida if Al Gore had managed to carry his own native state of Tennessee. But at the same time that Bush was losing in traditional Republican enclaves in the northeast and the coastal areas, Gore was running up an uncommon series of losses in states that were typically reliable for the Democrats. Surely, it was no random event that Gore lost, in a string, West Virginia and Arkansas, as well as Tennessee and Kentucky. With his usual, penetrating wryness, Robert George surveyed the map and observed that the marked split between Connecticut and Vermont, on one side, and Wyoming and West Virginia, on the other, no doubt indicated that the inhabitants were intensely divided over the various schemes of co-payments and deductibles for prescription drugs! Of course, no one could have thought that the dramatic difference between the Red and the Blue counties – the terrains marked off on the map as Bush and Gore country – had anything do with such divisions over health care or endangered species. But what they really had to do with was strangely unmentionable in our politics.

Among the Republicans in the House, the campaign of 2000 was entrusted to Thomas Davis from Fairfax, Virginia. Name a congressional district, and Tom Davis could tell you the river that ran through it, but more than that, he would fasten on the features in the landscape that shaped the politics of the area. (This was an attribute seasoned in the bone with him, as I had learned more than 30 years earlier, when he had been my student at Amherst and written his senior thesis.) When it came to politics, Davis looked with the eyes of a utter realist, unclouded by the hopes that might distract the vision of others. When he surveyed the map after the election, he was struck by the radical break from the alignments of the past: Some of the wealthiest counties in the country, on the east and west coasts, no longer voted along the lines of class. What caught Davis's eye were counties of this kind, solidly Republican in 1988 for George Bush, the father, and yet lost a dozen years later by George Bush the son: There was Bucks County, Pennsylvania, carried by the elder Bush by over 60 percent, but lost by the younger by a vote of about 132,000 to 121,000. In Nassau County, New York, the elder Bush had over 300,000 votes and 57 percent, while the younger lost the county by a vote of about 319,000 to 214,000. Bergen County, New Jersey, heretofore a firm Republican enclave, gave the first Bush 58 percent of the vote, but flipped over to Al Gore with a margin of about 190,000 to 143,000.[35]

Clearly, these counties were not voting their interest in taxes and regulation; they were voting for an ethic of the Left that included

---

[35] These figures were taken from Tom Davis's notes, assembled at the Republican campaign committee for the House.

the environment, and sexual liberation, under the euphemism of "privacy." And the issue that marked the key – the issue that was most central to the concerns for privacy and sexual freedom – was the issue that everyone seemed to insist was only peripheral to our politics. The dreaded "A-word" was not to be mentioned: The subject of abortion was to be avoided, in political discussions, and in polite settings. Yet, its intractable presence was conveyed at every turn in coded expressions: Stockbrokers of middle years, Republican in all of their reflexes on the economy and taxes, would now express a concern for "appointments to the courts." Yes, they were concerned about the economy, but they would confess a profound concern, also, for protecting the interests of their daughters. And the assumption was that their daughters had a deep interest now in that right to abortion.

A hesitant George W. Bush had regarded the A-word as mainly unmentionable in a national campaign; and yet he understood the reach of the question. He had absorbed, more than his father, a sense of how the "culture of life" bore on the deeper currents of the country. But he had to be acutely aware of the attitudes that prevailed in those upper-class Protestant circles from which he himself had sprung. Part of the art of George W. Bush is that he sought to balance all of these things, and yet keep a Republican party that was even more fully in the cast of the conservative party that Ronald Reagan had built. George W. Bush reflected that party far more than his father. But he also understood that Reagan had knitted together the new and the old. The Republican party was in substantial degree pro-life and "socially conservative," but it was not entirely. The drive for "planned parenthood," for contraception and abortion, had been powered in the past by the same Protestant elites who had formed the core of the Republican party. That remnant of the party had held on, but it was starting to break off now in a dramatic way. The shifts in Massachusetts, Connecticut, and New Jersey were critical – and threatening to the future of the party.

As Bush moved into the first spring of his presidency, the tensions of Bush versus Gore – the electoral contest and the litigation – would continue to generate turbulence and shocks in our politics. With a closely divided Senate, a handful of so-called moderate or liberal Republicans in the Northeast could effectively deny the Republicans, in fact, the control they could nominally claim. James Jeffords, Lincoln Chaffee, Olympia Snowe, and Arlen Specter, joined by three or four others, could do immense mischief by threatening to defect on any issue. If the Democrats preserved a high level of cohesion, the defection of these Republicans could conceivably defeat nominees to the courts unless some assurance was given that *Roe v. Wade* would stand in no danger of being overruled. As it turned out, the defection of Jeffords and Chaffee was quite enough to defeat George W. Bush's main initiative, an across the board tax cut of $1.6 billion. The tax cut had to be scaled back to around $1.3 billion, and subject to so many phase-ins, drawn over several years – so incremental and so small that conservative backers began to doubt its utility.

The sequel would soon become the subject of legend. As a congressman, Jeffords was often found voting against Ronald Reagan, and as the pattern of his disloyalty accumulated, a certain chill set in. There would be much talk later on the question of "who lost Jeffords?" But it could be that the emerging political map had far more to do with his departure from the party than any slights from the White House. Jeffords was persistently at odds with his party, not on marginal things, but on questions of the highest moment. On no matter was he more at odds than abortion. He stood for abortion, not merely as a private choice, but as public good, to be promoted and encouraged with public monies. He had learned over time that he could survive with his positions as a maverick in Vermont, as the state became a magnet for the wealthy and the liberal, moving in from more benighted regions. But now, as he surveyed the emerging electoral map, it should have been evident to him that New England had become a safe place for Democrats and liberals, and for a cultural politics tilted even more strongly to the Left.

First he threatened, and then he announced, his defection from the party in the spring. That was enough to tip the control of the Senate to the Democrats, and Jeffords received in return the premium of being preserved in a chairmanship of his choice. By June a transfer of control was effected, so that for the first time since 1994, or Clinton's first term, the Democrats had control over the flow of business in the Senate. The Democratic leader, Tom Daschle of South Dakota, would then determine just which measures would make it onto the floor for a vote. That change promised to make the most profound difference now for the Born-Alive Infants Protection Act. There was every expectation that the bill would be introduced again, for the conviction behind the bill, and the passion for bringing it to the floor, had not abated in the House. But assuming now that the bill would be introduced and passed, with the same level of support, there was no expectation any longer that the bill could be brought to the floor of the Senate. Rick Santorum of Pennsylvania had offered to introduce the measure in the Senate, but Santorum would no longer have any assurance that he could get the bill onto the floor – unless he brought it in through the back door as a rider to another bill. But then it could lose its meaning by being immersed in a bill on transportation or agriculture that would obscure, not highlight, its significance.

Just how Santorum's genius would come into play was anyone's guess; but the situation did require now an added degree of cleverness. In the meantime, the planning in the House moved forward. Bradley Clanton remained as counsel to the Subcommittee on the Constitution. The text of the bill would be brought back again, but now the findings would be attached as a preamble, from the very beginning, and arranged to build a case. As the staff arrayed them now, the findings took on a cumulative force as they were unfolded. They were also bolstered by a notable addition, an event that took place after the hearings on the bill in July. Six days after the hearings in the subcommittee, a panel of the federal appellate court in the Third Circuit struck down the law on partial-birth abortion in New Jersey. Coming, as it did, after the Stenberg case at the end of June, the decision in *Planned Parenthood v. Farmer* had become a foregone conclusion. But the opinion, written by Judge Maryann Trump Barry, displayed a strikingly different temper. Judge Barry suggested that the decision would have come out in the same way, even if the appellate court had not been given direction by the Supreme Court. Barry had been appointed by President Reagan, but later elevated to the court of appeals by Bill Clinton. Through the layers of legal reasoning, her views on abortion were unmistakable, and it was instantly clear that those views overrode any reasoning merely legal. The right to abortion took on the quality of a touchstone: The terms of the law would have to be recast if they somehow got in the way of that cardinal right. And so, with language rather colored, Judge Barry expressed her contempt for the effort to draw a line between the child in the womb and the child at the point of birth. That distinction has been known to common sense for millennia, but to raise that distinction here, she thought, involved "semantic machinations, irrational line-drawing, and an obvious attempt to inflame public opinion":

> the Legislature would have us accept, and the public believe, that during a 'partial-birth abortion' the fetus is in the process of being 'born' at the time of its demise. It is not. A woman seeking an abortion is plainly not seeking to give birth.[36]

If there was ever a decision that embodied the very vices it was decrying, this must surely have been it. For the argument now was that it was all, in the end, a matter of perceptions, of "semantics" and "line-drawing": There were no objective facts – no birth, no "child" being killed at the point of birth, because the mother, after all, had elected an abortion. Once she had made that fateful choice, there was no child to be killed, no birth to take place. For as Judge Barry said, the pregnant woman was "plainly not seeking to give birth." This decision must mark the emergence of a kind of postmodern jurisprudence: What the judge "saw" in the case would depend entirely on the theories she was willing to install. But it also confirmed what even many pro-life lawyers had refused to believe: Judge Haynsworth's opinion in *Floyd v. Anders* was not an anomaly or an aberration; it was being established now as the reigning orthodoxy among many federal judges. And that recognition would be incorporated in the findings of the committee.

The findings began by noting, as a principle long settled, that "infants who are born alive, at any stage of development, are persons who are entitled to the protections of the law." But they quickly noted that "recent decisions by the United States Supreme Court and the United States Court of Appeals for the Third Circuit have expanded *Roe v. Wade*, however, and brought this well-settled principle into question." After that allusion to the Farmer case, the findings cited the significance of the decision in *Stenberg v. Carhart*. It was observed that the location of the child, mostly outside the birth canal, did nothing to affect the claim of the child to the protections of the law. The more decisive fact was that the child had been marked for an abortion.

The findings went on to report on the Farmer case, and to cite some of Judge Barry's most quotable lines. As the staff construed Judge

---

[36] *Planned Parenthood v. Farmer*, 220 F. 3d 127, at 143 (July 26, 2000).

Barry, "an infant who is killed during a partial-birth abortion is not entitled to the protections of the law because '[a] woman seeking an abortion is plainly not seeking to give birth.'" From that anchoring point, the findings then drew out these further implications from the decision in the Farmer case:

(6) Under the logic of these decisions, once a child is marked for abortion, it is wholly irrelevant whether that child emerges from the womb as a live baby. That child may still be treated as though he or she did not exist, and would have not the slightest rights under the law – no right to receive medical care, to be sustained in life, or to receive any care at all.

(7) And if a child who survives an abortion and is born alive would have no claim to the protections of the law, there would, then, be no basis upon which the government may prohibit an abortionist from completely delivering an infant before killing the child or allowing the child to die. The 'right to abortion,' under this logic, means nothing less than the right to a dead baby, no matter where the killing takes place.

The staff then recalled the testimony of Jill Stanek. There was undeniable evidence now that babies were deliberately delivered alive, with the intention of performing an even safer "abortion" by allowing them to die. With those points in place, the staff brought the chain of propositions down to this culminating statement:

(9) Thus, having created in *Roe v. Wade* a legal regime in which a child's status under the law was dependent upon that child's location in relation to the body of his or her mother – "born" or "unborn" – the Federal judiciary has now rejected that regime as irrational, creating instead an expanded *Roe v. Wade* regime in which a child's entitlement to the protections of the law depends upon whether the child's mother intends to abort the child or to give birth.

The findings presented then a bill of charges against the law shaped in the decisions of federal judges. By drawing out the premises behind those decisions, the findings formed a moral critique that supplied, in turn, a justification for this new act of legislation. The findings would put in place new premises for the law. And finally, the committee would draw out, in summation, the purposes to which the findings now pointed:

PURPOSE – It is the purpose of this Act –

(1) to repudiate the flawed notion that a [born-alive] child's entitlement to the protections of the law is dependent upon whether that child's mother or others want him or her;
(2) to repudiate the flawed notion that the right to an abortion means the right to a dead baby, regardless of where the killing takes place;
(3) to affirm that every child who is born alive – whether as a result of induced abortion, natural or induced labor, or cesarean section – bears an intrinsic dignity as a human being which is not dependent upon the desires, interests, or convenience of any other person, and is entitled to receive the full protections of the law;
(4) to establish firmly that, for purposes of Federal law, the term "person" includes an infant who is completely expelled or extracted from his or her mother and who is alive – regardless of whether or not the baby's development is believed to be, or is in fact, sufficient to permit long-term survival, and regardless of whether the baby survived an abortion.

For those who had worked, over the years, for this bill, the findings offered the most gratifying confirmation that the staff had absorbed fully, deeply, the rationale and the logic behind the bill. Quite as gratifying was the report that the main sponsors of the bill were as committed as Charles Canady had been to bringing the bill to the floor with the findings that explained and justified the legislation. Canady's place had been taken as Chairman of the Subcommittee on the Constitution by Steve Chabot of Ohio, who had also served, with Canady, as one of the House managers during the impeachment of President Clinton. Chabot took up the baton with enthusiasm, he introduced again the Born-Alive Infants Protection Act, and he sought sponsors from colleagues on both sides of the party aisle. His "Dear Colleague" letter eventually attracted about 70 congressmen, willing to be listed as cosponsors for the bill. An encounter with friends on Capitol Hill brought the report that sponsors such as Joe Pitts (R–PA) and Sue Myrick (R–NC) were not only committed to the bill, but committed as well to the findings, and the willingness to stir the debate.

But with the shift in control of the Senate, there was a concern that the sponsors in the Senate might be tempted to jettison the findings as the price of bringing the bill to the floor. Yet, as it turned out, there was no need to wait for the bill to reach the Senate – no need for the Democrats to exert themselves to cast up impediments. Nor would there be a need for the Democrats to pay any price, in fact, for removing this difficulty from their path. The Republican Chairman of the Judiciary Committee, James Sensenbrenner of Wisconsin, was willing to perform this service for them on his own. Through a flick of the wrist, or a show of his prerogative as chairman, he simply announced to the staff that the findings would be deleted. The bill would go to hearings, to markup, and to the floor in the same, spare version that had gone to the floor in September. The staff pleaded the case, and so did the chairman of the subcommittee, Steve Chabot. But it was to no avail. As the saying went around the Hill, Sensenbrenner was a man "who did not take easily to advice." He was the heir to a fortune, a man of independent means. He had a reputation of being quite conservative politically, and he had been known in the past as a firm pro-lifer. What then was the problem? In one plausible account, Sensenbrenner was concerned that he not turn in a performance as chairman that seemed less effective in any way than the record made by his predecessor, Henry Hyde. Hyde and Canady had brought that bill in with a vote of 380–15. Sensenbrenner did not wish to preside over an erosion of support. He, too, wanted a massive win on the floor, which might even strengthen the case for getting the bill onto the floor of the Senate.

In fairness, it must be said for the leadership that they could not welcome another conflagration with that nervous band of "pro-choice" Republicans. Of course, some of those members, wobbling in the last Congress, were no longer there. Steven Kuykendall, in San Diego, had indeed been hanging by a thread, and he lost his bid for reelection by one percentage point (48–47). But that shrinking of the Republican majority was also part of the problem. What if a contingent of "pro-choice" Republicans in the Northeast threatened to "do a Jeffords"? Could Nancy Johnson not run as easily now as a Democrat in Connecticut as a Republican? These were not worries to be disregarded. And yet, the leadership did not show any panic. The sponsors of the bill thought they could reasonably make the case for their colleagues to back them in going to the floor with the findings, and in my own conversations, taking soundings on the Hill, the Republican leadership was quite as willing to go to the floor with the most coherent version of the bill. The point was worth recalling that it had required no small exertions to have brought matters to this point: It had taken a few years to persuade people in the pro-life movement that this modest bill could actually accomplish something. It had taken eight more years before the National Right to Life Committee was willing to sign on and weigh in seriously with its support. It was, altogether, a notable convergence of sentiment, years in the making, and it seemed unbelievable that it should all be waved aside now, as a matter of little consequence, by one man, even if he was the chairman of the committee. Sensenbrenner seemed more concerned than anyone else to avoid any erosion in the massive support for the bill. But to the others who had worked on the bill, a box score of 380–15 was less important. There was room to spare; the managers could afford to lose some votes. From our perspective it hardly made sense to see the bill passed without the kind of discussion that would bring out the very meaning of the bill.

But then, while this agonizing was taking place, Rick Santorum "pulled the trigger." That phrase came back to me because it was used by the redoubtable Jeffrey Bell as he accompanied me to a meeting with Santorum in the summer of 1998. I had been making the case in print for a return to the proposal to save the child who survived the abortion, and Bell was helping in the search for a sponsor who would actually introduce such a bill. Bell helped to arrange this particular meeting because, as he remarked, among the Republicans in the Senate, Santorum had the nerve and the temperament to "pull the trigger," to make the decisive move. Santorum also understood the argument at its core. That point came out quite dramatically in the fall of 1999, when he was debating, on the floor of the Senate, the bill on partial-birth abortion. He fell into a colloquy with Barbara Boxer of California, and put the question to her: When was the first moment when the child came within the protections of the law? Boxer replied, "I think when you bring your baby home, when your baby

is born – . . . the baby belongs to your family and has the rights."
Santorum, perhaps out of a sense of chivalry, presumed that she had
simply misspoken: Surely, she did not really think that the child became
human – and subject to the protections of the law – only when it
was taken home from the hospital. He pressed the question: Would it
be an acceptable abortion if the baby's toe were still in the birth canal?
Boxer replied, "absolutely not" – but then she became caught in the
coils of the argument. As Santorum brought out her contradictions, she
sought to ease out of the chamber. He would keep drawing her back,
however, with further questions, until she simply receded, sputtering
with anger ("You had the same conversation with a colleague of mine,
and I never saw such a twisting of his remarks").[37]

Past the spectacle of the show, it was clear to onlookers that
Santorum was putting the question that emerged most distinctly from
the bill to protect the child who had survived the abortion. There was
no question but that Santorum understood, as well as any Senator on
the scene, the logic and purpose behind the Born-Alive act. But with
the shift in control of the Senate, Santorum had to calculate the
moment for a rider. In June, the word came in from his staff that he
was considering the offering of the bill as a rider to the Patients' Bill
of Rights, a bill picking up momentum in the Senate, as the lead
measure pushed by the new Democratic majority. Without rules of
"germaneness," Santorum could have offered the proposal as a rider
to an appropriations bill, but here was a bill, after all, about patients.
And the purpose of the Born-Alive bill was to give the standing of
"patients" to children who had survived abortions. If there was a
serious concern about "rights," it was certainly apt to consider the
right of innocent patients not to have their lives imperiled through the
withdrawal of the medical care that would be given to other patients.
Yet, the action on the Patients' Bill of Rights was complicated; and
the word came from the senator's staff that it might not in fact become
practicable to offer the rider. But then suddenly, before one looked
up, it was done. The news came to me through a fax on June 29 that
Santorum had pulled the trigger. He introduced the Born-Alive Act
as an amendment to the Patients' Bill of Rights – and it created imme-
diately a crisis among the Democrats.

[37] *Congressional Record*, 106th Cong., 1st sess., p. S12879 (October 20, 1999).

Deborah Stabenow, the new senator from Michigan, reacted instantly: She couldn't vote for that bill, she said; it sought to establish that the unborn child was a "person" in the law even before birth. In all strictness, of course, the bill did no such thing, as Santorum quickly pointed out to her. But in a way, she was right, and her reaction confirmed the character of the bill: The deeper principles in the bill made it harder to deny that the child had a claim to the protection of the law even before birth. That the opposition should recognize so clearly the reach of the bill must stand as proof of a critical kind that people were indeed quite sensitive to the arguments in principle about abortion at all stages. They knew that they could not concede the human standing of the child marked for abortion without generating some unsettling questions about the child still in the womb. In any case, the problem posed by the bill was recognized at once, and it called for a quick conference. The Democrats huddled in a corner of the chamber, and they soon settled on Jerry Nadler's game plan for guidance. They would affably waive any objection to the bill, and hope then to deprive of it any significance. They might also seek to delete the rider later in a conference. But Santorum, sensing that move, called for a roll call vote, and the bill glided through with a vote of 98–0.

Once again there had been an encounter with Barbara Boxer, but the exchange this time had a notably different, and suspiciously amiable, quality: "I say to my friend from Pennsylvania, our side has no disagreement with this whatsoever." Whatsoever? The assent was hardly possible if she had listened to anything Santorum had just said, for as compressed as he was, he had made his case, and there was virtually nothing in his remarks that she could ever second. Santorum condensed the case for the bill to two points:

No. 1, because of the treatment of children who are delivered as a result of an abortion that was botched. We have ample testimony to, unfortunately, show that children born alive as a result of induced abortions are not cared for and are discarded, not cared for as appropriate to their gestational age. So we think it is important to make it clear there is Federal protection; that the laws of the land apply to even children who are born as a result of abortion – born alive.

The second reason is because of our courts in this country, particularly the Supreme Court, where two Supreme Court Justices in the most recent abortion decision, the Nebraska decision, stated that any proce-

dure that the doctor would permit is OK in this country. [He was referring here to the concurrence of Justices Stevens and Ginsburg.] This is
just two of the nine. But they said the Federal Government and our
Constitution does not allow regulation of any procedure that the doctor
believes is in the best health interests of the mother. That, to me, leaves
open the possibility, if the doctor decides in the health interest of a
mother that the best thing is to deliver the baby alive and then kill the
baby, two Justices on this Court would suggest that would be OK
because we cannot regulate any procedure, and they use 'any procedure,'
that the doctor believes is in the best interests of the mother.

So I think it is important for us to draw a line at least here.[38]

The entire rationale of the bill was contained there. Barbara Boxer
could be so breezy in expressing her assent only by deliberately ignor-
ing the reasons put before her and by putting, in their place, a construction entirely of her own:

> Of course, we believe everyone born should deserve the protections of
> this bill. . . . Who could be more vulnerable than a newborn baby? So,
> of course, we agree with that.

> But we go further. We believe everyone deserves the protection of this
> bill: babies, infants, children, families, all the way up until you are fight-
> ing for your life because you may have a dreaded disease; you may be
> elderly. Everyone deserves the HMOs to act in the right way and to put
> your vital signs ahead of their dollar signs. That is key.[39]

Yes, of course, she preferred to talk about the attack on Health
Maintenance Organizations (HMOs), but she evidently preferred also
to understand Santorum's bill as a bill that recognizes rights only on
the part of children born alive. That was not exactly what Santorum was
saying, and yet without the findings attached to the bill – the findings
that made Santorum's own premises clearer – there was little to disturb
Boxer's construction of the bill. On the other hand, was it Santorum's
fault that the Democrats seemed not to have noticed that the bill also
carried a "rule of construction" that decisively offset Boxer's account?
The text of the bill stipulated that nothing in it "shall be construed to
affirm, deny, expand, or contract any legal status or legal right applicable to any member of the species homo sapiens at any point prior to
being 'born alive.'" In other words, the bill explicitly avoided any sense

[38] *Congressional Record* (June 29, 2001), p. S7128.   [39] *Ibid.*

that the child was protected because it became a "person" or a bearer of rights only when it was born. Santorum was content to leave this modest bill gently presented. But the bill, if enacted, opened into a wider understanding of the rights that were available even to the child in the womb. And that is where Rick Santorum found the promise of the bill. Even if the Democrats insisted that the bill had nothing to do with abortion, that claim was belied by the clear language of the bill. That bill, enacted into law, would in fact plant premises. It would be there, establishing that the law could indeed protect the child marked for abortion; and that step, finally filled in, would provide the ground for other, serious steps in the future.

Over on the other side of the Capitol, there had been no tumult or overturning in the control of the House, and so it was rather expected that it would be, in the House, "deja vu all over again." It was expected that the bill would pass easily, and so the Democrats called no opposing witnesses. But at the same time, the witnesses in favor of the bill would be restricted to three. I would go in again, but as the sole advocate speaking from the perspective of constitutional law and moral philosophy. Jill Stanek would appear again, with an updated report on the experience at Christ Hospital. Dr. Watson Bowes, a neonatologist, from Chapel Hill, North Carolina, would appear for the sake of answering questions about the treatment of newborns. He would also explain that the standards in the bill were the same standards used for years in his hospital and in other states.

The level of tension was diminished, because the Democrats had decided to waive their opposition. Still, there was an undercurrent of hostility. Jerrold Nadler's staff had tracked down an article of mine from 1988, and Nadler sought to stir a bit of friendly mischief by suggesting that I was indeed one of those curious characters who actually thought that life did begin at conception. But apart from that, there was a certain degree of good-natured banter. I took the occasion to address, more systematically, the question that Mel Watt had put to me the year before, and at that moment, Congressman Watt walked into the hearing room. He seemed genuinely to be taken by the fact that I had made a special point of addressing the question he had raised. I explained again, more slowly, the problem of the ball and the inclined plane – the difference between a principle and the instances in which a principle may be manifested. But I also made a connection to civil rights: I pointed to the puzzlement that some professors of law had professed to suffer over the question of how the Court had made its way from racial segregation in public schools, to segregation in swimming pools. Once again, if we were clear on the principle, I suggested, we would have been clear that the principle would cover the numberless instances in which racial discrimination could be found. As that argument bore on the legislation before us, I drew out the implications in this way:

> Our contention in this bill is that there is no defensible ground in principle to remove a newborn from the protections of the law because she happened to survive an abortion. Nothing in that accident could possibly affect in any way the innocence of the child, her standing as a human being, or her claim to receive the same protections that extend to any other newborn. The people who do not share our position would be free, of course, to challenge our reasoning on all of these points. But if they cannot quarrel with that reasoning, then we would simply suggest that there is no conceivable set of circumstances in which the innocence of the child would be impaired. And therefore, we can see no conceivable set of circumstances that could justify removing that child from the protections of the law.[40]

Whether the angels of benevolence had passed over the land, or whether there was a new mood of sweet reason, Congressman Watt now seemed appeased and satisfied. He remarked, I can understand that – and go along with it. But then, he quickly recovered political reflexes, and sought to change the subject to racial reparations! Since he had made a gesture of comity, implicitly conceding my argument, he evidently sought to see if he could lure me in, with a comparable gesture, to fall in with one of his own enthusiasms. The conversation had turned curiously amiable, and as I began to respond to one of his questions, a cell phone suddenly went off, in the hands of Representative Melissa Hart (R–PA). Startled by the bells going off, I asked, "Did I win something?" In the laughter of the room, Mel Watt joined,

---

[40] The *Born-Alive Infants Protection Act 2001*, Hearings on H.R. 2175, Subcommittee on the Constitution, Committee on the Judiciary, U.S. House of Representatives, July 12, 2001, p. 40.

and remarked, "If you did, I think I must have too, because this happens to me all the time."

The bill was destined then to move without resistance through the markup. There was some talk that it would get to the floor in August. But the Congress was taken up with the problem of stem-cell research and cloning, and those bills now promised to be far more divisive. The president was also readying his own statement on the matter of stem-cell research. The administration and the Republican leadership in the House decided to concentrate on this issue, and steer it through without getting distracted by other matters before the Congress adjourned for the summer recess. The Born-Alive bill would be put off until September. As I returned to Amherst in the fall, and classes resumed, it was expected that the bill would be brought to the floor in the middle of September. But in a year characterized by sudden, unexpected turns, with plans upended, a quiet, clear Tuesday on September 11 suddenly brought news that upended the whole country. All plans, all schedules, would be put aside; everything would have to be seen anew. There was the task first of coming to terms with a brutal, and clever, terrorist assault. There would be the search for victims, the assembling of evidence, the marshaling of the country. And for at least another month, the administration would have to put virtually everything else aside as this issue of terrorism and war would become the architectonic issue: From the decisions made on this issue, everything else would now radiate. All other schedules, for all other things, would clearly be subordinated. From one perspective, there could be a new surge of willingness to affirm the importance of life and the intrinsic dignity of the human person, even for that unborn person still in the womb. But on the other hand, that question, which ran to the root of the matter of human life, its moral standing, its claims to respect and protection – that question could just as plausibly be put aside at this moment as somehow too important, too vexing, morally. Precisely because it was so freighted with moral significance and divisive, it might not be absorbed in the current, fragile state of America in its political life. If Republicans made the effort now to attach the findings, the result might not be a willingness, on all sides, to affirm the concern for the sanctity of human life. It was quite as plausible that the response would be, "Why are you raising this issue now, just as Democrats are making gestures of coming behind the president and muting their opposition?"

My own suspicion was that the moral arguments, crystallized in the bill, would be lost in the clamor of the moment. The bill was still scheduled to go to the floor, and the prospect was that it would move through readily, without friction or carping. But its significance could well have been muted along with everything else. Yet once again, nothing new under the sun: It was ever the task of statesmen, or political men and women, to read the moment and the circumstances. The laws may teach, but there are moments when even the sharpest lessons could be lost in the drama and thunder of many other, momentous events. Under these conditions, even people who had worked hard to advance the bill at every stage could find a ground of consolation, or even an advantage, if this bill, so ripened, were nevertheless put off for another day. For the postponement to another day could offer the chance of getting it right: There could be another chance to overcome the petulance of James Sensenbrenner and make the case anew, make the case even more strongly, for going to the floor, not only with the bill, but with the findings that gave to the bill its real significance.

On the other hand, political men, attuned to the moment, were also attuned to the possibility of acting when the Republicans still had control of the House. In the aftermath of the terrorist attack, and the massive surge of support for George W. Bush, the Republican prospects for holding the Congress could have been heightened at the same time. Not as much perhaps, but a rising tide lifts all boats. Still, in a year characterized by the most dramatic reversals and surprises, of culture wars and litigation, and of war, real and savage, loosed upon American civilians in their own streets and buildings, no one could look ahead complacently with political reckonings of any kind. From this nettle, uncertainty, it was hardly a surprise that the Republican leaders in the House might grasp this one reliable shoot, this bill in hand, carefully crafted, while it was within reach.

In one of his stand-up routines, Woody Allen once apologized for not leaving his audience with something positive. As a compensation, he wondered if they would accept "two negatives." Over these pages, part analysis, part argument, part memoir, I have sought to bring out a critical change that has taken place among the members of the political class. They are the people who "form the regime." They fill the offices of state, they have a commanding presence in the legal profession and the key positions in the media. When they are in politics, they have sprung from the most notable colleges and universities, and from the leading schools of law. But to compare them to the statesmen and jurists of the founding generation is to become aware at once of the most striking differences in the furnishings of mind. And by that, as I have sought to show, we would mean more than stylistic grace. At every turn, it is a difference in understanding, a difference in substance. It involves the capacity to look plainly at what is before us, to grasp a "nature of things" that is not wholly malleable, and to recognize that we stand as an enduring part of that nature. In the classic teaching, shared by the American Founders, there were rights and wrongs that found their ground in that nature. There was indeed a moral "up and down," and ways of life that were rightful for human beings. The first generation of jurists and statesmen, worldly as they were, suffered no embarrassment as they spoke about the rightful and wrongful ways of ordering political life.

To speak of the American regime in any coherent way, one must be led back to the notion of natural rights. That notion has fallen into a certain skeptical doubt among the educated classes. But it has simply fallen to us to learn again – and learn each time painfully – that we will not be able to give a coherent account of this regime, and the rights it was meant to secure, if those doctrines of natural rights are not in fact true. Part of the sobriety of the founders was that they understood, with the ancients, that the polity arose from the nature of that forked creature, situated somewhere between the beasts and the angels. They understood that he will always be affected by his interests and his self-love, and it would require a rare character, closer to the angels, who would be governed, unceasingly, by a devotion to principle. In each generation, the leading statesmen have found paths leading them away from the principles of the founding even as they have earnestly sought ends they regarded as good and just. And so it should come as no surprise that even the children of this regime may nevertheless talk themselves out of the principles of the founders, and the doctrines of natural right, even as they get on with the business of life, serenely certain that they have been working to expand the domain of rights.

I have sought to show here that for the current generation, the most decisive vehicle for that transformation has come with the doctrines of "choice" over abortion. Nothing would seem, on the surface, a more natural expression of that personal liberty, that freedom from constraint, that seemed to lie at the core of the idea of America. And that conviction can only be given a deeper resonance when attention is fixed on the persons we can readily see: not the offspring, small as a dot, or as ungainly as an embryo, looking more like a tadpole; but rather the people who find their lives complicated and strained, their prospects endangered, by the advent of a child coming at the wrong time, and forcing the end of their own days as children. But as people have persuaded themselves that they have, in abortion, a deep right of personal freedom, they have had to talk themselves into a logic that must detach them, inescapably, from the logic of natural rights. And as I have contended, the people who have talked themselves into that logic have put themselves in a position in which they cannot really vindicate any of their rights, including even that right to abortion. For with the shift in logic – with that move decisively away from "natural rights" – they can no longer offer a moral justification for any of their rights.

I have argued then that the "right to abortion" functions as a kind of key in understanding the political class, and what it reveals is quite sobering for all parts of that political class, the Right as well as the Left. The experience in managing the Born-Alive Act yielded a rather melancholy report on the other side of the political class. It brought, as I have said, a sobering account, even of those people who have aligned themselves against an activist judiciary and the ethic of imposing, through the courts, the regime of abortion. To borrow a phrase from Plato, they may be men and women of "right opinion" (at least, in my judgment), but it does not follow that because they are reserved about a right to abortion, they are in a position to restore a public teaching of natural right. As we have seen, some of them have been enthralled by the maxims of "conservative jurisprudence." They may utterly deny that there is a constitutional right to abortion, and some of them may even hold moral and religious convictions opposed to abortion. Yet, by their own admission they are skeptical of natural rights, and some have even professed a willingness to uphold policies of abortion on demand if they are enacted in the positive law through the democratic process. Once again, the malady I have described here, the erosion of conviction, or the falling away from natural rights, has been diffused now through all parts of the political class. That movement has no doubt been fed by the same forces in the culture that have undermined confidence in reason itself, or in the conviction that it is indeed possible to have *rational* knowledge of the things that are morally right or wrong.

The experience of the Born-Alive Act, as it encountered the divided soul of the Republican party, gave us the equivalent of a light cast on the retina. For the physician, that simple test yields a vast amount of information about the state of the organism. For the writer, and the generous people who worked with him in the academy and the staffs of Congress, the experience yielded a vast amount of information about our political friends, and not all of it comforting. Of course, we figured to be disappointed when our friends did not read the political moment as we did. We thought it a grave mistake when they held back from attaching the findings to the bill, and when they gave in to a show of tantrums rather than using their experience to steady their colleagues. But those were judgments of tactics, and when it came to making guesses, our friends might well have been right and we wrong. Nor was it always a matter of measuring moral fiber, for the people who disagreed with us had been willing to absorb more than their share of battering on other occasions. What was far more telling, though, and dismaying, was the erosion of the sense that reasons truly mattered. There was hardly a trace of recognition that the giving of reasons was important even for the actor himself in getting clear on the grounds of his own judgments. But then there was the loss, too, of the sense in which reason works in the alchemy of politics: Compelling people to give reasons, to justify their positions, may often produce the most notable crises, as allies come to discover that the principles that divide them run far deeper than the agreement they share on the surface. In the play of politics, we keep discovering that the two sides are always connected: The willingness to be scrappy and have the debate will usually mark a certain conviction, mingled at times with a curiosity to see how the arguments may actually hold up when they are challenged. On the other side, there should be no surprise that the waning of confidence in giving reasons will go hand in hand with a certain aversion to engaging in the argument. We were convinced that the reasons mattered profoundly, that the central task was to draw out those reasons in a debate, and all of that meant a willingness to accept a fight – or even pick one.

Or perhaps that was the problem: the tendency to confuse the staging of a debate with the spectacle of a brawl. As the first George Bush had said in his inaugural address, "[the people] did not send us here to bicker."[41] With that phrase he managed to reduce to matters of trivia, or bad temper, the serious differences in principle that separated the political parties. In an age of moral relativism and logical positivism, moral argument could readily be reduced to expressions of emotion or translated simply into matters of personal "likes" or "dislikes." It did not help when a certain "feminization" of politics took place, and candidates seemed wary of offending "soccer Moms" in the suburbs by coming on as "too negative." Political argument could be reduced, in this perspective, to the roughhouse games played by aggressive young males. George W. Bush seemed quite reluctant to stage a fight, but at a certain point that desire to remain civil fed a willingness to keep backing away from an argument. Or it led him to feign the possibilities of collaboration with people who had not the faintest interest in anything that would redound to his credit.

The Born-Alive Infants Act was a measure that produced real strain and anxiety among the Democrats and the defenders of abortion until the Republicans went to their rescue. The conservative side of the political class could have made deft use of that bill in one or both of two ways: It could have used the bill to draw out people on the other side, to induce them to make explicit the premises that stood behind the "right to abortion." That exposure would have brought them embarrassment (as Jerrold Nadler clearly understood) – and it would have delivered some surprising news to large portions of the public. And/or: the bill could have been used by the president in disarming the opposition. He might well have melted the intransigence of many Republicans in the northeast who had been willing to vote against him solely on this issue.[42] If he had managed to lure some of them back,

[41] George H. W. Bush, Inaugural Address, January 20, 1989.

[42] On this matter, I do not fall back on speculation. My estimate here has been confirmed in my own experience, in addressing audiences that are wary about arguments over abortion, or even hostile to the pro-life side. I was invited by some of my former students to offer a talk on this bill, in April 2000, at the law school

states such as Connecticut, Vermont, and New Jersey could have come into more serious play in the next election. But the remarkable thing is that the Republican version of the political class actually did neither of things. They neither staged the argument, to embarrass their adversaries, nor used this measure as a device for disarming the opposition and setting a new course on abortion.

In each case, it was not a matter of deception or ill will, but the loss of the sense that reasons may somehow matter. It truly did not seem to occur to most politicians that something momentous – and something with political bite – could occur if one put the simple question to the partisans of abortion, "Why are you willing to protect the child born alive? You say that the bill is not needed because the laws in the States already protect that child. But why do the laws do that? And should they? The answer surely cannot be, 'the child deserves to be protected because we have always done that.' To remark that something has been long done is not to supply a justification for continuing to do it. And besides, that same answer could have been given in answer to the question of why we protect the child in the womb – up until January 22, 1973." To their credit, NARAL knew, acutely, that the reasons mattered. And so did the "moderate" Republicans, who were willing to close down the House rather than vote to say that a child had an intrinsic dignity that became, in turn, the source of rights of intrinsic dignity. The reactions from NARAL and the moderate Republicans offered dramatic evidence that the effort to make reasons explicit can be utterly explosive in politics. And yet, even with the evidence plainly before them, many key Republicans, in the Congress and the White House, saw no particular utility in pressing

at Duke University. My students made it a point to draw in, for the talk, people they knew at the medical school, and several others whom they knew to be strongly in favor of abortion. In the eyes of the audience I did indeed find wariness and traces of hostility. But those looks quickly gave way to a certain concentration as I set forth the logic of the problem, and people became engaged in the puzzle of the bill. Soon the hostility completely dissolved. Several young women, who professed themselves to be pro-choice, voiced their objections to the fact that congressmen might try to block us from getting a vote on the bill. But even more telling, I thought, one young woman, who had worked for Senator Jeffords and lobbied for Planned Parenthood, remarked that this bill sounded quite "sensible" to her, and she would support it. If these were the attitudes of people adamantly pro-choice, it is not hard to imagine what George W. Bush, in his most fetching style, could have accomplished with this approach, even in Connecticut and other parts of New England.

the other side, through the simplest and most earnest move of all: to insist that they make explicit the reasons behind their judgments.

Of course, there may be at work here the kinds of differences that separate, say, the lawyer from the philosopher. A pro-life lawyer looked at Judge Haynsworth's opinion in *Floyd v. Anders,* noted that the case was eventually dropped, and Haynsworth's opinion never endorsed by the Supreme Court. But had the Court ever explicitly rejected his reasoning? The lawyers were more inclined to look at the results, or to the conduct mandated by the law, without inquiring too deeply into the reasons that prescribe that conduct. But even the social scientist wishes to know how the action looked "from the inside," in the understanding of the man who acted. And as we saw earlier, the philosopher understands that even acts that appear outwardly the same could spring from maxims, or principles, that are strikingly different. For the philosopher, the meaning of the act would depend entirely on the understanding that animated the actor, and the reasons that formed that understanding. In the classic understanding of politics, the polis would teach through the laws. But the laws would teach, they would shape the souls of the populace, to the extent that the public came to understand, and absorb, the reasons that moved the legislators; the reasons that formed, for them, the justification for the law they were enacting.

Certainly it would be foolish to overlook the mixture of motives among those men and women who have made politics their vocation in our own day. Laws may be proposed even without any interest, especially eager, to enforce them. They might be proposed, and even enacted, to strike a posture. In some instances, they could be enacted mainly to run up a box score, to show accomplishments for the committee, and the chairman, who managed their passage. But if all of our legislation and politics were handled in that way, it would not only be a politics without substance. It would be a politics shorn precisely of that dimension of reason and principle that gives law its justification, and politics its real meaning. Aristotle famously remarked that the law is reason without passion. At the heart of the law is the sense of principle – the understanding of right and wrong from which the law emanates when it truly merits the name of law. A political class that has lost the sense that reason matters is a political class that may serve in positions as officers of state, and yet its members will have lost their vocation. At times, the need to clarify the principles entails the need to stage the confrontation or the debate, and that may indeed involve the need to pick a fight. A political class that is persistently reluctant to show that spirited nature will produce, not merely a politics that is banal, but one that is denatured. In removing the conflict, or removing the argument, one may remove as well the moral substance.

Aristotle also remarked, in one of his most memorable observations, that if the art were in the material, then ships would be springing, fully crafted, from trees.[43] But ships were not part of the world of "causation," produced through the workings of the laws of nature. Ships were part of a world governed by design, by the awareness of ends, and the shaping of reasons. We may be bringing forth now a political class more and more detached from the sense that there is any particular importance in compelling the other side to come out with their reasons, and claim them as their own. To a political class molding itself in that way, we may not only ask, where is the reason that gives meaning to political life, but where, in all of that, is the *art*? Where do we find the distinctive hand that shows your work – the work of one who had "grasped his warrant," as Henry James once put it, and embodied the art he claimed to practice? Where do we find the design that marked your understanding, the touch that reflected the experience you had cultivated? And where, finally, do we find the impression, lingering through time, that you were here?

---

[43] "If the shipbuilding art were in the wood, it would produce the same results by nature." Aristotle, Physics, 199b 28, in *The Complete Works of Aristotle*, Jonathan Barnes, ed. (Princeton: Princeton University Press, 1984), p. 340.

Index

abortion, right to, 67–70
 surveys of opinion on, 80–1, 85–7, 148–9
 and principled reasoning, 83–5
 and test of "mental health," 87–8
 popular referenda, before *Roe v. Wade*, 148
 public funding, 186
 as public good, not merely private choice, 187
 constitutional ground for Congress to legislate on the subject, 213ff.
 and informed consent, 224
 restoring to conversation and public argument, 226
 and the unmentionable "A-word," 273
 at odds with "natural rights," 179–84, 234, 289–90
Abraham, (Sen.) Spence, 102n.32
Adkins v. Children's Hospital (1923), 53, 218n.33
alchemists, 130
Allen, Woody, 287
American Medical Association (AMA), opposition to partial-birth abortions, 119, 121, 127, 134
Americans United for Life (AUL), 245
Antijural jurisprudence, 138–46
Aquinas, Thomas, 17, 83
Aristotle, 3, 5, 17, 38, 38n.1, 68, 144, 293–4

Arkes, Hadley, 21n.17, 47n.21, 51n.26, 60n.36, 75n.2, 76n.4, 83n.13, 84n.14, 109n.38; 156, 159n.23, 178n.52, 186n.6, 191–2n.11, 196n.15, 205n.26, 210n.29, 216n.30, 221n.39, 229n.46, 262, 267
 and the proposal of the "modest first step," 87, 19, 89–94, 96ff., 135, 138n.28
 pointing out the trend of cases on partial-birth abortion in the courts, 243
 bringing back the "modest" proposal in 1998, then 2000, 235
 leading the testimony for the Born-Alive Infants Protection Act of 2000 [H.R.4292], 248, 249–51
 exchange with Rep. Watt in hearings in House, 256–9
 leading testimony on the bill in 2001, Subcommittee on the Constitution, U.S. House of Representatives, 285
 at Duke University law school, 291n.42
Article III, Sec. 2, of the Constitution, on altering the jurisdiction of the courts, 215
Association of American Law Schools, 156n.21
Augustine, St., 39
Auschwitz, 159

295